THE AMPSCRIPT GUIDE

The Definitive Scripting Manual for Salesforce Marketing Cloud

Eliot Harper and Adam Spriggs

Published by AttributeValue Pty Limited, Melbourne, Australia

Text printed in the United States on FSC certified Accent Opaque 70lb paper by Edition One Books, Berkeley, CA.

ISBN 978-0-6482872-0-9

NATIONAL LIBRARY OF AUSTRALIA

A catalogue record for this book is available from the National Library of Australia

THE AMPSCRIPT GUIDE

This book is an accompaniment to the online edition. Visit **https://ampscript.guide** to access searchable content, code examples and up-to-date documentation.

Table of Contents

Foreword

The fourth industrial revolution is driving new data, devices, and consumer expectations. Today's digital marketer needs to adapt and put the consumer at the center of every experience. Marketers must know their consumers like never before, engage with them across the entire journey, and personalize every interaction.

AMPscript is a powerful scripting language that is unique to Salesforce Marketing Cloud. It provides a standard personalization language across all digital marketing channels, enabling rapid development. AMPscript empowers organizations to respond to changing consumer and market needs with highly relevant messages.

This book will show you how to quickly and easily leverage AMPscript to improve your marketing results, and have fun while you're doing it.

Joanna Milliken
SVP, Product Management
Salesforce

Introduction

Digital marketing is changing. Again.

The lines between digital marketing and Customer Relationship Management (CRM) is blurring because the need for highly personalized, relevant communication is greater than ever before. The unique needs and desires of customers and prospects need be understood through CRM, then realized through marketing communication. Relevance is now the key to effective customer experiences, customer engagement, and revenue generation.

With these shifting trends, today's challenge in digital marketing is to create and deliver sophisticated personalization from different data sources across multiple channels. But creating highly complex marketing communication can take a significant amount of effort, time and expertise.

AMPscript has been designed with these challenges in mind. It's an extensive scripting language for Salesforce Marketing Cloud that enables highly sophisticated personalization, while also integrating with CRM platforms and external data sources.

Our goal in writing this book is to help Marketing Cloud users realize and leverage this powerful language to its full potential. This comprehensive reference manual provides documentation on every AMPscript function, with supporting code examples for real-world scenarios.

AMPscript can seem intimidating when you're getting started, particularly if you aren't familiar with scripting languages. But it doesn't have to be. The language is actually based on a simple syntax that is easy to learn and quick to code.

We encourage you to familiarize yourself with the concepts and fundamentals in the Language chapter, then explore the different functions and try them using the supplied code examples.

We hope you enjoy reading and working with this book as much as we've enjoyed writing it.

Eliot and Adam

Language

Overview
AMPscript is a scripting language for Salesforce Marketing Cloud. You can use it to create highly sophisticated, personalized content through an extensive set of functions. The language follows a simple syntax and semantics, making it quick to learn and easy to code.

Unlike other general-purpose languages such as JavaScript, Perl and Python, AMPscript is a server-side scripting language that has been developed for a specific runtime environment (Salesforce Marketing Cloud), where scripts are interpreted and executed when the content is rendered.

AMPscript is a language in two parts: a syntax and library of functions. With an understanding of these, it's possible to quickly gain proficiency in the language, without prior programming or scripting experience, and create highly personalized, dynamic content for direct marketing campaigns.

Syntax
As AMPscript is a server-side language, the code can be included in any location in an email, web page, SMS or push message. Similar to other scripting languages, AMPscript is interpreted and not compiled, which means that it's interpreted in the order it is written. So if you are using AMPscript to include personalized content in an email, the AMPscript code will need to be defined before or at the point where the personalized content should appear.

AMPscript code is contained within a character sequence that opens and closes with double percentage marks (`%%`) and either contains an inner bracket delimiter (`[` and `]`), for AMPscript blocks, or an equality character (`=`), for inline AMPscript. All AMPscript code must be surrounded by matching opening and closing delimiter patterns, otherwise the code will be ignored.

AMPscript Blocks

AMPscript blocks are used to define code for interpretation but do not display output where the code appears in the email or on the page. There are some exceptions to this rule through the provision of two functions, Output and OutputLine, which enable variable values to be output at the location where the code block appears.

Example 1

In this example, a constant value is set based on the current month when the email is sent, within an AMPscript block. The output value of the heading can then be displayed on the page or in the message using inline AMPscript.

```
%%[

var @month
set @month = xtmonthnumeric
if @month == 9
   set @heading = "Our End of Financial Year Offers"
else
   set @heading = "Our Seasonal Offers"
endif

]%%
```

Example 2

A section of AMPscript code does not necessarily need to be contained within an individual block. It can span multiple blocks, as the page or message is interpreted in a consolidated order.

This example uses a statement spanning three AMPscript blocks to determine a heading to display on the page or in the message.

```
%%[ if xtmonthnumeric == 9 then ]%%

<h2>Our End of Financial Year Offers</h2>

%%[ else ]%%

<h2>Our Seasonal Offers</h2>

%%[ endif ]%%
```

Inline AMPscript

Inline AMPscript provides a convenient method of interpreting and executing a function within message content. Unlike AMPscript blocks, inline AMPscript can only be used with a single function, and the function output is displayed where the inline AMPscript code appears. However, nested functions are supported.

Example 1

This example retrieves an attribute value (for example, a Subscriber Attribute, or a field from a Sendable Data Extension) if the attribute is available in the context of the send, and the value is rendered where the inline delimiters appear.

```
<p>You have %%=AttributeValue("Points Balance")=%% status
points.</p>
```

Example 2

In this example, an AMPscript block is used to set a points balance from a field in a Sendable Data Extension, then the Subscriber's membership level is determined based on the balance value. The member level is then set as a variable which is output using inline AMPscript.

```
%%[

var @pointsBalance, @memberLevel
set @pointsBalance = AttributeValue("Points Balance")

if @pointsBalance < 3000 then
   set @memberLevel = "Standard"
else
   set @memberLevel = "VIP"
endif

]%%

<p>You are a valued %%=v(@memberLevel)=%% member.</p>
```

Example 3
This example outputs the same result as the previous example but includes nested functions using inline AMPscript.

```
<p>You are a valued %%=IIF(AttributeValue("Points Balance") <
3000, "Standard", "VIP")==%% member.</p>
```

Tag-Based Syntax

As an alternative to the AMPscript block syntax, the HTML script tag is also supported. This syntax can be beneficial when developing in both Server-Side JavaScript (SSJS) and AMPscript, as it provides a standardized syntax for interpreting both server-side scripting languages.

Additional **`runat`** and **`language`** attributes must be included in the opening script tag for the containing code to be interpreted as AMPscript, as indicated in the example below.

```
<script runat="server" language="ampscript">

/* AMPscript code */

</script>
```

Functions

In programming, a *function* is a named section of a program that takes some input values (or *arguments*) to perform a specific task and produce an output value. While other scripting languages offer user-defined functions (for example, JavaScript), AMPscript uses a declarative approach through predefined functions which are primarily oriented to displaying, transforming and storing customer data and marketing content.

AMPscript functions are *pure functions*, which mean they take some input and return an output based on the input. Pure functions form the foundation of functional programming and are independent, which means that you can move them around your code, making it easy to refactor or adapt. This programming style simplifies the development process for users as it doesn't follow an explicit control flow or an imperative sequence, which in turn allows flexibility in development through applying 'creative' design patterns to achieve an outcome result.

AMPscript and Excel

AMPscript functions work in much the same way as they do in Microsoft Excel; that is, parameters are set for a predefined function, which are interpreted and, in turn, return a value. Several AMPscript functions are identical to Excel functions – while some functions are named differently, they share the same parameters and output the same result as Excel.

The example below compares the **SUM** Excel function with the **Add** AMPscript function, where a range of numbers are passed as arguments to the function. In this case, both functions will output the value **10**.

```
Excel SUM function

=SUM(1,2,3,4)

AMPscript Add Function

%%=Add(1,2,3,4)=%%
```

There are a total of 15 comparable functions between Excel and AMPscript which accept the same parameters and output the same result, as indicated in the table below.

Excel Function	AMPscript function
CHAR	Char
CONCATENATE	Concat
FIND	IndexOf
IF	IIf
ISBLANK	Empty
LEN	Length
LOWER	Lowercase
MOD	Mod
NOW	Now
PROPER	ProperCase
RANDBETWEEN	Random
SUBSTITUTE	Replace
SUM	Add
TRIM	Trim
UPPER	Uppercase

Variables

Similar to other programming and scripting languages, AMPscript supports *variables*. In programming, variables provide a convenient method of setting a function or value once, then reusing that variable by referencing it within code. This is in much the same way that Cascading Style Sheets (CSS) classes are defined once and then the defined style properties are applied to one or more elements by including the class name in a class attribute. However, variables not only allow fixed values (or constants) to be defined once, but also AMPscript functions, and in turn, the output value of the variable can change depending on the context for which it's interpreted.

Naming Convention

Variables are essentially 'named containers', where a user-defined name is applied to a defined entity, either a constant or function. Variable names are case-insensitive and can include characters or numbers, but not spaces or commas. Variable names must begin with **`@`** and include at least one other letter, number or underscore. You should consider naming variables with a human-readable taxonomy that has meaning or context to others, so your code is easy to interpret and does not require reverse engineering to comprehend its purpose.

For example, if you are setting a variable that derives a propensity score value from customer data, you should consider using a name like **`@propensityScore`**, not **`@ps`**. Also, it can be helpful to apply camel-case notation for variable names that are comprised of more than one word by capitalizing subsequent words. For example, a variable named **`@preferredContactNumber`** is easier to read than **`@preferredcontactnumber`**.

For example, if you are setting a variable that derives a propensity score value from customer data, you should consider using a name like **`@propensityScore`**, not **`@ps`**. Also, it can be helpful to apply camel-case notation for variable names that are comprised of more than one word by capitalizing subsequent words. For example, a variable named **`@preferredContactNumber`** is easier to read than **`@preferredcontactnumber`**.

Declaring Variables

Before a variable can be *set*, it must be declared. Variables are declared with the **`var`** keyword, followed by one or more comma-delimited variable names. For example, if you need to define a member's first name, last name and membership expiry date, the variables could be declared as:

```
var @firstName, @localDate, @promotionEndDate
```

Declaring a variable adds an entry to an internal Variables Dictionary, using the variable name as the key and **null** as the value. If an entry for that name already exists, the value of the variable will be reset to **null**.

> **NOTE:** AMPscript is a loosely typed language and as a result, the interpreter does not enforce variables to be declared. However, it's best practice to do so, to ensure the variable name is added to the Variables Dictionary.

Setting Variables

Once a variable is declared, it can be set. Variables are set using a syntax that comprises of four elements:

1. the **set** keyword
2. the variable name
3. a single equals symbol (=)
4. a personalization string, constant or AMPscript function (which can contain nested functions).

Refer to the example below, where variables are set as a personalization string (**@firstName**), AMPscript function (**@localDate**) and constant (**@promotionEndDate**):

```
%%[

var @firstName, @localDate, @promotionEndDate

set @firstName = FirstName
set @localDate = SystemDateToLocalDate(Now())
set @promotionEndDate = '10/15/2018'

]%%
```

Scope

Once a variable is set, its scope is set globally; that is, it can be referenced later in the code to display the output, or used in conditional expressions. However, variables can also be changed after they have been set. For example, a promotion end date is set from a field in a Sendable Data Extension using a personalization string, but for specific customers, there is a requirement to adjust this value later in the code:

```
%%[

var @promotionEndDate, @memberStatus
set @promotionEndDate = '10/15/2018'
set @memberStatus = status

if @memberStatus == 'gold' then
   set @promotionEndDate = '11/15/2018'
endif

]%%
```

Variables can also be set on themselves in a function; that is, if the variable has previously been declared, then it can be used as an argument to a function, based on its previous value. So the above code could also be expressed as:

```
%%[

var @promotionEndDate, @memberStatus
set @promotionEndDate = '10/15/2018'
set @memberStatus = status

if @memberStatus == 'gold' then
   set @promotionEndDate = DateAdd(@promotionEndDate, 1,
'M')
endif

]%%
```

Also, once a variable has been set, it can be reset by declaring the value again. In the example below, if the current date is less than (after) a membership end date, then a **`null`** value will be set for membership status.

```
%%[

var @membershipEndDate, @memberStatus
set @membershipEndDate = '10/15/2018'
set @memberStatus = status

if Now() < @membershipEndDate
   var @memberStatus
endif

]%%
```

The only exception to this scope rule is when a variable is used within a **`for`** block. In this scenario, the variable is locked from modification within the process loop.

Order of Operations

Like other scripting languages, AMPscript is interpreted from top to bottom, which means that variables have to be declared and set before they can be used. However, email components are interpreted in the following order:

1. email preheader
2. HTML body
3. text body
4. subject line.

For example, a variable can be declared and set in an HTML body (within an AMPscript block), then used in a subject line:

```
<!--Appears in Body-->
%%[

var @subjectLine

if AttributeValue('Member Status') == 'VIP' then
  set @subjectLine = 'An exclusive offer for VIP members'
else
  set @subjectLine = 'A special offer for our members'
endif

]%%
```

```
<!--Appears in Subject Line-->
%%=v(@subjectLine)=%%
```

Using Variables

Variables aren't required in AMPscript. It's possible to achieve the same result by just using functions, conditional statements and operators. However, without variables:

- functions and constants would need to be defined multiple times, often resulting in more code and making it harder to maintain
- each duplicated AMPscript function needs to be interpreted again, resulting in potential performance issues when sending emails or rendering content.

The example below indicates the inclusion of two variables in AMPscript to retrieve a points balance and display a corresponding status level.

```
%%[

var @pointsBalance, @status
set @pointsBalance = Lookup("Points
Balance","Balance","MemberId", _subscriberKey)

if @pointsBalance < 100 then
   set @status = "bronze"
elseif @pointsBalance > 100 and @pointsBalance < 500
   set @status = "bronze"
else
   set @status = "gold"
endif

]%%

You are a valued %%=v(@status)=%% member.
```

When writing AMPscript, it's good practice to optimize your code through setting variables for commonly used functions.

Comments

Comments can be included in AMPscript blocks. They are contained within an opening **/*** and closing ***/** syntax pair and provide the ability to include a readable explanation or annotation for users. Any comments are ignored by

Marketing Cloud and will not be interpreted. They can be used on a single line or traverse multiple lines.

Example 1

This is an example of a single-line comment:

```
%%[

  var @agentId
  set @agentId = 32 /* our agent identifier */

]%%
```

Example 2

Here is an example of a comment traversing multiple lines:

```
%%[

   /* The following code block declares
   and sets a variable to a constant */

  var @agentId
  set @agentId = 32

]%%
```

> **NOTE:** Comments are not supported in inline AMPscript.

Function Calls

Functions are interpreted, or 'called' either within an AMPscript block or inline AMPscript, at the location where they appear on the page or in the message. However, functions don't need to be contained in the same AMPscript block. For example, when using conditional statements, the conditional expression can span multiple blocks:

```
%%[ if Lookup('Points Balance','Balance','MemberId',
_subscriberKey) < 100 then ]%%

You are a valued bronze member.
```

```
%%[
elseif Lookup('Points Balance','Balance','MemberId',
_subscriberKey) > 100
and Lookup('Points Balance','Balance','MemberId',
_subscriberKey) < 500 then
]%%

You are a valued silver member.

%%[ else ]%%

You are a valued gold member.

%%[ endif ]%%
```

In the same way, Process Loops can (and typically do) span multiple blocks, as indicated below.

```
<h2>Your Order Items</h2>
<ul>
%%[
var @orderId, @rows, @row, @rowCount, @counter

set @orderId = AttributeValue("OrderId")
set @rows = LookupRows("Orders","OrderId", @orderId)
set @rowCount = rowcount(@rows)

if @rowCount > 0 then

  for @i = 1 to @rowCount do

   var @name, @value
   set @row = row(@rows, @counter)
   set @name = field(@row,"Name")
   set @value = field(@row,"Value")

]%%

   <li>%%=v(@name)=%%, $%%=v(@value)=%%</li>

   %%[ next @i ]%%
```

```
%%[ else ]%%

   <li>No items ordered</li>

%%[ endif ]%%
</ul>
```

Constants

In programming, a constant is a value that never changes. In AMPscript, these predefined or hard-coded values are used to set a fixed value for evaluation or lookup. They can be a constant, numeric, string or a Boolean value.

Numeric Constants

Numeric constants consist of an unquoted set of numerals. They can also include one decimal point and can be prefixed with a minus symbol to indicate negative values. Numeric constants cannot contain commas, as indicated below:

```
%%[

var @discountAmount
set @discountAmount = -10.50

]%%
```

String Constants

String (or text) constant values must use double or single quotes, as indicated in the example here:

```
%%[

var @statusTier
set @statusTier = "Gold"

]%%
```

If quotation marks appear within the text, string constants can escape the delimiting quote when their quote type is switched (to single or double). Alternative quote characters, such as smart quotes, are not supported.

```
%%[

var @bonusProduct
```

```
set @bonusProduct = 'Our "Uber" Umbrella'

]%%
```

Boolean Constants

Boolean constant values must use **`true`** or **`false`** values and are case-insensitive, as shown in the example below:

```
%%[

var @statusTier, @freeShipping
set @statusTier = AttributeValue("Tier Level")

if @statusTier == "Gold" then /* string constant */
  set @freeShipping = true /* Boolean constant */
endif

]%%
```

Attributes

Attribute Strings and other Personalization Strings can also be used with AMPscript. However, in this case, the double percentage delimiters (**`%%`**) should not be included.

If the Attribute includes a space character or hyphen, the string must be contained in brackets when used in an AMPscript function.

In the example below, a Sendable Data Extension includes the fields 'MemberID', 'First Name' and 'Order-Amount':

```
%%[

var @memberId, @firstName, @orderAmount

set @memberId = MemberID
set @firstName = [First Name]
set @orderAmount = [Order-Amount]

]%%
```

If a personalization string is included in AMPscript but is not available in the message context (for example, the corresponding field does not appear in the Sendable Data Extension), then an error will be returned. However, when personalization strings are included as an input argument in an AttributeValue function, then the function will output a null value if the attribute is not available.

Statements

The **if** statement allows the conditional evaluation of one or more expressions, which, if it evaluates to **true**, will process the block of code within it.

An **if** statement, at a minimum, must contain three elements:

1. an opening **if** statement
2. a **then** statement preceding the expression for evaluation
3. a closing **endif** statement.

Expressions within an **if** statement can include the following types:

- Constants
- Variables
- Attributes
- Personalization Strings
- Function Calls

Example 1

In the following example, the **@group** variable will only be **set** if the value of **@ age** is greater than or equal to 18:

```
%%[

var @age, @group
set @age = 12

if @age >= 18 then
  set @group = "adult"
endif

]%%
```

An **else** statement can also be included in conjunction with an **if** statement, to specify a block of code, if the same condition evaluates to false.

Example 2

In the following example, if the value of **@age** is greater than or equal to 18, then the **@group** variable will only be **set** to **adult**, otherwise it will be set to **child**.

```
%%[

var @age, @group
set @age = 12

if @age >= 18 then
  set @group = "adult"
else
  set @group = "child"
endif

]%%

<p>Group is %%=v(@group)=%%</p>
```

Output

The first expression evaluates to **false**, so the following output will be displayed:

```
<p>Group is child</p>
```

An **elseif** statement can be used to specify a new expression to evaluate, if the preceding condition evaluates to **false**. If multiple **elseif** statements are included, each expression is evaluated in the order that they are displayed, until an expression evaluates to **true**.

Example 3

```
%%[

var @age, @group
set @age = 12

if @age < 1 then
  set @group = "infant"
elseif @age < 3 then
  set @group = "toddler"
elseif @age < 18 then
  set @group = "child"
else
  set @group = "adult"
endif

]%%

<p>Group is %%=v(@group)=%%</p>
```

Output

In the above example, the first two expressions evaluate to **false**, but the third evaluates to **true**, so the following result will be displayed:

```
<p>Group is child</p>
```

Comparison Operators

Comparison operators are used to compare two values, or operands. The result of the evaluation will return a Boolean result. There are six comparison operators available in AMPscript.

The operands need to be the same type; for example, string, date, number or Boolean:

Operator	Description
==	is equal to
!=	is not equal to
>	is greater than
<	is less than
>=	is greater than or equal to
<=	is less than or equal to

String operands can only use `==` or `!==` operators for comparison. String comparisons are evaluated as case-insensitive, so **`"GOLD" == "gold"`** will evaluate to **`true`**.

Example 1

The example below indicates a string comparison (in the AMPscript block) and a Boolean comparison (in inline AMPscript):

```
%%[

var @statusTier, @freeShipping
set @statusTier = AttributeValue("Tier Level")
set @goldStatus = "Gold"

if @statusTier == "Gold" then
  set @freeShipping = true
endif

]%%

<p>You %%=Iif(@freeShipping != true, "do not
qualify","qualify")=%% for free shipping.</p>
```

Output

If the value of the 'Tier Level' attribute is equal to 'Silver', then the following output will be displayed:

```
<p>You do not qualify for free shipping.</p>
```

If the value of the 'Tier Level' attribute is equal to 'Gold', then the following output will be displayed:

```
<p>You qualify for free shipping.</p>
```

Example 2

```
%%[

var @scheduledDate, @currentDate, @dispatched
set @scheduledDate = AttributeValue("Scheduled Shipment
Date")
set @currentDate = SystemDateToLocalDate(Now())

if @scheduledDate < @currentDate then
  set @dispatched = true
endif

]%%
```

```
<p>Your order has %%=Iif(@dispatched == true, "shipped","not
shipped")=%%.</p>
```

Output

If the value of the 'Scheduled Shipment Date' attribute is earlier than the current date (for example, '2/15/2015'), then the following output will be displayed:

```
<p>Your order has shipped.</p>
```

If the value of the 'Scheduled Shipment Date' attribute is later than the current date (for example, '1/11/2025'), then the following output will be displayed:

```
<p>Your order has not shipped.</p>
```

Logical Operators

While Comparison Operators can only compare two values, logical operators can be used to join multiple conditions.

Two types of operators are supported; **`or`** and **`and`**. Two or more logical operators can be used to evaluate an expression.

> **NOTE:** when using Einstein Email Recommendations in AMPscript statements to compare a constant, product, or catalog attribute, use **||** for an **`or`** logical operator and **`&&`** for an **`and`** logical operator.

Example 1

```
%%[

var @statusTier, @amount, @freeShipping
set @statusTier = "Gold"
set @amount = 125

if @statusTier == "Gold" and @amount > 100 then
  set @freeShipping = true
endif

]%%

<p>You %%=Iif(@freeShipping == true, "qualify","do not
qualify")=%% for free shipping.</p>
```

Output

In the above example, both expressions evaluate to **`true`**, therefore the following output will be displayed:

```
<p>You qualify for free shipping.</p>
```

Example 2

```
%%[

var @statusTier, @amount, @freeShipping
set @statusTier = "Gold"
set @amount = 90

if @statusTier == "Gold" or @amount > 100 then
  set @freeShipping = true
endif

]%%

<p>You %%=Iif(@freeShipping == true, "qualify","do not
qualify")=%% for free shipping.</p>
```

Output
In the above example, the first expression evaluates to **true** and the second evaluates to **false**. However as an **or** operator is used to join the expressions, the following output will be displayed:

```
<p>You qualify for free shipping.</p>
```

Controlling Expression Evaluation

Parentheses can be used to control the order of operation for evaluating expressions.

Example 1
In this scenario, free shipping should only be offered to bronze or silver members who spend over $500.

```
%%[

var @statusTier, @amount, @freeShipping
set @statusTier = "Bronze"
set @amount = 300

if @statusTier == "Bronze" or @statusTier == "Silver" and
@amount > 500 then
  set @freeShipping = true
```

```
endif

]%%

<p>You %%=Iif(@freeShipping == true, "qualify","do not
qualify")=%% for free shipping.</p>
```

Output

The join operators in the above **`if`** statement will be evaluated as a single expression and will produce the following result:

```
<p>You qualify for free shipping.</p>
```

Example 2

By modifying the first example to include parentheses, the expression evaluation can be controlled into two expressions.

```
%%[

var @statusTier, @amount, @freeShipping
set @statusTier = "Bronze"
set @amount = 300

if (@statusTier == "Bronze" or @statusTier == "Silver") and
@amount > 500 then
  set @freeShipping = true
endif

]%%

<p>You %%=Iif(@freeShipping == true, "qualify","do not
qualify")=%% for free shipping.</p>
```

Output

While the first expression evaluated to **`true`**, the **`@amount`** was less than **`500`**, so the following message is displayed:

```
<p>You do not qualify for free shipping.</p>
```

Not Operator

A **not** operator can be used to reverse the logic of a Boolean evaluation.

Example 1

```
%%[

var @statusTier, @amount, @freeShipping
set @statusTier = "Gold"
set @amount = 125

if @statusTier == "Gold" and not @amount > 100 then
  set @freeShipping = true
endif

]%%

<p>You %%=Iif(@freeShipping == true, "qualify","do not
qualify")=%% for free shipping.</p>
```

Output

In the above example, the logic evaluation of the second expression is reversed, so the following output will be displayed:

```
<p>You not qualify for free shipping.</p>
```

Example 2

The **not** operator can also be used to reverse the evaluation of an AMPscript function:

```
<p>Dear %%=Iif(not Empty(FirstName), FirstName,
"Member")=%%,</p>
```

Output

In this example, if the 'FirstName' attribute is not empty, then the attribute will be displayed; otherwise the constant value 'Member' will be displayed:

```
<p>Dear Member,</p>
```

Process Loops

A process loop enables code or content within a block to be repeated until an ending index expression is reached. There are seven required parts in a process loop:

1. an opening **`for`** statement
2. a loop counter, defined as a variable
3. a starting index expression
4. a direction keyword; either **`to`** (to increase) or **`downto`** (to decrease)
5. an ending index expression
6. a **`do`** keyword
7. a **`next`** keyword

The opening **`for`** statement initializes the process loop. The scope of counter variable is different from other AMPscript variables (which have a local scope). This variable is set as a global scope and is locked from modification within the process loop.

> **NOTE:** The counter variable is locked from modification within a process loop. Any attempt to declare it will result in a validation or runtime error.

The start and end index expressions must evaluate to an integer (not a decimal) and can use one of the following input types:

1. a numeric constant
2. an attribute or Data Extension value
3. a variable
4. a function

The direction keyword determines whether the value of the variable increases or decreases by one with each iteration of the **`for`** loop. The variable value sets or increments by one after each iteration of the loop.

The **`next`** statement closes the **`for`** loop. When the **`next`** keyword is reached, the system compares the end index expression to the value of the counter variable. If the value is not equal to the end index, the loop will repeat until the end index is reached.

Example 1

The following example sets the starting index as **1** and the ending index as **5**:

```
%%[

var @counter
for @counter = 1 to 5 do

]%%

   %%=v(@counter)=%%

%%[ next ]%%
```

Output

```
1
2
3
4
5
```

Example 2

Optionally, the **next** statement can be followed with the counter variable name:

```
%%[

var @counter

for @counter = 5 downto 1 do

]%%

   %%=v(@counter)=%%

%%[ next @counter ]%%
```

Output

```
5
4
3
2
1
```

Example 3

A common use case for AMPscript process loops is to look up multiple values from a Data Extension for a Contact or Subscriber; for example order line items to include in an order confirmation email.

The following code retrieves 'Name' and 'Price' fields from a Data Extension for rows that match an order number attribute. The number of matching rows is counted using the RowCount function and the field values are displayed as list items for the returned rows.

```
<ul>

%%[

var @lineItems, @countLineItems, @orderNumber, @counter

set @orderNumber = AttributeValue('Order Number')
set @lineItems = LookupRows('Order Line Items','Order
Number',@orderNumber)
set @countLineItems = RowCount(@lineItems)

if @countLineItems > 0 then

  for @counter = 1 to @countLineItems do
    var @lineItem, @name, @price

    set @lineItem = row(@lineItems, @counter)
    set @name = field(@lineItem,'Name')
    set @price = field(@lineItem,'Price')
]%%

  <li>%%=v(@name)=%%, %%=v(@price)=%%</li>

%%[ next @counter ]%%
```

```
%%[ else ]%%
%%[ RaiseError('No Rows Found!') ]%%
%%[ endif ]%%

</ul>
```

Output

```
<ul>
  <li>Mens Large Jacket, $85.50</li>
  <li>Red Socks, $9.60</li>
  <li>Grey Wool Scarf, $32.80</li>
</ul>
```

Dynamic Link Tracking

AMPscript enables dynamic content to be included as an alias attribute in html anchor links within HTML email content. In turn, these values are available in email engagement reports.

Example

In this example, a 'Country' value is retrieved from a 'Members' Data Extension based on a matching 'Subscriber Key' value. In turn, click engagement can be tracked based on a Subscriber's country.

```
<a href="https://limedash.com"
alias="%%=Lookup('Members','Country','Subscriber Key',
_subscriberKey)=%%">Offer</a>
```

> **NOTE:** Marketing Cloud limits the number of unique resolved alias values to 100. If the number of unique alias names is greater than 100, the additional links will only be tracked by the link name, not by the alias name.

Execution Context

When creating web-based content — either landing pages, Web Collect or Smart Capture forms — the execution context of the page ('load' or 'post') can be detected by the global, read-only variable **`@@ExecCtx`**.

The variable returns the execution context of the page request. If the page request does not specify a context, the variable defaults to **`load`**.

> **NOTE:** In current release of Marketing Cloud, the **`@@ExecCtx`** variable will always return **`load`**, irrespective of the context. This is a known issue and should be resolved in a future release.

Example

In the following example, a form is displayed when the page is loaded:

```
%%[ if @@ExecCtx == "load" then ]%%

    <form action="%%=RequestParameter('PAGEURL')=%%"
method="post">
        <label>Name</label><input type="text"
name="name"><br>
        <label>Email</label><input type="text"
name="email"><br>
        <input type="submit">
    </form>
%%[ elseif @@ExecCtx == "post" then ]%%
%%[
   var @name, @email
   set @name = RequestParameter('name')
   set @email = RequestParameter('email')
   UpsertData("Form Submissions",1,"email",@email,"name",@name)
]%%
    <p>Your form has been submitted</p>
%%[ endif ]%%
```

Output

When the form is submitted, the execution context will be **`post`** and the following actions will occur:

1. The form data will be upserted to a 'Form Submissions' Data Extension
2. The message 'Your form has been submitted' will be displayed on the page, instead of the form.

Script Blocks

Script blocks can also be included within code blocks to whether the containing code should be interpreted. Two attributes can be included in a script block: **`name`** and **`type`**.

Example 1

In the example below, the **`HTTPGet`** function will only be executed if the execution context is 'post'.

```
%%[

[type="post"] HTTPGet("https://limedash.com/webhook")

]%%
```

Example 2

In the example below, the **`HTTPGet`** function will only be executed if the execution context is 'post' and the name **`callback`** is specified.

```
%%[

[name="callback";type="post"] HTTPGet("https://limedash.com/
webhook")

]%%
```

> **NOTE:** Script blocks must be completed within the same script block section. For example, if the script block includes an **`if`** statement, the **`endif`** statement must reside within the same script block.

Personalization Strings

Overview

Most digital marketing platforms offer personalization strings, which may be referred to as *merge fields*, *merge tags* or *substitution strings*, depending on the platform. This support allows a string-based identifier, enclosed in a delimiter, to be included on a page or in a message, and when the content is published or sent, the string is substituted with Subscriber data or a defined, system-derived value.

Marketing Cloud supports two types of personalization strings: attribute-based and system-based. Personalization strings are not part of the AMPscript language. However, they can be used with AMPscript within conditional statements, variable definitions or function arguments.

Syntax

Personalization strings are enclosed within double percentage delimiters; for example, **`%%string%%`**. However, these delimiters should not be included when used in an AMPscript function (refer to Attributes). The containing string is case-insensitive.

> **NOTE:** If the attribute name contains a non-alphanumeric character, then it must be enclosed in square brackets.

```
%%[

var @firstName, @age
set @firstName = [First Name]
set @age = Age

]%%
```

Attribute Strings

Attribute data strings are used to personalize content based on the context of the Contact or Subscriber that they are sent to. These values are derived from a field or attribute related to the Contact or Subscriber that the message is sent to. These can include the following data sources:

- Email Subscriber Profile Attributes
- Sendable Data Extension Fields
- Journey Builder Entry Source Attributes
- MobileConnect List Attributes
- MobilePush Attributes
- Journey Builder Entry Source.

System Strings

Marketing Cloud includes a library of system-based personalization strings which can be included in a message or on a page to output a value, based on the context of the Subscriber, Contact or a message.

Email Date Strings

> **NOTE:** Date-based personalization strings use the system time (the data center location of your Marketing Cloud account) and appear in US format. However, these values can be transformed using AMPscript date functions.

String	Description	Example Output
`xtmonth`	Full name of the month when email is sent	`January`
`xtmonthnumeric`	Current month as a number	`1`
`xtday`	Current day of the month when the email was sent	`15`
`xtdayofweek`	Current day of the week when the email was sent	`Monday`
`xtyear`	Current year when the email was sent	`2018`
`xtshortdate`	Current date when the email was sent in short format	`01/15/2018`
`xtlongdate`	Current date when the email was sent in long format	`Monday, January 15, 2018`

Example

This example will update a date field in a Data Extension with the system time when an email is sent, which can be used as a suppression Data Extension for future sends:

```
InsertDE("Sent Subscribers","Member ID", _subscriberkey,"sent
date",xtshortdate)
```

Email Data Strings

String	Description	Example Output
`emailname_`	Name assigned to the email	`Spring Newsletter`
`_messagecontext`	the context in which the Subscriber viewed the message or page. Either: **`SEND`** – an email that is sent to a Subscriber **`PREVIEW`** – an email that is previewed within the email editor **`VAWP`** – an email opened as 'view as web page' (from a **`view_email_url`** link in an email) **`FTAF`** – an email that is sent as a 'Forward to a Friend' message **`LANDINGPAGE`** – content is viewed on a landing page, microsite page or CloudPage code resource **`VALIDATION`** – email is validated using the validation option in Marketing Cloud **`LINKRESOLUTION`** – a URL in an email that is resolved as a click-through link **`SMS`** – an SMS message that is sent to a Subscriber **`SOCIAL`** – email content that is shared using the Social Forward feature	Refer to Description
`_replycontent`	Used in a Triggered Send Email that has been set as the 'Triggered send to forward' option in a Sender Profile when Reply Mail Management is configured. Returns the email body that was included in the reply message.	Refer to Description
`_IsTestSend`	Resolves to **`true`** if the email was sent as a Test Send from Email Studio, otherwise the value is **`false`**	`false`
`jobid`	Returns the unique job identifier related to the email send	`3210123`
`_PreHeader`	The preheader attribute assigned to the email. This string only returns a value when used in an AttributeValue function. For example, **`%%=AttributeValue ("_Preheader")=%%`**	`30% off store-wide, this weekend only!`

Subscriber Data Strings

String	Description	Example Output
`emailaddr`	The email address of the Subscriber	`leon@limedash.com`
`firstname_` or `firstname`	The Subscriber's first name from the 'FirstName' Subscriber Profile Attribute	`Leon`
`lastname_` or `lastname`	The Subscriber's last name from the 'LastName' Subscriber Profile Attribute	`Green`
`subscriberid`	A system-defined numeric identifier representing a Subscriber	`1234`
`_subscriberkey`	A user-defined unique identifier representing a Subscriber	`M123456`
`listid`	The corresponding list identifier of the Subscriber; returns the All Subscribers list id if the email is not sent to a specific list	`12345`
`list_`	The `listid` value suffixed with an underscore character and the email type (either `TEXT` or `HTML`)	`12345_HTML`
`listsubid`	A system-defined identifier representing the Subscriber's relationship to the list	`987654321`
`_messagetypepreference`	The Subscriber's preferred email type, as defined as in the HTML Emails Attribute in the Subscriber record; either `TEXT` or `HTML`	`HTML`
`_listname`	The user-defined list name; returns an empty value if the All Subscribers list is used	`VIP Members`
`_emailid`	The system-defined numeric identifier of the email	`33345`
`_JobSubscriberBatchID`	A numeric identifier of the batch associated with a Triggered Email; this value defaults to 0 for a List send	`5554321`

String	Description	Example Output
`_DataSourceName`	The value of the List, Group, Sendable Data Extension or Data Extension Filter related to the email send; returns an empty value if the All Subscribers list is used	`VIP Members`

Sender Data Strings

String	Description	Example Output
`replyname`	The email From name, retrieved from the Sender Information in the Sender Profile, or the selected user profile	`Limedash Corporation`
`replyemailaddress`	The email From email address, retrieved from the Sender Information in the Sender Profile, or the selected user profile	`marketing@email.limedash.com`
`memberid`	The member identifier (MID) of the Business Unit which the email is sent from	`6541234`
`member_busname`	The 'Company Name' value defined for the Business Unit which the email is sent from	`Limedash Corporation, Inc.`
`member_addr`	The 'Street Address' value defined for the Business Unit which the email is sent from	`4463 Shinn Street`
`member_city`	The 'City' value defined for the Business Unit which the email is sent from	`New York`
`member_state`	The 'State/Province' value defined for the Business Unit which the email is sent from	`NY`
`member_postalcode`	The 'Zip/Postal Code' value defined for the Business Unit which the email is sent from	`10019`
`member_country`	The 'Country' value defined for the Business Unit which the email is sent from	`United States`

Email URL Data Strings

String	Description	Example Output
`view_email_url`	URL to view the email	`http://view.s6.exacttarget.com/?qs=17f9ecc7fcd5...`
`ftaf_url`	URL to a Forward to a Friend form page	`http://view.s6.exacttarget.com/ftaf.aspx?qs=17f9ecce47fcd...`
`subscription_center_url`	URL of the Subscriber's Subscription Center	`http://cl.s6.exct.net/subscription_center.aspx?qs=8ecce2c86ef063c...`
`profile_center_url`	URL of the Subscriber's Profile Center	`http://cl.s6.exct.net/profile_center.aspx?qs=8ecce2c86ef063c31effc761`
`unsub_center_url`	URL of the Subscriber's One-Click Unsubscribe page	`http://cl.s6.exct.net/unsub_center.aspx?qs=8ecce2c86ef063c3...`
`double_opt_in_url`	Inserts a double opt-in link in an email if this feature is enabled	`http://cl.exct.net/sub_confirm.asp?lst=1234&eml=...`

MobileConnect Data Strings

MobileConnect messages use *nouns* and *verbs*. A verb is a keyword used in a Mobile Originated (MO) message. Nouns are strings that appear after the keyword. In the example below, **`OFFER`** is the keyword, or verb, of the message and **`Curt Harris`** forms the message nouns.

```
OFFER Curt Harris
```

String	Description	Example Output
`MOBILE_NUMBER`	The mobile number of the Contact, prefixed with an area code	`17182097651`
`SHORT_CODE`	The associated short or long code used to send the message	`111322` (*short code*) or `19172759833` (*long code*)
`MSG(0)`	The entire message	`OFFER Curt Harris`
`MSG(0).VERB`	The message keyword	`OFFER`
`MSG(0).NOUNS`	The part of the message after the verb	`Curt Harris`
`MSG(0).NOUN([n])`	Returns the 'n' noun in the current message using a zero-based index, (`0` returns the first noun, `1` returns the second noun etc.)	`MSG(0).NOUN(0) = Curt`
`MMS_CONTENT_URL([n])`	Similar to **`MSG(0)`** but used for MMS messages. Returns the URL of the MMS content from the incoming MO message, where 'n' is the zero-based index of the MMS content contained in the MO message. A value of `0` indicates the MMS content in the current MO message.	`http://exacttarget.com/mms.aspx?qs=17f9ecce47fcd`

Example

This example code is used in a text response template and inserts the message into a Data Extension when a Contact replies to a text response message.

```
%%[

InsertData('SMS
Responses','mobile',MOBILE _NUMBER,'keyword',MSG(0).VERB,
'response',MSG(0).NOUNS)

]%%
```

GroupConnect Data Strings

The following strings apply only to GroupConnect messages and cannot be used in other Marketing Cloud applications. Some strings are specific to integration with the LINE messaging application.

String	Description	Example Output
`LINE_ADDRESS_ID`	Unique LINE ID of a person	`eliotharper`
`LINE_JOB_ID`	Unique LINE job identifier	`b409facab49447eb8 f1d489e5473bf5e`
`LINE_SUBSCRIBER_ID`	Corresponding Subscriber identifier in Marketing Cloud	`8765432`
`TEXT`	The entire message	`OFFER Lily Baker`
`VERB`	The first word in the message	`OFFER`
`TEXT.NOUN`	All words after the verb	`Lily Baker`
`TEXT.NOUN([n])`	Returns the 'n' noun in the current message using a zero-based index, (0 returns the first noun, 1 returns the second noun etc.)	`MSG(0).NOUN(0)` = `Lily`
`STKR.STKPKGID`	Package ID associated with the specified sticker (for LINE messages containing a sticker)	`1234`
`STKR.STKID`	ID associated with the specified sticker (for LINE messages containing a sticker)	`5678`
`STKR.STKTXT`	Text associated with the specified sticker (for LINE messages containing a sticker)	`happy`

Website Data Strings

The following strings apply only to landing pages, microsites and CloudPages and cannot be used in other Marketing Cloud applications.

String	Description	Example Output
microsite_base_url[default]ID[/default]	URL to a microsite landing page. Replace **ID** with the unique ID value for the landing page. This string is for classic landing pages and does not function in CloudPages.	**https://pub.s1.exacttarget.com/page.aspx?qs=1550dccf35ce...**
PAGEURL	URL of current landing page with URL parameters	**https://pub.s1.exacttarget.com/lcuh4w3abc?subscriber=12345**

Email Analytics Strings

String	Description	Example Output
`linkname`	The value entered in the `alias` link attribute. If no value is specified, it contains the complete URL.	`CTA`
`_ImpressionRegionID`	Returns the ID of the Impression Region. Contains 0 if there are no active Impression Regions.	`1`
`_ImpressionRegionName`	Returns the name of the active Impression Region defined in the email.	`heading`
`AdditionalInfo_`	The value entered into the Additional Info field when sending an email. This value is appended to email links as a URL parameter. This feature requires the Web Analytics Connector to be enabled.	`summeroffer`
`__AdditionalEmailAttribute[n]`	The values entered into the Additional Email Attributes fields when sending an email, where `[n]` is an integer from 1 to 5 (up to five Additional Email Attributes are supported). These values are appended to email links as a URL parameter. This feature requires the Web Analytics Connector to be enabled.	`segment1`

Einstein Email Data Strings

The following strings can be used for formatting and sanitizing Einstein Email Recommendation data. These strings differ from other system personalization strings in that they behave similar to a function, where the string value is interpreted based on arguments within the string construct.

String	Description	Example Output
`RegularPriceMain`	Outputs the integer part (before the decimal) of the field mapped to `RegularPrice` or `Price` for streaming updates	`65`
`SalePriceMain`	Outputs the integer part (before the decimal) of the field mapped to `SalePrice`	`42`
`RegularPriceFractional`	Outputs the fractional part (integer after the decimal) of the field mapped to `RegularPrice` or `Price` for streaming updates	`99`
`SalePriceFractional`	Outputs the fractional part (integer after the decimal) of the field mapped to `SalePrice` for streaming updates	`50`
`ToFloat`	Converts the value of a string field in a Catalog to a floating-point number	`12.25`
`[a]LongestWordLength`	Calculates the longest word in an attribute and outputs the length of that word as a number, where `[a]` is the attribute	For a Description attribute with the string 'Also available in black', `%%DescriptionLongestWordLength%%` will output 9.

String	Description	Example Output
`[a]LengthNum`	Returns the length of a Catalog attribute, where **[a]** is the attribute	For a Description with the string 'One size only', **%%Description LengthNum%%** will output **13**.
`First[n]`	Outputs the first characters of value, where **[n]** is an integer	**%%SKUFirst5%%** will output **ABC123**
`Split[d]At[i]`	Splits a value and returns the given index, where **[d]** is the delimiter and **[i]** is a zero-based index. The delimiter can be longer than one character and the index can be negative.	For a Size attribute with the string 'small;medium;large' , **%%Split;At1%%** will output **medium**.
`[a]Replace[r]With[w] End`	Globally replaces a given string with another string from a Catalog attribute, where **[a]** is the attribute, **[r]** is the string to match and **[w]** is the string to replace	For a Color attribute with the string 'Purple', **%%Color ReplacePurpleWith LavenderEnd%%** will output **Lavender**.
`[a]UpTo[n]By[d] With[o]End`	Outputs the value of a Catalog attribute up to an index with an appended string (if included), where **[a]** is the attribute, **[i]** is a whole number of characters to evaluate, **[d]** is the delimiter and **[o]** is the optional string into append. Values shorter than the limit output unaltered and values without a delimiter that match within the limit output blank.	For a Size attribute with the string 'small;medium;large', **%%SizeUpTo14By; With~End%%** will output **small;medium~**.

Chaining

When using Einstein Email Data Strings, strings can be chained together into a single string. The example below illustrates that for a **`ProductName`** attribute with a value **`Vintage Cruiser Bike`**, **`Vintage`** is changed to **`Classic`** and the product name is displayed in uppercase.

```
%%ProductNameReplaceVintageWithClassicEndToUpCase%%
```

This string renders the following output:

```
CLASSIC CRUISER BIKE
```

Marketing Cloud API Functions

Overview

These AMPscript functions provide a means for interacting with the Marketing Cloud SOAP API in the context of a microsite page, CloudPage or MobileConnect SMS message. While they are more verbose than the regular AMPscript functions, these API functions do provide some additional granularity of interaction with the platform.

It is helpful to be familiar with the SOAP API Objects and Methods, specifically the SOAP Envelopes in order to get the most out of these functions.

You might these functions them when you need to retrieve data from a Data Extension beyond the criteria limitations of the regular Data Extension Lookup functions or interact with other Marketing Cloud objects that do not have a corresponding AMPscript function (for example, AccountUser, ListSubscriber, DataFolder, QueryDefinition, ContentArea, etc.).

> **NOTE:** In order to utilize these functions, Web Services must be enabled in your Marketing Cloud account. These functions do not work in the context of an email.

AddObjectArrayItem

This function adds an object to a Marketing Cloud API Object array.

Arguments

`AddObjectArrayItem(1,2,3)`

Ordinal	Type	Required	Description
1	API Object	True	The API Object that contains the array
2	String	True	The array property associated with the item to be added
3	String	True	The item to add to the array

Example

The following example retrieves all of the **`DataFolder`** objects in a Marketing Cloud account. The **`AddObjectArrayItem()`** lines are used to add the object attributes to retrieve in the request (**`ID`** and **`Name`**).

```
%%[

var @rr, @ID, @Name
set @rr = CreateObject("RetrieveRequest")
SetObjectProperty(@rr, "ObjectType", "DataFolder")
AddObjectArrayItem(@rr, "Properties", "ID")
AddObjectArrayItem(@rr, "Properties", "Name")

set @dataFolders = InvokeRetrieve(@rr, @rrStatus,
@rrRequestID)

output(concat("rrStatus: ", @rrStatus))
output(concat("<br>rrRequestID: ", @rrRequestID))

for @i = 1 to RowCount(@dataFolders) do

  set @dataFolder = Row(@dataFolders, @i)
  set @ID = Field(@dataFolder, "ID")
  set @Name = Field(@dataFolder, "Name")

  output(concat("<br>ID: ", @ID, ", Name: ", @Name))

next @i

]%%
```

Output

```
rrStatus: OK
rrRequestID: 9a64813a-0aa1-497b-8cb6-c6030531b3b1
ID: 13738, Name: my emails
ID: 13739, Name: simple automated emails
ID: 13740, Name: my templates
ID: 13741, Name: my lists
ID: 13742, Name: my tracking
ID: 13743, Name: my contents
ID: 13744, Name: my documents
ID: 13745, Name: my surveys
ID: 13746, Name: my images
ID: 13747, Name: Portfolio
ID: 13748, Name: my groups
ID: 13749, Name: my subscribers
ID: 13750, Name: Forward to a Friend
ID: 13751, Name: Forward to a Friend
ID: 13752, Name: Suppression Lists
ID: 13753, Name: Triggered Sends
ID: 13754, Name: User-Initiated
ID: 13755, Name: Data Extensions
ID: 13756, Name: Publication Lists
ID: 13757, Name: my microsites
ID: 13758, Name: microsite layouts
ID: 13760, Name: Query
ID: 13761, Name: Data Filters
ID: 13762, Name: Filter
ID: 13763, Name: Social
ID: 13764, Name: A/B Testing
ID: 13765, Name: my workflows
ID: 25111, Name: Journey Builder Sends
ID: 58137, Name: HiddenCategory
ID: 58138, Name: SystemHiddenDataFilters
ID: 58139, Name: SystemHiddenDataFiltersForGE
ID: 58140, Name: SystemHiddenFilterActivities
ID: 58141, Name: SystemHiddenFilterActivitiesForGE
ID: 58142, Name: my automations
ID: 58547, Name: Salesforce Single Sends
ID: 58548, Name: Salesforce Mass Sends
ID: 58549, Name: Salesforce Sends
ID: 58550, Name: Salesforce Data Extensions
```

CreateObject

This function instantiates the specified Marketing Cloud API Object.

> **NOTE:** Instantiated objects do not persist after the first subsequent Invoke function call (for example, **`InvokeRetrieve()`**, **`InvokeUpdate()`**, etc.).

Argument

`CreateObject(1)`

Ordinal	Type	Required	Description
1	String	True	The name of the API Object to instantiate

Example

The following example retrieves all of the **`DataExtenion`** objects in a specific DataFolder (**`CategoryID`**). The **`CreateObject()`** line specifies the object to instantiate.

```
%%[

var @rr, @CategoryID, @Name, @CustomerKey
set @rr = CreateObject("RetrieveRequest")
SetObjectProperty(@rr, "ObjectType", "DataExtension")
AddObjectArrayItem(@rr, "Properties", "CategoryID")
AddObjectArrayItem(@rr, "Properties", "Name")
AddObjectArrayItem(@rr, "Properties", "CustomerKey")

set @sfp = CreateObject("SimpleFilterPart")
SetObjectProperty(@sfp, "Property", "CategoryID")
SetObjectProperty(@sfp, "SimpleOperator", "equals")
AddObjectArrayItem(@sfp, "Value", "13755")

SetObjectProperty(@rr,"Filter", @sfp)

set @rows = InvokeRetrieve(@rr, @rrStatus, @rrRequestID)

output(concat("rrStatus: ", @rrStatus))
output(concat("<br>rrRequestID: ", @rrRequestID))
```

```
for @i = 1 to RowCount(@rows) do

  set @row = Row(@rows, @i)
  set @CategoryID = Field(@row, "CategoryID")
  set @Name = Field(@row,"Name")
  set @CustomerKey = Field(@row, "CustomerKey")

  output(concat("<br>CategoryID: ", @CategoryID, ", Name: ",
@Name, ", CustomerKey: ", @CustomerKey))

next @i

]%%
```

Output

```
rrStatus: OK
rrRequestID: 677010b6-69d4-4839-bf59-b342d3440ca5
CategoryID: 13755, Name: LoyaltyMembers, CustomerKey:
LoyaltyMembers
CategoryID: 13755, Name: CouponCodes, CustomerKey:
CouponCodes
```

InvokeCreate

This function executes the creation of the instantiated Marketing Cloud API Object. The function returns a status code, message and an error code.

API error codes are outlined in the official documentation.

Arguments

`InvokeCreate(1,2,3,4)`

Ordinal	Type	Required	Description
1	API Object	True	The API Object to be created
2	Variable	True	The AMPscript variable in which the resulting status message is stored
3	Variable	True	The AMPscript variable in which the resulting error code is stored
4	API Object	False	The optional CreateOptions API Object

Example

The following example creates a new **DataFolder** object in the specified parent folder. The attributes of the object are specified with the **SetObjectProperty()** function.

```
%%[

var @df, @parentFolder, @createStatusCode,
@createStatusMessage, @createErrorCode
set @df = CreateObject("DataFolder")
SetObjectProperty(@df, "Name", "Test Folder")
SetObjectProperty(@df, "Description", "Test Folder
Description")
SetObjectProperty(@df, "CustomerKey", "Test Folder")
SetObjectProperty(@df, "ContentType", "email")
SetObjectProperty(@df, "IsActive", "true")
SetObjectProperty(@df, "IsEditable", "true")
SetObjectProperty(@df, "AllowChildren", "true")

set @parentFolder = CreateObject("DataFolder")
SetObjectProperty(@parentFolder, "ID", "13738") /* CategoryID
of "my emails" folder */

SetObjectProperty(@df, "ParentFolder", @parentFolder)

set @createStatusCode = InvokeCreate(@df,
@createStatusMessage, @createErrorCode)

]%%
createStatusCode: %%=v(@createStatusCode)=%%
<br>createStatusMessage: %%=v(@createStatusMessage)=%%
<br>createErrorCode: %%=v(@createErrorCode)=%%
```

Output

```
createStatusCode: OK
createStatusMessage: Folder created successfully.
createErrorCode: 0
```

If the **DataFolder** already exists, it will return an error:

```
createStatusCode: Error
createStatusMessage: ParentFolder ID: "13738" already has a
child Folder named "Test Folder". Please select a different
Name.
createErrorCode: 396007
```

InvokeDelete

This function executes the deletion of the instantiated Marketing Cloud API Object. In order to delete an object, you must specify a **ID**, **ObjectID** or **CustomerKey** property for the object. API error codes are outlined in the official documentation.

Arguments

InvokeDelete(1,2,3,4)

Ordinal	Type	Required	Description
1	API Object	True	The API Object to be deleted
2	Variable	True	The AMPscript variable in which the resulting status message is stored
3	Variable	True	The AMPscript variable in which the resulting error code is stored
4	API Object	False	The optional DeleteOptions API Object

Example

The following example deletes an existing **DataFolder** object. The **CustomerKey** property indicates the **DataFolder** to delete. It returns a status code, message and an error code.

```
%%[

var @df, @deleteStatusCode, @deleteStatusMessage,
@deleteErrorCode
set @df = CreateObject("DataFolder")
SetObjectProperty(@df, "CustomerKey", "Test Folder")

set @deleteStatusCode = InvokeDelete(@df,
@deleteStatusMessage, @deleteErrorCode)

]%%
deleteStatusCode: %%=v(@deleteStatusCode)=%%
<br>deleteStatusMessage: %%=v(@deleteStatusMessage)=%%
<br>deleteErrorCode: %%=v(@deleteErrorCode)=%%
```

Output

```
deleteStatusCode: OK
deleteStatusMessage: Folder deleted successfully.
deleteErrorCode: 0
```

If the **DataFolder** is not found, it will return an error:

```
deleteStatusCode: Error
deleteStatusMessage: Folder with CustomerKey: "Test Folder "
could not be found.
deleteErrorCode: 396009
```

InvokeExecute

This function executes the instantiated Marketing Cloud API Object. It returns a **`RequestID`** value (because it is executed asynchronously), an API Object containing a status message and an error code value.

Arguments

`InvokeExecute(1,2,3)`

Ordinal	Type	Required	Description
1	API Object	True	The API Object to be executed
2	String	True	The AMPscript variable in which the resulting status message is stored
3	Variable	True	The AMPscript variable in which the resulting RequestID is stored

Example

The following example logs an unsubscribe event for a specific email Subscriber.

```
%%[

set @er = CreateObject("ExecuteRequest")
SetObjectProperty(@er,"Name","LogUnsubEvent")

set @prop = CreateObject("APIProperty")
SetObjectProperty(@prop, "Name", "SubscriberKey")
SetObjectProperty(@prop, "Value", "9496")
AddObjectArrayItem(@er, "Parameters", @prop)

set @prop = CreateObject("APIProperty")
SetObjectProperty(@prop, "Name", "Reason")
SetObjectProperty(@prop, "Value", "Hates getting emails")
AddObjectArrayItem(@er, "Parameters", @prop)

set @invokeStatusObj = InvokeExecute(@er,
@invokeStatusMessage, @invokeRequestId)

SET @invokeResponse = Row(@invokeStatusObj, 1)
SET @invokeStatus = Field(@invokeResponse,'StatusMessage')
SET @invokeErrorCode = Field(@invokeResponse,'ErrorCode')

]%%
```

```
invokeStatusMessage: %%=v(@invokeStatusMessage)=%%
<br>invokeRequestId: %%=v(@invokeRequestId)=%%
<br>invokeStatus: %%=v(@invokeStatus)=%%
<br>invokeErrorCode: %%=v(@invokeErrorCode)=%%
```

Output

```
invokeStatusMessage: OK
invokeRequestId: 89d0a3ad-00b8-4347-858b-41b672984359
invokeStatus: Event posted
invokeErrorCode: 0
```

InvokePerform

This function performs the instantiated Marketing Cloud API Object. It returns a status code value and a status message.

> **NOTE:** Only certain API Objects can be performed. Current objects are listed in documentation for the Perform API Method.

Arguments

`InvokePerform(1,2,3)`

Ordinal	Type	Required	Description
1	API Object	True	The API Object to be performed
2	String	True	The action to perform on the object. Must be a valid action for the object specified in the first argument.
3	Variable	False	The AMPscript variable in which the resulting status message is stored

Example

The following example retrieves the **ObjectID** of a **QueryDefinition** and then performs it.

```
%%[

var @rr, @objectID, @queryDefinitions
set @rr = CreateObject("RetrieveRequest")
SetObjectProperty(@rr, "ObjectType", "QueryDefinition")
AddObjectArrayItem(@rr, "Properties", "ObjectID")

set @sfp = CreateObject("SimpleFilterPart")
SetObjectProperty(@sfp, "Property", "CustomerKey")
SetObjectProperty(@sfp, "SimpleOperator", "equals")
AddObjectArrayItem(@sfp, "Value", "LoyaltyMembers")

SetObjectProperty(@rr,"Filter", @sfp)

set @queryDefinitions = InvokeRetrieve(@rr, @rrStatus,
@rrRequestID)

output(concat("rrStatus: ", @rrStatus))
output(concat("<br>rrRequestID: ", @rrRequestID))

if rowcount(@queryDefinitions) > 0 then

  var @queryDefinition, @ObjectID, @obj

  set @queryDefinition = Row(@queryDefinitions, 1)
  set @ObjectID = Field(@queryDefinition, "ObjectID")

  set @obj = CreateObject("QueryDefinition")

  SetObjectProperty(@obj, "ObjectID", @ObjectID)
  Set @performStatusCode = InvokePerform(@obj, "start",
@performStatusMessage)

endif

]%%
<br>queryDefinitions: %%=rowcount(@queryDefinitions)=%%
<br>performStatusCode: %%=v(@performStatusCode)=%%
<br>performStatusMessage: %%=v(@performStatusMessage)=%%
```

Output

```
rrStatus: OK
rrRequestID: 3a78779e-6ed3-44b1-a381-3d5134949445
queryDefinitions: 1
performStatusCode: OK
performStatusMessage: QueryDefinition perform called
successfully
```

InvokeRetrieve

This function retrieves the instantiated Marketing Cloud API Object **`RetrieveRequest`**. It returns a status message and a **`RequestID`** value.

Arguments

`InvokeRetrieve(1,2,3)`

Ordinal	Type	Required	Description
1	API Object	True	The API Object to be retrieved
2	String	False	The AMPscript variable in which the resulting status message is stored
3	Variable	False	The AMPscript variable in which the resulting RequestID is stored

Example

The following example retrieves a list of column names in the **`LoyaltyMembers`** Data Extension.

Data Extension: *LoyaltyMembers*

Name	Data Type	Length	Primary Key	Nullable	Default Value
EmailAddress	EmailAddress	254	N	N	
SubscriberKey	Text	254	Y	N	
FirstName	Text	50	N	Y	
LastName	Text	50	N	Y	
Region	Text	50	N	Y	
Rank	Number		N	Y	
Created	Date		N	Y	Current Date
Updated	Date		N	Y	

```
%%[

var @rr, @ID, @Name
set @rr = CreateObject("RetrieveRequest")
SetObjectProperty(@rr, "ObjectType", "DataExtensionField")
AddObjectArrayItem(@rr, "Properties", "Name")

set @sfp = CreateObject("SimpleFilterPart")
SetObjectProperty(@sfp, "Property", "DataExtension.
CustomerKey")
SetObjectProperty(@sfp, "SimpleOperator", "equals")
AddObjectArrayItem(@sfp, "Value", "LoyaltyMembers")

SetObjectProperty(@rr,"Filter", @sfp)

set @dataExtensions = InvokeRetrieve(@rr, @rrStatus,
@rrRequestID)

output(concat("rrStatus: ", @rrStatus))
output(concat("<br>rrRequestID: ", @rrRequestID))

for @i = 1 to RowCount(@dataExtensions) do

  set @dataExtension = Row(@dataExtensions, @i)
  set @Name = Field(@dataExtension, "Name")

  output(concat("<br>Name: ", @Name))

next @i

]%%
```

Output

```
rrStatus: OK
rrRequestID: d85dedfd-0833-4fe2-bcb1-3a25ad059759
Name: Updated
Name: Created
Name: FirstName
Name: SubscriberKey
Name: Rank
Name: Region
Name: LastName
Name: EmailAddress
```

InvokeUpdate

This function executes an update on the instantiated Marketing Cloud API Object. It returns a status code, message and an error code.

API error codes are outlined in the official documentation.

Arguments

`InvokeUpdate(1,2,3,4)`

Ordinal	Type	Required	Description
1	API Object	True	The API Object to be updated
2	Variable	False	The AMPscript variable in which the resulting status message is stored
3	Variable	False	The AMPscript variable in which the resulting error code is stored
4	API Object	False	The optional UpdateOptions API Object

Example

The following example executes an insert or update on a Subscriber record, setting the Status to **`Active`**. The **`EmailAddress`** and **`SubscriberKey`** are required for creating a new Subscriber.

```
%%[

var @sub, @updateStatusCode, @updateStatusMessage,
@updateErrorCode
set @sub = CreateObject("Subscriber")
SetObjectProperty(@sub, "EmailAddress", "doug@limedash.com")
SetObjectProperty(@sub, "SubscriberKey", "8473")
SetObjectProperty(@sub, "Status", "Active")

set @updateOptions = CreateObject("UpdateOptions")
set @saveOptions = CreateObject("SaveOption")
SetObjectProperty(@saveOptions,"SaveAction","UpdateAdd")
SetObjectProperty(@saveOptions,"PropertyName","*")
AddObjectArrayItem(@updateOptions,"SaveOptions",
@saveOptions)

set @updateStatusCode = InvokeUpdate(@sub,
@updateStatusMessage, @updateErrorCode, @updateOptions)
```

```
]%%
updateStatusCode: %%=v(@updateStatusCode)=%%
<br>updateStatusMessage: %%=v(@updateStatusMessage)=%%
<br>updateErrorCode: %%=v(@updateErrorCode)=%%
```

Output

```
updateStatusCode: OK
updateStatusMessage: Updated Subscriber.
updateErrorCode: 0
```

SetObjectProperty

This function sets a property value for an object created with the CreateObject function.

Arguments

`SetObjectProperty(1,2,3)`

Ordinal	Type	Required	Description
1	API Object	True	The API Object for which the property is set
2	String	True	The name of the property to set
3	String	True	The value of the property

Example

The following example executes an insert or update on a Subscriber record, setting the Status to **`Active`**. The **`SetObjectProperty()`** function is used to set the properties to add to or update the **`Subscriber`** object.

```
%%[

var @sub, @updateStatusCode, @updateStatusMessage,
@updateErrorCode
set @sub = CreateObject("Subscriber")
SetObjectProperty(@sub, "EmailAddress", "barb@limedash.com")
SetObjectProperty(@sub, "SubscriberKey", "5767")
SetObjectProperty(@sub, "Status", "Active")

set @updateOptions = CreateObject("UpdateOptions")
set @saveOptions = CreateObject("SaveOption")
SetObjectProperty(@saveOptions,"SaveAction","UpdateAdd")
SetObjectProperty(@saveOptions,"PropertyName","*")
```

```
AddObjectArrayItem(@updateOptions,"SaveOptions",
@saveOptions)

set @updateStatusCode = InvokeUpdate(@sub,
@updateStatusMessage, @updateErrorCode, @updateOptions)

]%%
updateStatusCode: %%=v(@updateStatusCode)=%%
<br>updateStatusMessage: %%=v(@updateStatusMessage)=%%
<br>updateErrorCode: %%=v(@updateErrorCode)=%%
```

Output

```
updateStatusCode: OK
updateStatusMessage: Updated Subscriber.
updateErrorCode: 0
```

Contact Model Functions

Overview
Marketing Cloud includes a contact model for organizing and creating data relationships for Contacts. This model is administered in Contact Builder, which provides a single view of all Contacts.

Contact Model functions enable interaction with Contact attributes. Currently, one Contact Model function is available.

UpsertContact
This function 'upserts' a Contact in Marketing Cloud. If the Contact does not already exist, then a new record is created. If the Contact exists, then the record is updated.

The function will output `1` if an error occurred when upserting the Contact and `0` if the upsert was successful.

> **NOTE:** This function currently only supports mobile Contacts. Other channels should be supported in a future release.

Arguments

`UpsertContact(1,2,3,4,5,[6a,6b]...)`

Ordinal	Type	Required	Description
1	String	True	The Contact channel. Only `mobile` is supported at this time.
2	String	True	Attribute to match the Contact. Only `phone` is supported at this time.
3	Integer	True	Phone number with country area code
4	String	True	Attribute name to upsert (see Attributes)
5	String or Integer	True	Attribute value to upsert
6a	String	False	Additional attribute name to upsert (see note)
6b	String or Integer	False	Additional attribute value to upsert (see note)

> **NOTE:** Additional attribute name and value pairs can be appended as arguments.

Attributes

You can include user-created attributes and system attributes when upserting mobile Contacts.

User-Created Attributes

To view available user-created attributes or to create new attributes, follow these steps:

1. Open Contact Builder Application.
2. Select the MobileConnect Data Attribute Group from the constellation view in Data Designer.
3. View the user-created attributes in the MobileConnect Demographics Attribute Set, or click 'Create Attribute' to add additional attributes.

System Attributes

The following system attributes are currently supported by this function.

Name	Attribute
City	`_City`
State	`_State`
Zip	`_ZipCode`
First Name	`_FirstName`
Last Name	`_LastName`
UTC Offset	`_UTCOffset`

Example

The following example inserts or updates a mobile Contact record.

```
%%[
var @upsert
set @upsert = UpsertContact("mobile",
                             "phone",13153695271,
                             " _City","Old Forges",
                             " _State","NY",
                             " _ZipCode",13420,
                             " _FirstName","Scott",
                             " _LastName","Jones",
                             " _UTCOffset",-5
                            )
]%%
result: %%=v(@upsert)=%%
```

Output

A value of **0** is set by the function, indicating that no errors occurred.

```
result: 0
```

Content Functions

Overview

The Content AMPscript functions provide a means to interact, reference and output content in a Marketing Cloud account. These elements include Content Areas, Content Builder content blocks, objects in your Portfolio, files from internal or external file locations, and message context data.

AttachFile

This function attaches the specified file to the outbound message or displays a link to the file when included in a landing page. This function returns no output.

The following file types can be attached to email messages in Marketing Cloud:

Extension	Description
`.doc`	Microsoft Word document
`.docx`	Microsoft Word document
`.gif`	GIF image
`.ics`	ICS file
`.jpeg`	JPEG image
`.jpg`	JPEG image
`.mp4`	MPEG-4 video file
`.pdf`	PDF document
`.png`	PNG image
`.ppt`	Microsoft PowerPoint document
`.pptx`	Microsoft PowerPoint document
`.rar`	WinRAR Compressed Archive

Extension	Description
`.tif`	TIFF image
`.tiff`	TIFF image
`.xls`	Microsoft Excel document
`.xlsx`	Microsoft Excel document
`.zip`	ZIP archive

NOTE: Marketing Cloud Support must provision this function for use in your account. There is typically an additional charge per attachment sent. Contact your Salesforce Account Executive to complete the process.

NOTE: If the specified file cannot be found at send time, the send will throw a runtime error and abort.

NOTE: The AttachFile function does support files referenced using the **`HTTPS`** protocol.

NOTE: If you are attaching an external file and the remote server does not respond within 30 seconds, the send will be scheduled to retry 15 minutes later.

NOTE: Local assets in shared Content Builder or Portfolio locations are not supported.

Arguments

`AttachFile(1,2,3,4,5,6,7)`

Ordinal	Type	Required	Description
1	String	True	Type of location containing the file to attach. Valid values include: ▪ `ContentBuilder` ▪ **`FTP`** ▪ **`HTTP`** ▪ **`Portfolio`** (Classic Content)
2	String	True	Path or key of the asset to attach. Specify the following for the preceding location: ▪ **`ContentBuilder`** – Customer/External Key of asset ▪ **`FTP`** – Name of file in the Enhanced SFTP Import Folder ▪ **`HTTP`** – HTTP/HTTPS URL of the asset ▪ **`Portfolio`** – Customer/External Key of asset in Classic Content
3	String	False	Alias assigned to file when attached. If no value is specified, the name of the file is used. If you do not specify an alias for **`HTTP`** type asset, the **`Content-Disposition`** from the HTTP header will be used. If no **`Content-Disposition`** is provided, a system-generated value will be returned.
4	Boolean	False	Show link to file in the *View as a Web Page* context. Default value is **`false`**. This argument can only be used with the **`HTTP`** location type.
5	String	False	URL of the attachment to use in the *View as a Web Page* context. Default value is **`false`**. This argument can only be used with the **`HTTP`** location type.
6	String	False	Link name for file in the *View as a Web Page* context. This argument can only be used with the **`HTTP`** location type.

Ordinal	Type	Required	Description
7	Number	False	Number of days the link to download the file appears in the *View as a Web Page* context. This argument can only be used with the **`HTTP`** location type.

> **NOTE:** Arguments 4 – 7 are unavailable in the current release of Marketing Cloud. This should be resolved in a future release.

Example 1

This example attaches a Content Builder asset by Customer/External Key:

```
%%[

var @customerKey, @fileAlias
set @customerKey = "LoyaltyMembersCB"
set @fileAlias = "LoyaltyMembers _ContentBuilder.zip"

AttachFile("ContentBuilder", @customerKey, @fileAlias)

]%%
```

Example 2

This example attaches a file from the Marketing Cloud **`Import`** folder:

```
%%[

var @fileName, @fileAlias
set @fileName = "LoyaltyMembers.zip"
set @fileAlias = "LoyaltyMembers _FTP.zip"

AttachFile("FTP", @fileName, @fileAlias)

]%%
```

Example 3

This example attaches a file from an external website via HTTP/HTTPS:

```
%%[

var @fileName, @fileAlias
set @fileName = "https://limedash.com/drop/LoyaltyMembers.
zip"
set @fileAlias = "LoyaltyMembers.zip"

AttachFile("HTTP", @fileName, @fileAlias)

]%%
```

Example 4

This example attaches a file from the Portfolio asset by Customer/External Key:

```
%%[

var @externalKey, @fileAlias
set @externalKey = "LoyaltyMembers"
set @fileAlias = "LoyaltyMembers _Portfolio.zip"

AttachFile("Portfolio", @externalKey, @fileAlias)

]%%
```

BarcodeURL

This function generates a barcode image URL using the specified arguments.

Arguments

`BarcodeURL(1,2,3,4,5,6,7,8,9)`

Ordinal	Type	Required	Description
1	String	True	Value to convert into a barcode
2	String	True	Type of barcode to generate. Valid barcode symbology values include: ▪ `Codabar` ▪ `Code11` ▪ `Code128A` ▪ `Code128Auto` ▪ `Code128B` ▪ `Code128C` ▪ `Code39` (Code 3 of 9) ▪ `Code39Ext` ▪ `Code93` ▪ `Code93Ext` ▪ `DataMatrix` ▪ `Ean13` ▪ `Ean8` ▪ `Industr25` ▪ `Interl25` ▪ `Mat25` (Matrix 2 of 5) ▪ `MSI` ▪ `OneCode` ▪ `PDF417` ▪ `PlainText` ▪ `Planet` ▪ `Postnet` ▪ `Telepen` ▪ `UPCa` ▪ `UPCe`
3	Number	True	Barcode image width in pixels
4	Number	True	Barcode image height in pixels
5	String	False	Checksum value for barcode
6	Boolean	False	Display value from Ordinal 1 under barcode

Ordinal	Type	Required	Description
7	String	False	Alternate text to display under the barcode if Ordinal 6 is **`false`**
8	Number	True	Orientation of barcode in degrees. Valid values are **`0`**, **`90`**, **`180`** and **`270`**
9	Boolean	True	Use a transparent background color

NOTE: **`Codabar`** requires an **`A`** prefix and a **`B`** suffix.

NOTE: **`Mat25`**, **`OneCode`**, **`PlainText`** , **`Planet`**, **`Postnet`** and **`Telepen`** symbologies do not render properly in the current release of Salesforce Marketing Cloud. This should be resolved in a future release.

Example

```
%%[

var @Codabar
var @Code11
var @Code128A
var @Code128Auto
var @Code128B
var @Code128C
var @Code39
var @Code39Ext
var @Code93
var @Code93Ext
var @DataMatrix
var @Ean13
var @Ean8
var @Industr25
var @Interl25
var @Mat25
var @MSI
var @OneCode
var @PDF417
var @PlainText
var @Planet
var @Postnet
```

```
var @Telepen
var @UPCa
var @UPCe

var @val_generic
var @val_codabar
var @val_ean13
var @val_ean8
var @val_mat25
var @val_onecode
var @val_planet
var @val_postnet
var @val_telepen

set @val_generic = "12345678901"
set @val_codabar = "A2030405060B"
set @val_ean13 = "1234567890123"
set @val_ean8 = "12345678"
set @val_mat25 = "0123456785678"
set @val_onecode = "0123456709498765432101234567891"
set @val_plaintext = "12345678901"
set @val_planet = "55555-1234"
set @val_postnet = "55555-1234"
set @val_telepen = "ABC123"

set @Codabar = BarcodeURL(@val_codabar, "Codabar", 100, 50)
set @Code11 = BarcodeURL(@val_generic, "Code11", 100, 50)
set @Code128A = BarcodeURL(@val_generic, "Code128A", 100, 50)
set @Code128Auto = BarcodeURL(@val_generic, "Code128Auto",
100, 50)
set @Code128B = BarcodeURL(@val_generic, "Code128B", 100,
50)
set @Code128C = BarcodeURL(@val_generic, "Code128C", 100, 50)
set @Code39 = BarcodeURL(@val_generic, "Code39", 100, 50)
set @Code39Ext = BarcodeURL(@val_generic, "Code39Ext", 100,
50)
set @Code93 = BarcodeURL(@val_generic, "Code93", 100, 50)
set @Code93Ext = BarcodeURL(@val_generic, "Code93Ext", 100, 50)
set @DataMatrix = BarcodeURL(@val_generic, "DataMatrix",
100, 100)
set @Ean13 = BarcodeURL(@val_ean13, "Ean13", 100, 50)
set @Ean8 = BarcodeURL(@val_ean8, "Ean8", 100, 50)
```

```
set @Industr25 = BarcodeURL(@val_generic, "Industr25", 100, 50)
set @Interl25 = BarcodeURL(@val_generic, "Interl25", 100, 50)
set @Mat25 = BarcodeURL(@val_mat25, "Mat25", 100, 50)
set @MSI = BarcodeURL(@val_generic, "MSI", 100, 50)
set @OneCode = BarcodeURL(@val_onecode, "OneCode", 100, 50)
set @PDF417 = BarcodeURL(@val_generic, "PDF417", 100, 50)
set @PlainText = BarcodeURL(@val_generic, "PlainText", 100, 50)
set @Planet = BarcodeURL(@val_planet, "Planet", 100, 50)
set @Postnet = BarcodeURL(@val_postnet, "Postnet", 100, 50)
set @Telepen = BarcodeURL(@val_telepen, "Telepen", 100, 50)
set @UPCa = BarcodeURL(@val_generic, "UPCa", 100, 50)
set @UPCe = BarcodeURL(@val_generic, "UPCe", 100, 50)

]%%
<table border="1" cellpadding="3" cellspacing="0"
style="font: 11px sans-serif; ">
<tr><th>Symbology</th><th>Sample</th><th>Output</th></tr>
<tr><td>Codabar</td><td>%%=v(@val_codabar)=%%</td><td>
<img src="%%=v(@Codabar)=%%"></td></tr>
<tr><td>Code11</td><td>%%=v(@val_generic)=%%</td><td>
<img src="%%=v(@Code11)=%%"></td>
<tr><td>Code128A</td><td>%%=v(@val_generic)=%%</td><td>
<img src="%%=v(@Code128A)=%%"></td></tr>
<tr><td>Code128Auto</td><td>%%=v(@val_generic)=%%
</td><td><img src="%%=v(@Code128Auto)=%%"></td></tr>
<tr><td>Code128B</td><td>%%=v(@val_generic)=%%</td><td>
<img src="%%=v(@Code128B)=%%"></td></tr>
<tr><td>Code128C</td><td>%%=v(@val_generic)=%%</td><td>
<img src="%%=v(@Code128C)=%%"></td></tr>
<tr><td>Code39</td><td>%%=v(@val_generic)=%%</td><td>
<img src="%%=v(@Code39)=%%"></td></tr>
<tr><td>Code39Ext</td><td>%%=v(@val_generic)=%%</td><td>
<img src="%%=v(@Code39Ext)=%%"></td></tr>
<tr><td>Code93</td><td>%%=v(@val_generic)=%%</td><td>
<img src="%%=v(@Code93)=%%"></td></tr>
<tr><td>Code93Ext</td><td>%%=v(@val_generic)=%%</td><td>
<img src="%%=v(@Code93Ext)=%%"></td></tr>
<tr><td>DataMatrix</td><td>%%=v(@val_generic)=%%</td><td>
<img src="%%=v(@DataMatrix)=%%"></td></tr>
<tr><td>Ean13</td><td>%%=v(@val_ean13)=%%</td><td>
<img src="%%=v(@Ean13)=%%"></td></tr>
```

```
<tr><td>Ean8</td><td>%%=v(@val_ean8)=%%</td><td>
<img src="%%=v(@Ean8)=%%"></td></tr>
<tr><td>Industr25</td><td>%%=v(@val_generic)=%%</td><td>
<img src="%%=v(@Industr25)=%%"></td></tr>
<tr><td>Interl25</td><td>%%=v(@val_generic)=%%</td><td>
<img src="%%=v(@Interl25)=%%"></td></tr>
<tr><td>Mat25</td><td>%%=v(@val_mat25)=%%</td><td>
<img src="%%=v(@Mat25)=%%"></td></tr>
<tr><td>MSI</td><td>%%=v(@val_generic)=%%</td><td>
<img src="%%=v(@MSI)=%%"></td></tr>
<tr><td>OneCode</td><td>%%=v(@val_onecode)=%%</td><td>
<img src="%%=v(@OneCode)=%%"></td></tr>
<tr><td>PDF417</td><td>%%=v(@val_generic)=%%</td><td>
<img src="%%=v(@PDF417)=%%"></td></tr>
<tr><td>PlainText</td><td>%%=v(@val_generic)=%%</td><td>
<img src="%%=v(@PlainText)=%%"></td></tr>
<tr><td>Planet</td><td>%%=v(@val_planet)=%%</td><td>
<img src="%%=v(@Planet)=%%"></td></tr>
<tr><td>Postnet</td><td>%%=v(@val_postnet)=%%</td><td>
<img src="%%=v(@Postnet)=%%"></td></tr>
<tr><td>Telepen</td><td>%%=v(@val_telepen)=%%</td><td>
<img src="%%=v(@Telepen)=%%"></td></tr>
<tr><td>UPCa</td><td>%%=v(@val_generic)=%%</td><td>
<img src="%%=v(@UPCa)=%%"></td></tr>
<tr><td>UPCe</td><td>%%=v(@val_generic)=%%</td><td>
<img src="%%=v(@UPCe)=%%"></td></tr>
</table>
```

Output

Symbology	Sample	Output
Codabar	A2030405060B	A2030405060B
Code11	12345678901	12345678901
Code128A	12345678901	12345678901
Code128Auto	12345678901	12345678901
Code128B	12345678901	12345678901
Code128C	12345678901	1234 5678 901
Code39	12345678901	12345678901
Code39Ext	12345678901	12345678901
Code93	12345678901	12345678901
Code93Ext	12345678901	12345678901
DataMatrix	12345678901	

Symbology	**Sample**	**Output**
Ean13	1234567890123	1234567890123
Ean8	12345678	12345678
Industr25	12345678901	12345678901
Interl25	12345678901	12345678901
Mat25	123456785678	Live Content
MSI	12345678901	12345678901
OneCode	0123456709498765432101234567891	Live Content
PDF417	12345678901	
PlainText	12345678901	Live Content
Planet	55555-1234	Live Content
Postnet	55555-1234	Live Content
Telepen	ABC123	Live Content
UPCa	12345678901	12345678901
UPCe	12345678901	12345678901

BeginImpressionRegion

This function marks the beginning of a region to be tracked within the impression tracking infrastructure. It has no output.

> **NOTE:** Impression Regions are implicitly closed at the end of the email. They can be (and typically are) closed explicitly with the EndImpressionRegion function.

Argument

`BeginImpressionRegion(1)`

Ordinal	Type	Required	Description
1	String	True	Name of the Impression Region to track

> **NOTE:** By default, the Impression Region name cannot be an AMPscript variable.

Example 1

```
%%=BeginImpressionRegion("PrimaryNavigation")=%%

<a href="https://limedash.com/shop" alias="Shop">Shop</a> |
<a href="https://limedash.com/contact" alias="Shop">Contact
</a>

%%=EndImpressionRegion(0)=%%
```

Example 2

While it is not explicitly supported, dynamically named Impression Regions can be created by forcing AMPscript to be evaluated using the TreatAsContent function.

```
%%=TreatAsContent(concat("%", "%=BeginImpressionRegion('",
"PrimaryNavigation _ ", _messagecontext, "')=%", "%"))=%%

<a href="https://limedash.com/shop" alias="Shop">Shop</a> |
<a href="https://limedash.com/contact" alias="Shop">Contact
</a>

%%=EndImpressionRegion(0)=%%
```

BuildOptionList

This function outputs **<option>** elements for use inside **<select>**, **<optgroup>** or **<datalist>** HTML elements.

> **TIP:** This function is best utilized in landing pages or CloudPages.

Arguments

`BuildOptionList(1,2,3,[4a,4b])`

Ordinal	Type	Required	Description
1	String	True	Default option value
2	String	True	Option value
3	String	True	Option name
4a	String	True	Additional option value (see note)
4b	String	True	Additional option name (see note)

> **NOTE:** Additional pairs of values and names can be appended as arguments.

Example

```
%%[

var @defaultRank, @optionList
set @defaultRank = AttributeValue("rank")
set @defaultRank = "4"
set @optionList  = BuildOptionList(@defaultRank,"1", "Good",
"2", "Better", "3", "Best", "4", "OK" )

]%%
default rank: %%=v(@defaultRank)=%%
<br>Ranking: <select name="rank">
%%=v(@optionList)=%%
</select>
```

Output

```
default rank: 4
<br>Ranking: <select name="rank">
<option value="1">Good</option>
<option value="2">Better</option>
<option value="3">Best</option>
<option value="4" selected="selected">OK</option>
</select>
```

BuildRowSetFromString

This function returns a row set by splitting a string by the specified delimiter string.

Arguments

`BuildRowSetFromString(1,2)`

Ordinal	Type	Required	Description
1	String	True	String to split into a row set
2	String	True	Delimiting string

Example

Values returned in the row set are not named. They are specified with an ordinal of **`1`** as illustrated in the following example:

```
%%[
var @regionList, @rows, @row, @rowCount, @region, @i

set @regionList = "North**South**East**West"

set @rows = BuildRowsetFromString(@regionList,"**")
set @rowCount = rowCount(@rows)

if @rowCount > 0 then

  for @i = 1 to @rowCount do

    var @emailAddress, @firstName, @rank
    set @row = row(@rows, @i) /* get row based on counter */
    set @region = field(@row,1)
```

```
    ]%%

    <br>Row %%=v(@i)=%%, region: %%=v(@region)=%%

    %%[

  next @i ]%%

%%[ else ]%%

No rows found

%%[ endif ]%%
```

Output

```
Row 1, region: North
Row 2, region: South
Row 3, region: East
Row 4, region: West
```

BuildRowSetFromXML

This function creates a row set from an XML string. It returns an error or an empty row set if no XML matches the specified XPATH.

The following nodes will return no value:

- CDATA
- Comment
- Document
- Document Fragments
- DocumentType
- Entities
- Entity References
- Notation
- ProcessingInformation
- Whitespace
- XmlDeclaration

> **NOTE:** Marketing Cloud supports the XPATH 1.0 specification.

Arguments

BuildRowSetFromXML(1,2,3)

Ordinal	Type	Required	Description
1	String	True	Source XML string to parse
2	String	True	XPATH string that specifies the root XML node from which to build the row set
3	Boolean	True	Return an empty row set if XPATH is not found in source string

Example 1

The following example retrieves XML node values:

```
%%[

var @xml, @isXML, @nodes, @rowCount

set @xml = ""
set @xml = concat(@xml, '<?xml version="1.0"
encoding="UTF-8"?>')
set @xml = concat(@xml, '<cart>')
set @xml = concat(@xml, '  <items>')
set @xml = concat(@xml, '    <item>')
set @xml = concat(@xml, '       <sku><![CDATA[123]]></sku>')
set @xml = concat(@xml, '       <name><![CDATA[Square]]>
</name>')
set @xml = concat(@xml, '       <url><![CDATA[https://
limedash.com?sku=123]]></url>')
set @xml = concat(@xml, '    </item>')
set @xml = concat(@xml, '    <item>')
set @xml = concat(@xml, '        <sku><![CDATA[456]]></sku>')
set @xml = concat(@xml, '        <name><![CDATA[Circle]]>
</name>')
set @xml = concat(@xml, '        <url><![CDATA[https://
limedash.com?sku=456]]></url>')
set @xml = concat(@xml, '    </item>')
set @xml = concat(@xml, '    <item>')
set @xml = concat(@xml, '        <sku><![CDATA[789]]></sku>')
set @xml = concat(@xml, '        <name><![CDATA[Triangle]]>
</name>')
```

```
set @xml = concat(@xml, '        <url><![CDATA[https://
limedash.com?sku=789]]></url>')
set @xml = concat(@xml, '    </item>')
set @xml = concat(@xml, '  </items>')
set @xml = concat(@xml, '</cart> ')

if indexOf(@xml,"<cart>") > 0 then

  set @nodes = BuildRowsetFromXML(@xml,"/cart/items/item",0)
  set @rowCount = rowcount(@nodes)

  if @rowCount > 0 then

    for @i = 1 to @rowCount do

      var @sku
      var @name
      var @url

      set @nodepath = concat("/cart/items/item[",@i,"]/")

      if rowcount(BuildRowsetFromXML(@xml,concat(@nodepath,
"sku"))) > 0 then
          set @sku =
Field(Row(BuildRowsetFromXML(@xml,concat(@nodepath,"sku"),0)
,1),'Value')
      endif

      if rowcount(BuildRowsetFromXML(@xml,concat(@nodepath,
"name"))) > 0 then
          set @name =
Field(Row(BuildRowsetFromXML(@xml,concat(@nodepath,"name"),0),
1),'Value')
      endif

      if rowcount(BuildRowsetFromXML(@xml,concat(@nodepath,
"url"))) > 0 then
          set @url =
Field(Row(BuildRowsetFromXML(@xml,concat(@nodepath,"url"),0),
1),'Value')
      endif
```

```
      if not empty(@sku) and not empty(@name) and not empty
(@url) then

      ]%%

       <br><a href="%%=redirectto(@url)=%%">%%=v(@name)=%%
(%%=v(@sku)=%%)</a>

      %%[

      endif

    next @i

  else

   output(concat("<br>no products found"))

  endif

else

  output(concat("<br>no XML found"))

endif

]%%
```

Output

```
<br><a href="https://limedash.com/?sku=123">Square (123)</a>
<br><a href="https://limedash.com/?sku=456">Circle (456)</a>
<br><a href="https://limedash.com/?sku=789">Triangle (789)</a>
```

Example 2

The following example retrieves values from the XML node attributes:

```
%%[

var @xml, @isXML, @nodes, @rowCount

set @xml = ""
set @xml = concat(@xml, '<?xml version="1.0"
encoding="UTF-8"?>')
set @xml = concat(@xml, '<cart>')
set @xml = concat(@xml, '  <item sku="123" url="https://
limedash.com?sku=123">Square</item>')
set @xml = concat(@xml, '  <item sku="246" url="https://
limedash.com?sku=246">Circle</item>')
set @xml = concat(@xml, '  <item sku="789" url="https://
limedash.com?sku=789">Triangle</item>')
set @xml = concat(@xml, '</cart> ')

if indexOf(@xml,"<cart>") > 0 then

  set @nodes = BuildRowsetFromXML(@xml,"/cart/item",0)
  set @rowCount = rowcount(@nodes)

  if @rowCount > 0 then

    for @i = 1 to @rowCount do

      var @sku
      var @name
      var @url

      set @nodepath = concat("/cart/item[",@i,"]/")

      if
rowcount(BuildRowsetFromXML(@xml,concat(@nodepath,"@sku"))) >
0 then
          set @sku =
Field(Row(BuildRowsetFromXML(@xml,concat(@nodepath,"@sku"),0)
,1),'Value')
      endif
```

```
      if
rowcount(BuildRowsetFromXML(@xml,concat(@nodepath,"@url"))) >
0 then
          set @url =
Field(Row(BuildRowsetFromXML(@xml,concat(@nodepath,"@url"),0)
,1),'Value')
      endif

      if rowcount(BuildRowsetFromXML(@xml,concat(@nodepath,
"text()"))) > 0 then
          set @name = Field(Row(BuildRowsetFromXML(@xml,
concat(@nodepath,"text()"),0),1),'Value')
      endif

      if not empty(@sku) and not empty(@name) and not empty
(@url) then

      ]%%

       <br><a href="%%=redirectto(@url)=%%">%%=v(@name)=%%
(%%=v(@sku)=%%)</a>

      %%[

      endif

    next @i

  else

   output(concat("<br>no products found"))

  endif

else

  output(concat("<br>no XML found"))

endif

]%%
```

Output

```
<br><a href="https://limedash.com/?sku=123">Square (123)</a>
<br><a href="https://limedash.com/?sku=456">Circle (456)</a>
<br><a href="https://limedash.com/?sku=789">Triangle (789)</a>
```

ContentArea

This function returns the content stored in the specified Content Area and optionally wraps the content in an Impression Region.

> **NOTE:** The ID for the Content Area can be found in the Properties dialog accessible from the Content Area folder listing page.

> **NOTE:** This function does not retrieve content stored in Content Builder.

Arguments

`ContentArea(1,2,3,4,5)`

Ordinal	Type	Required	Description
1	Number	True	The ID of the Content Area to return. This can be specified as a String or Number.
2	String	False	Name of the Impression Region to associate with the Content Area
3	Boolean	False	Return an error if the Content Area cannot be found
4	String	False	Default content to return if an error occurs from retrieving the Content Area specified in Ordinal 1
5	Number	False	Numeric status code resulting from the retrieve. A value of `0` indicates the retrieve was successful, while `-1` indicates that the content was not found or empty.

Example 1

A Content Area named **LoyaltyGreeting** (ID: **11437**) contains the following code:

```
%%[

var @firstName
set @firstName = properCase(AttributeValue("FirstName"))

]%%
Hello, %%=v(@firstName)=%%!
```

The Content Area can be referenced as:

```
%%[

var @contentAreaID
set @contentAreaID = 11437 /* my contents\LoyaltyGreeting */

]%%
%%=ContentArea(@contentAreaID)=%%
```

Output

```
Hello, Curt!
```

Example 2

A Content Area named **LoyaltyGreeting** (ID: **11437**) contains the following code:

```
%%[

var @firstName
set @firstName = properCase(AttributeValue("FirstName"))

]%%
Hello, %%=v(@firstName)=%%!
```

In the scenario where the Content Area ID does not exist, fallback content is handled using the value of the fourth argument, or by conditionally showing content based on the value of the **@retrieveStatus** variable.

```
%%[

var @contentAreaID, @content, @retrieveStatus
set @contentAreaID = 11434 /* does not exist */
set @content = ContentArea(@contentAreaID, "Greeting", 0,
"Hello!", @retrieveStatus)

output(concat(@content))

if @retrieveStatus < 0 then
  output(concat('<br><br><a href="https://limedash.com/
join">Join Now</a> &raquo;'))
endif

]%%
```

Output

```
Hello!

<a href="https://limedash.com/join">Join Now</a> &raquo;
```

ContentAreaByName

This function returns the content stored in the specified Content Area and optionally wraps the content in an Impression Region.

> **NOTE:** This function does not retrieve content stored in Content Builder.

Arguments

`ContentAreaByName(1,2,3,4,5)`

Ordinal	Type	Required	Description
1	Number	True	The full path of the Content Area to return
2	String	False	Name of the Impression Region to associate with this Content Area
3	Boolean	False	Return an error if the Content Area cannot be found
4	String	False	Default content if an error occurs retrieving the Content Area specified in Ordinal 1
5	Number	False	Numeric status code resulting from the retrieve. A value of `0` indicates the retrieve was successful, while `-1` indicates that the content was not found or empty.

Example 1

A Content Area named **`LoyaltyGreeting`** in the **`my contents`** folder contains the following code:

```
%%[

var @firstName
set @firstName = properCase(AttributeValue("FirstName"))

]%%
Hello, %%=v(@firstName)=%%!
```

The Content Area can be referenced as:

```
%%[

var @contentAreaPath
set @contentAreaPath = "my contents\LoyaltyGreeting"

]%%
%%=ContentAreaByName(@contentAreaPath)=%%
```

Output

```
Hello, Curt!
```

Example 2

A Content Area named **`LoyaltyGreeting`** in the **`my contents`** folder contains the following code:

```
%%[

var @firstName
set @firstName = properCase(AttributeValue("FirstName"))

]%%
Hello, %%=v(@firstName)=%%!
```

In the scenario where the Content Area does not exist, fallback content is handled with the value of the fourth argument, or by conditionally showing content based on the value of the **`@retrieveStatus`** variable:

```
%%[

var @contentAreaPath, @content, @retrieveStatus
set @contentAreaPath = "my contents\LoyaltyGreeting _Oops"
/* does not exist */
set @content = ContentAreaByName(@contentAreaPath,
"Greeting", 0, "Hello!", @retrieveStatus)

output(concat(@content))

if @retrieveStatus < 0 then
```

```
   output(concat('<br><br><a href="https://limedash.com/
join">Join Now</a> &raquo;'))
endif

]%%
```

Output

```
Hello!

<a href="https://limedash.com/join">Join Now</a> &raquo;
```

ContentBlockByID

This function returns the content stored in the specified Content Block and optionally wraps the content in an Impression Region.

> **NOTE:** The ID for the content block can be found in the Properties menu, accessible from the drop-down menu on the right-hand side of the Content Builder listing page.

> **NOTE:** This does not retrieve content stored in Classic Content.

Arguments

`ContentBlockByID(1,2,3,4,5)`

Ordinal	Type	Required	Description
1	Number	True	The ID of the content block to return. This can be specified as a String or Number.
2	String	False	Name of the Impression Region to associate with this Content Area
3	Boolean	False	Return an error if the content block cannot be found
4	String	False	Default content if an error occurs retrieving the content block specified in Ordinal 1
5	Number	False	Numeric status code resulting from the retrieve. A value of `0` indicates the retrieve was successful, while `-1` indicates that the content was not found or empty

Example 1

A Content Block named **LoyaltyGreeting** (ID: **5794**) contains the following code:

```
%%[

var @firstName
set @firstName = properCase(AttributeValue("FirstName"))

]%%
Hello, %%=v(@firstName)=%%!
```

The Content Block can be referenced as:

```
%%[

var @contentBlockID
set @contentBlockID = 5794 /* Content Builder\
LoyaltyGreeting */

]%%
%%=ContentBlockByID(@contentBlockID)=%%
```

Output

```
Hello, Curt!
```

Example 2

A Content Block named **LoyaltyGreeting** (ID: **5794**) contains the following code:

```
%%[

var @firstName
set @firstName = properCase(AttributeValue("FirstName"))

]%%
Hello, %%=v(@firstName)=%%!
```

In the scenario where a Content Block ID does not exist, fallback content is handled with the value of the fourth argument or by conditionally showing content based on the value of the **`@retrieveStatus`** variable:

```
%%[

var @contentBlockID, @content, @retrieveStatus
set @contentBlockID = 9794 /* does not exist */
set @content = ContentBlockByID(@contentBlockID, "Greeting",
0, "Hello!", @retrieveStatus)

output(concat(@content))

if @retrieveStatus < 0 then
  output(concat('<br><br><a href="https://limedash.com/
join">Join Now</a> &raquo;'))
endif

]%%
```

Output

```
Hello!

<a href="https://limedash.com/join">Join Now</a> &raquo;
```

ContentBlockByKey

This function returns the content stored in the specified Content Block and optionally wraps the content in an Impression Region.

> **NOTE:** The Customer Key for the Content Block can be found in the Properties menu, accessible from the drop-down menu, on the right-hand side of the Content Block listing page.

> **NOTE:** This does not retrieve content stored in Classic Content.

Arguments

`ContentBlockByKey(1,2,3,4,5)`

Ordinal	Type	Required	Description
1	Number	True	The Customer Key of the content block to return.
2	String	False	Name of the Impression Region to associate with this Content Area
3	Boolean	False	Return an error if the content block cannot be found
4	String	False	Default content if an error occurs retrieving the content block specified in Ordinal 1
5	Number	False	Numeric status code resulting from the retrieve. A value of 0 indicates the retrieve was successful, while **`-1`** indicates that the content was not found or empty.

Example 1

A Content Block named **`LoyaltyGreeting`** (Customer Key: **`2db254de-7b89-4daf-93af-0db2b5a00b83`**) contains the following code:

```
%%[

var @firstName
set @firstName = properCase(AttributeValue("FirstName"))

]%%
Hello, %%=v(@firstName)=%%!
```

The Content Block can be referenced as:

```
%%[

var @contentBlockKey
set @contentBlockKey = "2db254de-7b89-4daf-93af-0db2b5a00b83"
/* Content Builder\LoyaltyGreeting */

]%%
%%=ContentBlockByKey(@contentBlockKey)=%%
```

Output

```
Hello, Curt!
```

Example 2
A Content Block named **`LoyaltyGreeting`** (Customer Key: **`2db254de-7b89-4daf-93af-0db2b5a00b83`**) contains the following code:

```
%%[

var @firstName
set @firstName = properCase(AttributeValue("FirstName"))

]%%
Hello, %%=v(@firstName)=%%!
```

In the scenario where the Content Block Key does not exist, fallback content is handled with the value of the fourth argument or by conditionally showing content based on the value of the **`@retrieveStatus`** variable:

```
%%[

var @contentBlockKey, @content, @retrieveStatus
set @contentBlockKey = "2db254de-7b89-4daf-93af-0db2b5a00b99"
/* does not exist */
set @content = ContentBlockByKey(@contentBlockKey,
"Greeting", 0, "Hello!", @retrieveStatus)

output(concat(@content))

if @retrieveStatus < 0 then
```

```
  output(concat('<br><br><a href="https://limedash.com/
join">Join Now</a> &raquo;'))
endif

]%%
```

Output

```
Hello!

<a href="https://limedash.com/join">Join Now</a> &raquo;
```

ContentBlockByName

This function returns the content stored in the specified Content Block and optionally wraps the content in an Impression Region.

> **NOTE:** This does not retrieve content stored in Classic Content.

Arguments

`ContentBlockByName(1,2,3,4,5)`

Ordinal	Type	Required	Description
1	Number	True	The full path of the content block to return
2	String	False	Name of the Impression Region to associate with this Content Area
3	Boolean	False	Return an error if the Content Area cannot be found
4	String	False	Default content if an error occurs retrieving the content block specified in Ordinal 1
5	Number	False	Numeric status code resulting from the retrieve. A value of **0** indicates the retrieve was successful, while **-1** indicates that the content was not found or empty.

Example 1
A Content Block named **LoyaltyGreeting** in the **Content Builder** folder contains the following code:

```
%%[

var @firstName
set @firstName = properCase(AttributeValue("FirstName"))

]%%
Hello, %%=v(@firstName)=%%!
```

The Content Block can be referenced as:

```
%%[

var @contentBlockName
set @contentBlockName = "Content Builder\LoyaltyGreeting"

]%%
%%=ContentBlockByName(@contentBlockName)=%%
```

Output

```
Hello, Curt!
```

Example 2
A Content Block named **LoyaltyGreeting** in the **Content Builder** folder contains the following code:

```
%%[

var @firstName
set @firstName = properCase(AttributeValue("FirstName"))

]%%
Hello, %%=v(@firstName)=%%!
```

In the scenario where the Content Block does not exist, fallback content is handled with the value of the fourth argument or by conditionally showing content based on the value of the **@retrieveStatus** variable:

```
%%[

var @contentBlockName, @content, @retrieveStatus
set @contentBlockName = "Content Builder\
LoyaltyGreeting_Oops" /* does not exist */
set @content = ContentBlockByName(@contentBlockName,
"Greeting", 0, "Hello!", @retrieveStatus)

output(concat(@content))

if @retrieveStatus < 0 then
  output(concat('<br><br><a href="https://limedash.com/
join">Join Now</a> &raquo;'))
endif

]%%
```

Output

```
Hello!

<a href="https://limedash.com/join">Join Now</a> &raquo;
```

ContentImageByID

This function returns an HTML **`img`** tag with the specified Content Builder image. It also sets the **`title`**, **`alt`**, **`border`** and **`thid`** attributes on the **`img`** tag. The **`title`** and **`alt`** values are set to the name of the image as defined in Content Builder. The **`border`** is set to **`0`** in all circumstances. The **`thid`** is a proprietary Marketing Cloud attribute that contains the ID of the specified image in Content Builder.

> **NOTE:** The ID for the image can be found in the Properties menu, accessible from the drop-down menu on the right-hand side of the Content Builder asset listing page.

> **NOTE:** This function will only return Content Builder assets that are images. It will not return an Image Block from Content Builder.

Arguments

`ContentImageByID(1,2)`

Ordinal	Type	Required	Description
1	String	True	ID value of the image to return
2	String	True	ID value of the image to return if the image for the specified ID is not found

Example 1

```
%%[

var @imageID, @imageIDFallBack, @imageTag
set @imageID = "5940" /* limedash-logo-green */
set @imageIDFallBack = "5941" /* limedash-logo-gray */

set @imageTag = ContentImageByID(@imageID, @imageIDFallBack)

]%%
<a href="https://limedash.com">%%=v(@imageTag)=%%</a>
```

Output

```
<a href="https://limedash.com"><img title="limedash-
logo-green" alt="limedash-logo-green" src="http://image.
S7.exacttarget.com/lib/fe9213727567077b7d/m/1/087ae025-7205-
4121-8d5c-366f4a3dc117.png" border="0" thid="5940"></a>
```

Example 2

This example illustrates the output when the specified ID does not exist and the fallback image is returned:

```
%%[

var @imageID, @imageIDFallBack, @imageTag
set @imageID = "5999" /* does not exist */
set @imageIDFallBack = "5941" /* limedash-logo-gray */

set @imageTag = ContentImageByID(@imageID, @imageIDFallBack)

]%%
<a href="https://limedash.com">%%=v(@imageTag)=%%</a>
```

Output

```
<a href="https://limedash.com"><img title="limedash-logo-gray"
alt="limedash-logo-gray" src="http://image.S7.exacttarget.
com/lib/fe9213727567077b7d/m/1/8aabd3b9-cf2a-4d41-a56b-
bec76e2efd54.png" border=0 thid="5941"></a>
```

ContentImageByKey

This function returns an HTML **`img`** tag with the specified Content Builder image. It also sets the **`title`**, **`alt`**, **`border`** and **`thid`** attributes on the **`img`** tag. The **`title`** and **`alt`** values are set to the name of the image as defined in Content Builder. The **`border`** is set to **`0`** in all circumstances. The **`thid`** is a proprietary Marketing Cloud attribute that contains the ID of the specified image in Content Builder.

> **NOTE:** The ID for the image can be found in the Properties menu, accessible from the drop-down menu on the right-hand side of the Content Builder asset listing page.

> **NOTE:** This function will only return Content Builder assets that are images. It will not return Image Block from Content Builder.

Arguments

`ContentImageByKey(1,2)`

Ordinal	Type	Required	Description
1	String	True	Customer/External Key value of the image to return
2	String	True	Customer/External Key value of the image to return if the image for the specified Customer/External Key is not found

Example 1

```
%%[

var @imageKey, @imageKeyFallBack, @imageTag
set @imageKey = "limedash-logo-green" /* id: 5940  */
set @imageKeyFallBack = "limedash-logo-gray" /* id: 5941 */

set @imageTag = ContentImageByKey(@imageKey,
@imageKeyFallBack)

]%%
<a href="https://limedash.com">%%=v(@imageTag)=%%</a>
```

Output

```
<a href="https://limedash.com"><img title="limedash-
logo-green" alt="limedash-logo-green" src="http://image.
S7.exacttarget.com/lib/fe9213727567077b7d/m/1/087ae025-7205-
4121-8d5c-366f4a3dc117.png" border="0" thid="5940"></a>
```

Example 2

This example illustrates the output when the specified Customer/External Key does not exist and the fallback image is returned:

```
%%[

var @imageKey, @imageKeyFallBack, @imageTag
set @imageKey = "limedash-logo-pink" /* does not exist */
set @imageKeyFallBack = "limedash-logo-gray" /* id: 5941 */

set @imageTag = ContentImageByKey(@imageKey,
@imageKeyFallBack)

]%%
<a href="https://limedash.com">%%=v(@imageTag)=%%</a>
```

Output

```
<a href="https://limedash.com"><img title="limedash-logo-gray"
alt="limedash-logo-gray" src="http://image.S7.exacttarget.
com/lib/fe9213727567077b7d/m/1/8aabd3b9-cf2a-4d41-a56b-
bec76e2efd54.png" border=0 thid="5941"></a>
```

EndImpressionRegion

This function marks the end of a previously defined Impression Region set with the BeginImpressionRegion function. It has no output.

Argument

`EndImpressionRegion(1)`

Ordinal	Type	Required	Description
1	Boolean	False	Scope of regions closed by the function. A value of **`True`** closes all previous Impression Regions. A value of **`False`** closes only the preceding Impression Region. The default value is **`False.`**

Example

```
%%=BeginImpressionRegion("PrimaryNavigation")=%%

<a href="https://limedash.com/shop" alias="Shop">Shop</a> |
<a href="https://limedash.com/contact" alias="Shop">Contact
</a>

%%=EndImpressionRegion(0)=%%
```

GetPortfolioItem

This function returns Portfolio item content for the specified Customer/External Key.

> **NOTE:** Keys for the Portfolio item can be found by selecting the item on the listing page and clicking the Properties option in the toolbar.

> **NOTE:** This function is best suited for returning non-binary content from the Portfolio, like the Document and Code types.

Argument

`GetPortfolioItem(1)`

Ordinal	Type	Required	Description
1	String	True	Customer/External Key of the Portfolio item to return

Example

A **`LoyaltyRegions.txt`** file is uploaded to the Portfolio that contains the following content:

```
North
South
East
West
```

The content can be retrieved with this function:

```
%%[

var @portfolioItemKey
set @portfolioItemKey = "LoyaltyRegions"

]%%
Loyalty Regions: %%=GetPortfolioItem(@portfolioItemKey)=%%
```

Output

```
Loyalty Regions: North South East West
```

Image

This function returns an HTML **img** tag with the specified Portfolio image. It also sets the **title**, **alt**, **border** and **thid** attributes on the **img** tag. The **title** and **alt** values are set to the name of the image as defined in the Portfolio. The **border** is set to **0** in all circumstances. The **thid** is a proprietary Marketing Cloud attribute that contains the ID of the specified image in the Portfolio.

> **NOTE:** The Portfolio ID in the **thid** value is not visible in the Marketing Cloud interface.

> **NOTE:** Keys for the Portfolio item can be found by selecting the item in the listing page and then clicking the Properties option in the toolbar.

Arguments

Image(1,2)

Ordinal	Type	Required	Description
1	String	True	Customer/External Key value of the image to return
2	String	True	Customer/External Key value of the image to return if the image for the specified Customer/External Key is not found

Example 1

```
%%[

var @imageKey, @imageKeyFallBack, @imageTag
set @imageKey = "limedash-logo-green"
set @imageKeyFallBack = "limedash-logo-gray"

set @imageTag = Image(@imageKey, @imageKeyFallBack)

]%%
<a href="https://limedash.com">%%=v(@imageTag)=%%</a>
```

Output

```
<a href="https://limedash.com"><img title="limedash-
logo-green" alt="limedash-logo-green" src="http://image.
S7.exacttarget.com/lib/fe9213727567077b7d/m/1/087ae025-7205-
4121-8d5c-366f4a3dc117.png" border="0" thid="c87075e6-1959-
4e6c-8a08-775a40ca056e"></a>
```

Example 2

This example illustrates the output when the specified Customer/External Key does not exist and the fallback image is returned:

```
%%[

var @imageKey, @imageKeyFallBack, @imageTag
set @imageKey = "limedash-logo-pink" /* does not exist */
set @imageKeyFallBack = "limedash-logo-gray"

set @imageTag = Image(@imageKey, @imageKeyFallBack)

]%%
<a href="https://limedash.com">%%=v(@imageTag)=%%</a>
```

Output

```
<a href="https://limedash.com"><img title="limedash-logo-gray"
alt="limedash-logo-gray" src="http://image.S7.exacttarget.
com/lib/fe9213727567077b7d/m/1/8aabd3b9-cf2a-4d41-a56b-
bec76e2efd54.png" border=0 thid="fd7c5499-1409-44cb-90d7-
0873e7b51b20"></a>
```

TransformXML

This function applies an XSL transformation to the specified XML data.

> **TIP:** Generally speaking, XSL transformations are powerful and flexible when it comes to transforming XML, especially if you leverage AMPscript within them. However, it's advisable to limit the use of these in Marketing Cloud. The emails that use them can be particularly hard to maintain as the HTML code is not readily changeable in the Classic Content and Content Builder editors. It is recommended that the development of XSL emails should be done outside of Marketing Cloud using an appropriate IDE.

> **NOTE:** Marketing Cloud supports the XPATH 1.0 specification.

Arguments

`TransformXML(1,2)`

Ordinal	Type	Required	Description
1	String	True	XML content to transform
2	String	True	XSL document used to transform the XML content

Example

Here is a sample XSL file named **`LoyaltyRewards.xsl`** which is uploaded to the Portfolio. It has a Customer/External Key of **`LoyaltyRewards`**. This XSL file retrieves the elements from the XML, and outputs the repeating reward line items in a different order. It also totals all of the reward amounts and displays them in the last row of the table.

```
<?xml version="1.0"?>
<xsl:stylesheet xmlns:xsl="http://www.w3.org/1999/XSL/
Transform" version="1.0">
    <xsl:output method="html" indent="yes"/>
    <xsl:template match="/loyaltyRewards">
    <p>Hi, %%=properCase("<xsl:value-of
select="firstName"/>")=%%!</p>
    <p>Here's your reward statement:</p>
    <table cellspacing="0" cellpadding="5" border="1">
        <tr>
            <th>Reward Date</th>
```

```
            <th>Name</th>
            <th>Description</th>
            <th>Amount</th>
        </tr>
        <xsl:for-each select="rewards/reward">
            <xsl:sort select="./rewardDate"
order="descending" data-type="text"/>
            <tr>
                <td><xsl:value-of select="rewardDate"/></td>
                <td><xsl:value-of select="name"/></td>
                <td><xsl:value-of select="description"/></td>
                <td align="right"><xsl:value-of
select="amount"/></td>
            </tr>
        </xsl:for-each>
        <tr>
            <td colspan="3" align="right"><b>Total</b></td>
            <td align="right"><b><xsl:value-of
select="format-number(sum(rewards/reward/amount), '0.00')"/>
</b></td>
        </tr>
    </table>
  </xsl:template>
</xsl:stylesheet>
```

If an XML payload is specified, the TransformXML function will apply the logic in the XSL to the XML payload. The TreatAsContent function forces the AMPscript to be evaluated in the result.

```
%%[

var @xml, @xsl
set @xsl = GetPortfolioItem("LoyaltyRewards")

set @xml = AttributeValue("XML") /* value from attribute or
DE column in send context */
set @xml = "" /* or a literal value */
set @xml = concat(@xml,'<?xml version="1.0"?>')
set @xml = concat(@xml,'<loyaltyRewards>')
set @xml = concat(@xml,'
<emailAddress><![CDATA[suzy@limedash.com]]></emailAddress>')
```

```
set @xml = concat(@xml,'     <firstName><![CDATA[Suzy]]>
</firstName>')
set @xml = concat(@xml,'     <rewards>')
set @xml = concat(@xml,'          <reward>')
set @xml = concat(@xml,'
<rewardDate><![CDATA[2017-10-15]]></rewardDate>')
set @xml = concat(@xml,'
<name><![CDATA[Purchase]]></name>')
set @xml = concat(@xml,'
<description><![CDATA[Purchase cash back]]></description>')
set @xml = concat(@xml,'               <amount><![CDATA[3.21]]>
</amount>')
set @xml = concat(@xml,'          </reward>')
set @xml = concat(@xml,'          <reward>')
set @xml = concat(@xml,'
<rewardDate><![CDATA[2017-10-01]]></rewardDate>')
set @xml = concat(@xml,'               <name><![CDATA[Visit]]>
</name>')
set @xml = concat(@xml,'
<description><![CDATA[October visit reward]]></description>')
set @xml = concat(@xml,'
<amount><![CDATA[12.34]]></amount>')
set @xml = concat(@xml,'          </reward>')
set @xml = concat(@xml,'          <reward>')
set @xml = concat(@xml,'
<rewardDate><![CDATA[2017-12-01]]></rewardDate>')
set @xml = concat(@xml,'
<name><![CDATA[Referral]]></name>')
set @xml = concat(@xml,'
<description><![CDATA[Referral bonus]]></description>')
set @xml = concat(@xml,'
<amount><![CDATA[43.21]]></amount>')
set @xml = concat(@xml,'          </reward>')
set @xml = concat(@xml,'     </rewards>')
set @xml = concat(@xml,'</loyaltyRewards>')

]%%
%%=TreatAsContent(TransformXML(@xml,@xsl))=%%
```

Output

```
<p>Hi, Suzy!</p>
<p>Here's your reward statement:</p>
<table cellspacing="0" cellpadding="5" border="1">
  <tr>
    <th>Reward Date</th>
    <th>Name</th>
    <th>Description</th>
    <th>Amount</th>
  </tr>
  <tr>
    <td>2017-12-01</td>
    <td>Referral</td>
    <td>Referral bonus</td>
    <td align="right">43.21</td>
  </tr>
  <tr>
    <td>2017-10-15</td>
    <td>Purchase</td>
    <td>Purchase cash back</td>
    <td align="right">3.21</td>
  </tr>
  <tr>
    <td>2017-10-01</td>
    <td>Visit</td>
    <td>October visit reward</td>
    <td align="right">12.34</td>
  </tr>
  <tr>
    <td colspan="3" align="right"><b>Total</b></td>
    <td align="right"><b>58.76</b></td>
  </tr>
</table>
```

TreatAsContent

This function forces AMPscript and personalization strings to be evaluated in the specified input string.

Argument

`TreatAsContent(1)`

Ordinal	Type	Required	Description
1	String	True	String to evaluate

Example 1

```
%%[

var @contentMath
set @contentMath = "%%=add(1,3)=%%"

]%%
contentMath (static): %%=v(@contentMath)=%%
<br>contentMath (evaluated):
%%=treatascontent(@contentMath)=%%
```

Output

```
contentMath (static): (raw): %%=add(1,3)=%%
<br>contentMath (evaluated): 4
```

Example 2

A common use of the TreatAsContent function is to leverage the **`httpgetwrap|`** URL prefix in your Content Area. The intent of this prefix is to ensure Subscriber clicks are properly tracked in this external content.

There is a key consideration to using **`httpgetwrap`**: it only tracks the first 100 unique URLs in the send. If the prefix is being used in conjunction with the Web Analytics Connector, it's unlikely that click activity on these prefixed links will be completely tracked. If the business rule is not enabled, then these external links will not be tracked at all.

> **NOTE:** The **`httpgetwrap|`** prefix must be enabled by Marketing Cloud Support. The special business rule is called **`WRAP_HTTPGET_URLS`**.

```
%%[

var @contentWithLink
set @contentWithLink = 'Click here: <a
href="httpgetwrap|https://limedash.com">limedash.com</a>'

]%%
contentWithLink: %%=TreatAsContent(@contentWithLink)=%%
```

Output

```
contentWithLink: Click here: <a href="https://limedash.
com">limedash.com</a>
```

TreatAsContentArea

This function creates a static Content Area that is stored by key for the duration of the send. It will evaluate AMPscript included in the content retrieved, with a limit of 300 unique variations. If there are more than 300 unique variations, any subsequent versions will be rendered as the first.

> **TIP:** You may use this function instead of TreatAsContent if you are retrieving content that is the same for every Subscriber in your sending audience.

Arguments

`TreatAsContentArea(1,2,3)`

Ordinal	Type	Required	Description
1	String	True	Key value that identifies the content specified by the second argument
2	String	True	Content to be stored
3	String	False	Name of the Impression Region to wrap around content

Example

This example retrieves a test XML payload from a web service and replaces certain characters to display.

```
%%[

var @xmlContent
```

```
set @xmlContent = httpget("http://httpbin.org/xml")
set @xmlContent = replace(replace(@xmlContent, ">", "&gt;"),
"<", "&lt;")

]%%
xmlContent:
%%=TreatAsContentArea("XMLContent", @xmlContent, "XML
Content")=%%
```

Output

```
xmlContent:
&lt;?xml version='1.0' encoding='us-ascii'?&gt;

&lt;!--  A SAMPLE set of slides  --&gt;

&lt;slideshow
    title="Sample Slide Show"
    date="Date of publication"
    author="Yours Truly"
    &gt;

    &lt;!-- TITLE SLIDE --&gt;
    &lt;slide type="all"&gt;
      &lt;title&gt;Wake up to WonderWidgets!&lt;/title&gt;
    &lt;/slide&gt;

    &lt;!-- OVERVIEW --&gt;
    &lt;slide type="all"&gt;
        &lt;title&gt;Overview&lt;/title&gt;
        &lt;item&gt;Why &lt;em&gt;WonderWidgets&lt;/em&gt;
are great&lt;/item&gt;
        &lt;item/&gt;
        &lt;item&gt;Who &lt;em&gt;buys&lt;/em&gt;
WonderWidgets&lt;/item&gt;
    &lt;/slide&gt;

&lt;/slideshow&gt;
```

WAT

This function returns a specific set of Web Analytics Tracking parameters and values. Once the WAT parameters and values are returned, they can be manually appended to any URLs as needed. By default, parameter names and values must be static values.

Arguments

`WAT(1,2,n)`

Ordinal	Type	Required	Description
1	String	True	External key of the WAT parameter set
2	String	True	Value for parameter 1 in the set
n	String	False	Value for parameter 2 in the set (see note)

> **NOTE:** Additional parameter values can be appended as arguments.

The default Web Analytics Connector (WAC) configured by Marketing Cloud Support automatically appends a set of URL parameters and values to every link at email send time. This string can include in line personalization strings and AMPscript.

The WAC is enabled with the **`SPECIAL_LINK_PARAMS`** and **`ADDITIONAL_EMAIL_ATTRIBUTES`** business rules. The details are stored in a *Brand Tag* named **`email_XtraLinkParameters`**.

Like the WAC, the **`WAT`** function requires the **`SPECIAL_LINK_PARAMS`** business rule. In addition, a *Brand Tag* named **`ENHANCED_WEB_ANALYTICS_TRACKING`** must be enabled. Unlike the **`email_XtraLinkParameters`** set of parameters, these analytics strings are stored with *key* values:

```
verifyParams,?verify=%%=urlencode(lowercase(trim(WATP(1))))=%%
nameParams,?fName=%%=urlencode(WATP(1))=%%&lName=
%%=urlencode(WATP(2))=%%
```

At send time, WAT parameters and values are added before WAC parameters and values.

In this example, the WAT parameter and value is retrieved, set and appended to a login URL:

Example 1

```
%%[

var @loginURL

set @loginURL = concat("https://limedash.com/login",
WAT("verifyParams", "DfkSyhtdtYRBb"))

]%%
<a href="%%=redirectto(@loginURL)=%%" alias="Login">Login</a>
```

Output

```
<a href="https://limedash.com/login?verify=DfkSyhtdtYRBb"
alias="Login">Login</a>
```

To overcome for the static value limitation, the TreatAsContent function can be used to evaluate the WAT function prior to appending it to the URL:

Example 2

```
%%[

var @firstName
var @lastName
var @wat
var @profileURL

set @firstName = AttributeValue("FirstName") /* value from
attribute or DE column in send context */
set @firstName = "Nora" /* or a literal value */

set @lastName = AttributeValue("LastName") /* value from
attribute or DE column in send context */
set @lastName = "Taylor" /* or a literal value */
```

```
set @wat = treatascontent(concat('%%=WAT("nameParams","',
@firstName,'","', @lastName,'")=%%'))

set @profileURL = concat("https://limedash.com/profile", @wat)

]%%
<a href="%%=redirectto(@profileURL)=%%"
alias="Profile">Profile</a>
```

Output

```
<a href="https://limedash.com/profile?fName=Nora&lName=Taylor"
alias="Profile">Profile</a>
```

WATP

This function represents an ordinal placeholder for parameter values configured in the WAT string(s). It can only be set as part of the WAT string configuration by Marketing Cloud Support. Output is included in the result of the **WAT** function call. See the WAT example below for more context.

Argument

WATP(1)

Ordinal	Type	Required	Description
1	Number	True	Ordinal value that represents the position of the parameter value in the WAT string

Example

In the WAT string, the WATP parameters are ordinal placeholders for the parameter values. The first value gets **WATP(1)**, the second is **WATP(2)** and so on:

```
verifyParams,?verify=%%=urlencode(lowercase(trim(WATP(1))))=%%
nameParams,?fName=%%=urlencode(WATP(1))=%%&lName=%%=urlencode
(WATP(2))=%%
```

Data Extension Functions

Overview
This set of functions provides a means of interacting with rows in Data Extensions. Applications include:

- retrieving specific column values with simple criteria
- retrieving row sets with simple criteria
- executing predefined filters on data extension rows
- adding data extension rows
- updating column values in data extension rows
- retrieving row counts.

AMPscript functions that retrieve, update and delete rows in Data Extensions share a common characteristic: they can accept one or more column name/value pairs as parameters.

> **NOTE:** Not all of the Data Extension functions can be used in the context of an email. A few are only intended for landing pages, microsite pages or CloudPages, while others are only for use in SMS messages.

> **TIP:** If you are in a child business unit and are interacting with a Data Extension in the Shared Data Extension folder, you must reference the Data Extension name with a **`ENT.`** prefix (for example, **`ENT.DataExtensionName`**).

> **NOTE:** All Data Extensions have a hidden identity column called **`_CustomObjectKey`**. It's unique for each row in the Data Extension.

ClaimRow

This function returns a single row from a Data Extension and reserves the values to prevent them from being used by another operation. If a row is found and is unclaimed, the designated claimed column is set to **`true`** and data from that row is returned. If no unclaimed rows are available in the Data Extension, this function will return an error. Claimed rows can be used again if the designated claimed column changes back to **`false`**.

This function is primarily used for assigning unique coupon codes to an audience at send time and recording other pertinent data from the send context.

To utilize the ClaimRow function, you will need a Data Extension with some specific characteristics. At a minimum, your Data Extension must include the following:

1. a Boolean column that indicates claimed status, where **`true`** is claimed and **`false`** is unclaimed
2. a nullable column that represents the object or recipient claiming the row.

> **NOTE:** This function does not return a row set that can be checked using the RowCount function.

> **TIP:** You can also utilize the ClaimRow function in an SMS campaign.

> **TIP:** Ensure you upload sufficient coupon codes for your entire target audience. For recurring coupon campaigns, it's a good idea to have some method of monitoring unused coupon codes.

> **TIP:** Ensure the target of the coupon code (e-commerce site, point-of-sale or POS system etc.) is using the same set of coupon codes as your campaign.

> **TIP:** If you include a column named **`ClaimedDate`** in your Data Extension, the ClaimRow function will automatically populate it with the current date and time when a row is claimed.

Arguments

`ClaimRow(1,2,3,4,[5a,5b]...)`

Ordinal	Type	Required	Description
1	String	True	Data Extension from which to retrieve rows
2	String	True	Name of the column that identifies a row as claimed
3	String	True	Name of the Data Extension key column
4	String	True	Value of the Data Extension key column
5a	String	False	Additional name of the Data Extension key column (see note)
5b	String	False	Additional value of the Data Extension key column (see note)

> **NOTE:** The Data Extension name in the ClaimRow function cannot be an AMPscript variable.

> **NOTE:** Additional pairs of columns and values can be appended as arguments.

Example 1

The following illustrates the use of this function with the minimum number of arguments.

The sample Data Extension schema for this ClaimRow example is provided below.

Data Extension: *CouponCodes*

Name	Data Type	Length	Primary Key	Nullable	Default Value
CouponCode	Text	50	Y	N	
IsClaimed	Boolean		N	Y	False
EmailAddress	EmailAddress		N	Y	
ClaimedDate	Date		N	Y	

The *CouponCodes* Data Extension could include these initial rows:

CouponCode	IsClaimed	EmailAddress	ClaimedDate
SJOCYUNGIX	False		
ZURRPSIDQD	False		
LFZCWGPFCS	False		
KTZUYGCFOZ	False		
WDQHIUBVFS	False		

In this example, checking the **_messageContext** personalization string allows the coupon codes to be preserved while testing the AMPscript function. In this case, when no more coupons are available, the entire send is aborted with the **RaiseError** function.

```
%%[

var @em, @couponRow, @couponCode

if _messagecontext == "PREVIEW" then

    set @couponCode = "XX TEST XX"

else

    /* include the send context attributes or columns to
record here */
    set @em = AttributeValue("emailAddr")

    set @couponRow = ClaimRow("CouponCodes", "IsClaimed",
"EmailAddress", @em)

    if not empty(@couponRow) then

      set @couponCode = Field(@couponRow, "CouponCode")

    else

        /* You can do other error handling here */

        /* This aborts the entire send */
```

```
        RaiseError("No coupons available", false)

    endif

endif

]%%

Coupon code: %%=v(@couponCode)=%%
```

Output

If the AMPscript code referenced previously was executed in an email send to a single Subscriber, **doug@limedash.com**, the following would appear in the email:

```
Use this coupon code: SJOCYUNGIX
```

The result of the ClaimRow function would result in this claimed row in the *CouponCodes* Data Extension:

CouponCode	IsClaimed	EmailAddress	ClaimedDate
SJOCYUNGIX	True	doug@limedash.com	2017-10-10 12:34
ZURRPSIDQD	False		
LFZCWGPFCS	False		
KTZUYGCFOZ	False		
WDQHIUBVFS	False		

Example 2

The following illustrates the use of this function with additional arguments.

The sample Data Extension schema for this ClaimRow example is provided below.

Data Extension: *CouponCodes*

Name	Data Type	Length	Primary Key	Nullable	Default Value
CouponCode	Text	50	Y	N	
IsClaimed	Boolean		N	Y	False
EmailAddress	EmailAddress		N	Y	
Region	Text	50	N	Y	
ClaimedDate	Date		N	Y	

The *CouponCodes* Data Extension could include these initial rows:

CouponCode	IsClaimed	EmailAddress	Region	ClaimedDate
SJOCYUNGIX	False			
ZURRPSIDQD	False			
LFZCWGPFCS	False			
KTZUYGCFOZ	False			
WDQHIUBVFS	False			

In this example, checking the **`_messageContext`** personalization string allows the coupon codes to be preserved while testing the AMPscript function. In this case, when no more coupons are available, the entire send is aborted with the **`RaiseError`** function.

```
%%[

var @em, @region, @couponRow, @couponCode

if _messagecontext == "PREVIEW" then

    set @couponCode = "XX TEST XX"

else

    /* include the send context attributes or columns to
record here */
    set @em = AttributeValue("emailAddr")
    set @region = AttributeValue("Region")
```

```
    set @couponRow = ClaimRow("CouponCodes", "IsClaimed",
"EmailAddress", @em, "Region", @region)

    if not empty(@couponRow) then

      set @couponCode = Field(@couponRow, "CouponCode")

    else

        /* You can do other error handling here */

        /* This aborts the entire send */
        RaiseError("No coupons available", false)

    endif

endif

]%%

Coupon code: %%=v(@couponCode)=%%
```

Output

If the AMPscript code referenced previously was executed in an email send to a single Subscriber, **doug@limedash.com** with a **region** value of **Central**, the following would appear in the email:

```
Use this coupon code: SJOCYUNGIX
```

The result of the ClaimRow function would result in this claimed row in the *CouponCodes* Data Extension:

CouponCode	IsClaimed	EmailAddress	Region	ClaimedDate
SJOCYUNGIX	True	doug@limedash.com	Central	2017-10-10 12:34
ZURRPSIDQD	False			
LFZCWGPFCS	False			
KTZUYGCFOZ	False			
WDQHIUBVFS	False			

ClaimRowValue

Like the ClaimRow function, ClaimRowValue returns a single row from a Data Extension and reserves the values to prevent them from being used by another operation. If a row is found and is unclaimed, the designated claimed column is set to `true` and data from that row is returned. Unlike ClaimRow, if no unclaimed rows are available in the Data Extension, this function will return the value specified in the fourth parameter. Claimed rows can be used again if the designated claimed column changes back to `false`.

Generally speaking, you might choose to use the ClaimRowValue function over the ClaimRow function when you have a default value that can be presented to your Subscribers.

To utilize the ClaimRowValue function, you will need a Data Extension with some specific characteristics. At a minimum, your Data Extension must include the following:

1. a Boolean column that indicates claimed status, where `true` is claimed and `false` is unclaimed
2. a nullable column that represents the object or recipient claiming the row.

> **TIP:** You can also utilize the ClaimRowValue function in an SMS campaign.

> **TIP:** Ensure you upload sufficient coupon codes for your entire target audience. For recurring coupon campaigns, it's a good idea to have some method of monitoring unused coupon codes.

> **TIP:** Ensure the target of the coupon code (e-commerce site, point-of-sale or POS system etc.) is using the same set of coupon codes as your campaign.

> **TIP:** If you include a column named `ClaimedDate` in your Data Extension, the ClaimRowValue function will automatically populate it with the current date and time when a row is claimed.

Arguments

```
ClaimRowValue(1,2,3,4,5,6,[7a,7b]...)
```

Ordinal	Type	Required	Description
1	String	True	Data Extension from which to retrieve rows
2	String	True	Name of the column from which to retrieve the value
3	String	True	Name of the column that identifies a row as claimed
4	String	False	Default value to use if there are no available rows to claim
5	String	True	Name of the Data Extension key column
6	String	True	Value of the Data Extension key column
7a	String	False	Additional name of the Data Extension key column (see note)
7b	String	False	Additional value of the Data Extension key column (see note)

NOTE: Additional pairs of columns and values can be appended as arguments.

NOTE: The Data Extension name in the ClaimRowValue function cannot be an AMPscript variable.

Example 1

The following illustrates the use of this function with the minimum number of arguments.

A sample Data Extension schema for the ClaimRowValue example is provided below.

Data Extension: *CouponCodes*

Name	Data Type	Length	Primary Key	Nullable	Default Value
CouponCode	Text	50	Y	N	
IsClaimed	Boolean		N	Y	False
EmailAddress	EmailAddress		N	Y	
ClaimedDate	Date		N	Y	

The *CouponCodes* Data Extension could include these initial rows:

CouponCode	IsClaimed	EmailAddress	ClaimedDate
SJOCYUNGIX	False		
ZURRPSIDQD	False		
LFZCWGPFCS	False		
KTZUYGCFOZ	False		
WDQHIUBVFS	False		

In this example, checking the **`_messageContext`** personalization string allows the coupon codes to be preserved while testing the AMPscript function.

```
%%[

var @em, @defaultCoupon

set @defaultCoupon = "SAVE30"

if _messagecontext == "PREVIEW" then

    set @couponCode = "XX TEST XX"

else

    /* include the send context attributes or columns to
record here */
    set @em = AttributeValue("emailAddr")

    set @couponCode = ClaimRowValue("CouponCodes",
"CouponCode", "IsClaimed", @defaultCoupon, "EmailAddress",
@em)

endif

]%%

Coupon code: %%=v(@couponCode)=%%
```

Output

If the AMPscript code referenced previously was executed in an email send to a single Subscriber, **doug@limedash.com**, the following would appear in the email:

```
Use this coupon code: SJOCYUNGIX
```

The result of the ClaimRowValue function would result in this claimed row in the *CouponCodes* Data Extension:

CouponCode	IsClaimed	EmailAddress	ClaimedDate
SJOCYUNGIX	True	doug@limedash.com	2017-10-10 12:34
ZURRPSIDQD	False		
LFZCWGPFCS	False		
KTZUYGCFOZ	False		
WDQHIUBVFS	False		

If the same code is used and there were no available coupons for claiming, then the function would return the default value specified in the fourth parameter:

```
Use this coupon code: SAVE30
```

Example 2

The following illustrates the use of this function with additional arguments.

A sample Data Extension schema for the ClaimRow example is provided below.

Data Extension: *CouponCodes*

Name	Data Type	Length	Primary Key	Nullable	Default Value
CouponCode	Text	50	Y	N	
IsClaimed	Boolean		N	Y	False
EmailAddress	EmailAddress		N	Y	
Region	Text	50	N	Y	
ClaimedDate	Date		N	Y	

The *CouponCodes* Data Extension could include these initial rows:

CouponCode	IsClaimed	EmailAddress	Region	ClaimedDate
SJOCYUNGIX	False			
ZURRPSIDQD	False			
LFZCWGPFCS	False			
KTZUYGCFOZ	False			
WDQHIUBVFS	False			

In this example, checking the **`_messageContext`** personalization string allows the coupon codes to be preserved while testing the AMPScript function.

```
%%[

var @em, @region, @defaultCoupon

set @defaultCoupon = "SAVE30"

if _messagecontext == "PREVIEW" then

    set @couponCode = "XX TEST XX"

else

    /* include the send context attributes or columns to
record here */
    set @em = AttributeValue("emailAddr")
    set @region = AttributeValue("Region")

    set @couponCode = ClaimRowValue("CouponCodes",
"CouponCode", "IsClaimed", @defaultCoupon, "EmailAddress",
@em, "Region", @region)

endif

]%%

Coupon code: %%=v(@couponCode)=%%
```

Output

If the AMPscript code referenced previously was executed in an email send to a single Subscriber, **doug@limedash.com** with a **region** value of **Central**, the following would appear in the email:

```
Use this coupon code: SJOCYUNGIX
```

The result of the ClaimRowValue function would result in this claimed row in the *CouponCodes* Data Extension:

CouponCode	IsClaimed	EmailAddress	Region	ClaimedDate
SJOCYUNGIX	True	doug@limedash.com	Central	2017-10-10 12:34
ZURRPSIDQD	False			
LFZCWGPFCS	False			
KTZUYGCFOZ	False			
WDQHIUBVFS	False			

If the same code is used and there were no available coupons for claiming, then the function would return the default value specified in the fourth parameter:

```
Use this coupon code: SAVE30
```

DataExtensionRowCount

This function returns the number of rows in the specified Data Extension.

> **NOTE:** This function will not return row counts from the System Data Views.

Argument

`DataExtensionRowCount(1)`

Ordinal	Type	Required	Description
1	String	True	Data Extension from which to retrieve a row count

Example

Data Extension: *LoyaltyMembers*

Name	Data Type	Length	Primary Key	Nullable	Default Value
EmailAddress	EmailAddress	254	N	N	
SubscriberKey	Text	254	Y	N	
FirstName	Text	50	N	Y	
LastName	Text	50	N	Y	
Created	Date		N	Y	Current Date

The *LoyaltyMembers* Data Extension includes these rows:

EmailAddress	SubscriberKey	FirstName	LastName	Created
doug@limedash.com	8473	Doug	Smith	2017-10-21 12:01
suzy@limedash.com	5497	Suzy	Jackson	2017-10-20 11:01
dale@limedash.com	7114	Dale	Cameron	2017-10-19 10:01

Here is an example utilizing the preceding context:

```
%%[

var @rowCount
set @rowCount  = DataExtensionRowCount("LoyaltyMembers")

]%%
rowCount: %%=v(@rowCount)=%%
```

Output

```
RowCount: 3
```

DeleteData

This function deletes rows in a Data Extension that exactly match the specified column name and value pairs. It returns the number of rows deleted by the operation.

> **NOTE:** This function only works in a landing page, microsite page or CloudPage, or an SMS message in MobileConnect. Use DeleteDE if you need to delete rows from a Data Extension in an email.

Arguments

`DeleteData(1,2,3,[4a,4b]...)`

Ordinal	Type	Required	Description
1	String	True	Data Extension from which to delete rows
2	String	True	Name of the column that identifies the row to delete
3	String	True	Value that identifies the row to delete
4a	String	False	Additional column name that identifies the row to delete (see note)
4b	String	False	Additional value that identifies the row to delete (see note)

> **NOTE:** Additional pairs of columns and values can be appended as arguments.

Example 1

The following illustrates the use of this function with the minimum number of arguments.

Data Extension: *LoyaltyMembers*

Name	Data Type	Length	Primary Key	Nullable	Default Value
EmailAddress	EmailAddress	254	N	N	
SubscriberKey	Text	254	Y	N	
FirstName	Text	50	N	Y	
LastName	Text	50	N	Y	
Created	Date		N	Y	Current Date

The *LoyaltyMembers* Data Extension includes these rows:

EmailAddress	SubscriberKey	FirstName	LastName	Created
doug@limedash.com	8473	Doug	Smith	2017-10-21 12:01
suzy@limedash.com	5497	Suzy	Jackson	2017-10-20 11:01
dale@limedash.com	7114	Dale	Cameron	2017-10-19 10:01

Here is an example utilizing the preceding context:

```
%%[

var @deleteCount, @lookupValue

set @lookupValue = AttributeValue("emailaddr") /* value from
attribute or DE column in send context */
set @lookupValue = "suzy@limedash.com" /* or a literal value
*/

set @deleteCount =
DeleteData("LoyaltyMembers","EmailAddress", @lookupValue)

]%%
deleteCount: %%=v(@deleteCount)=%%
```

Output

```
deleteCount: 1
```

After the operation, the *LoyaltyMembers* Data Extension includes these rows:

EmailAddress	SubscriberKey	FirstName	LastName	Created
doug@limedash.com	8473	Doug	Smith	2017-10-21 12:01
dale@limedash.com	7114	Dale	Cameron	2017-10-19 10:01

Example 2
The following illustrates the use of this function with additional arguments.

Data Extension: *LoyaltyMembers*

Name	Data Type	Length	Primary Key	Nullable	Default Value
EmailAddress	EmailAddress	254	N	N	
SubscriberKey	Text	254	Y	N	
FirstName	Text	50	N	Y	
LastName	Text	50	N	Y	
Created	Date		N	Y	Current Date

The *LoyaltyMembers* Data Extension includes these rows:

EmailAddress	SubscriberKey	FirstName	LastName	Created
doug@limedash.com	8473	Doug	Smith	2017-10-21 12:01
suzy@limedash.com	5497	Suzy	Jackson	2017-10-20 11:01
dale@limedash.com	7114	Dale	Cameron	2017-10-19 10:01

Here is an example utilizing the preceding context:

```
%%[

var @deleteCount, @lookupValue1, @lookupValue2

set @lookupValue1 = AttributeValue("emailaddr") /* value
from attribute or DE column in send context */
```

```
set @lookupValue1 = "suzy@limedash.com" /* or a literal
value */

set @lookupValue2 = AttributeValue("FirstName") /* value from
attribute or DE column in send context */
set @lookupValue2 = "Suzy" /* or a literal value */

set @deleteCount =
DeleteData("LoyaltyMembers","EmailAddress",
@lookupValue1,"FirstName", @lookupValue2)

]%%
deleteCount: %%=v(@deleteCount)=%%
```

Output

```
deleteCount: 1
```

After the operation, the *LoyaltyMembers* Data Extension includes these rows:

EmailAddress	SubscriberKey	FirstName	LastName	Created
doug@limedash.com	8473	Doug	Smith	2017-10-21 12:01
dale@limedash.com	7114	Dale	Cameron	2017-10-19 10:01

DeleteDE

This function deletes rows in a Data Extension that exactly match the specified column name and value pairs. No output results from the use of this function.

> **NOTE:** This function only works in an email. Use DeleteData if you need to delete rows from a Data Extension in a landing page, microsite page or CloudPage, or in an SMS message in MobileConnect.

Arguments

`DeleteDE(1,2,3,[4a,4b])`

Ordinal	Type	Required	Description
1	String	True	Data Extension from which to delete rows
2	String	True	Name of the column that identifies the row to delete

Ordinal	Type	Required	Description
3	String	True	Value that identifies the row to delete
4a	String	False	Additional column name that identifies the row to delete (see note)
4b	String	False	Additional value that identifies the row to delete (see note)

> **NOTE:** Additional pairs of columns and values can be appended as arguments.

Example 1

The following illustrates the use of this function with the minimum number of arguments.

Data Extension: *LoyaltyMembers*

Name	Data Type	Length	Primary Key	Nullable	Default Value
EmailAddress	EmailAddress	254	N	N	
SubscriberKey	Text	254	Y	N	
FirstName	Text	50	N	Y	
LastName	Text	50	N	Y	
Created	Date		N	Y	Current Date

The *LoyaltyMembers* Data Extension includes these rows:

EmailAddress	SubscriberKey	FirstName	LastName	Created
doug@limedash.com	8473	Doug	Smith	2017-10-21 12:01
suzy@limedash.com	5497	Suzy	Jackson	2017-10-20 11:01
dale@limedash.com	7114	Dale	Cameron	2017-10-19 10:01

Here is an example utilizing the preceding context:

```
%%[

var @deleteCount, @lookupValue

set @lookupValue = AttributeValue("emailaddr") /* value from
attribute or DE column in send context */
```

```
set @lookupValue = "suzy@limedash.com" /* or a literal value
*/

DeleteDE("LoyaltyMembers","EmailAddress", @lookupValue)

]%%
```

Output

After the operation, the *LoyaltyMembers* Data Extension includes these rows:

EmailAddress	SubscriberKey	FirstName	LastName	Created
doug@limedash.com	8473	Doug	Smith	2017-10-21 12:01
dale@limedash.com	7114	Dale	Cameron	2017-10-19 10:01

Example 2

The following illustrates the use of this function with additional arguments.

Data Extension: *LoyaltyMembers*

Name	Data Type	Length	Primary Key	Nullable	Default Value
EmailAddress	EmailAddress	254	N	N	
SubscriberKey	Text	254	Y	N	
FirstName	Text	50	N	Y	
LastName	Text	50	N	Y	
Created	Date		N	Y	Current Date

The *LoyaltyMembers* Data Extension includes these rows:

EmailAddress	SubscriberKey	FirstName	LastName	Created
doug@limedash.com	8473	Doug	Smith	2017-10-21 12:01
suzy@limedash.com	5497	Suzy	Jackson	2017-10-20 11:01
dale@limedash.com	7114	Dale	Cameron	2017-10-19 10:01

Here is an example utilizing the preceding context:

```
%%[

var @deleteCount, @lookupValue1, @lookupValue2

set @lookupValue1 = AttributeValue("emailaddr") /* value
from attribute or DE column in send context */
set @lookupValue1 = "suzy@limedash.com" /* or a literal
value */

set @lookupValue2 = AttributeValue("FirstName") /* value from
attribute or DE column in send context */
set @lookupValue2 = "Suzy" /* or a literal value */

DeleteDE("LoyaltyMembers","EmailAddress",
@lookupValue1,"FirstName", @lookupValue2)

]%%
```

Output

After the operation, the *LoyaltyMembers* Data Extension includes these rows:

EmailAddress	SubscriberKey	FirstName	LastName	Created
doug@limedash.com	8473	Doug	Smith	2017-10-21 12:01
dale@limedash.com	7114	Dale	Cameron	2017-10-19 10:01

ExecuteFilter

This function executes the specified Data Extension Data Filter and returns a row set.

> **NOTE:** This function only works in a landing page, microsite page or CloudPage.

> **NOTE:** This function will not work on Profile Attribute Data Filters.

Argument

`ExecuteFilter(1)`

Ordinal	Type	Required	Description
1	String	True	Customer/External Key of the Data Filter to execute

Example

Data Extension: *LoyaltyMembers*

Name	Data Type	Length	Primary Key	Nullable	Default Value
EmailAddress	EmailAddress	254	N	N	
SubscriberKey	Text	254	Y	N	
FirstName	Text	50	N	Y	
LastName	Text	50	N	Y	
Created	Date		N	Y	Current Date

The *LoyaltyMembers* Data Extension includes these rows:

EmailAddress	SubscriberKey	FirstName	LastName	Created
doug@limedash.com	8473	Doug	Smith	2017-10-21 12:01
suzy@limedash.com	5497	Suzy	Jackson	2017-10-20 11:01
dale@limedash.com	7114	Dale	Cameron	2017-10-19 10:01
barb@plumcomma.com	5767	Barb	Brown	2017-10-18 09:01

Data Filter: `DataExtension_Test_Sample_Emails`

- Customer/External Key: **`DataExtension_Test_Sample_Emails`**
- **`Email Address`** contains **`limedash.com`**

Here is an example utilizing the preceding context:

```
%%[

var @rows, @row, @rowCount, @i

set @rows =
ExecuteFilter("DataExtension _Test _Example _Emails")
set @rowCount = rowcount(@rows)

if @rowCount > 0 then

  output(concat("rowCount: ", @rowCount))

  for @i = 1 to @rowCount do

    var @emailAddress
    set @row = row(@rows, @i) /* get row based on counter */
    set @emailAddress = field(@row,"emailAddress")

    ]%%

    <br>Row %%=v(@i)=%%, emailAddress is
%%=v(@emailAddress)=%%

    %%[

  next @i ]%%

%%[ else ]%%

No rows found

%%[ endif ]%%
```

Output

```
rowCount: 3
Row 1, emailAddress is doug@limedash.com
Row 2, emailAddress is suzy@limedash.com
Row 3, emailAddress is dale@limedash.com
```

ExecuteFilterOrderedRows

This function executes the specified Data Extension Data Filter and returns a row set with the specified number of rows. Rows are returned sorted by the column specified in the third parameter.

> **NOTE:** This function only works in a landing page, microsite page or CloudPage, or in an SMS message in MobileConnect.

> **NOTE:** This function will not work on Profile Attribute Data Filters.

Arguments

`ExecuteFilterOrderedRows(1,2,3)`

Ordinal	Type	Required	Description
1	String	True	Customer/External Key of the Data Filter to execute
2	Number	True	Number of rows to return. A value of 0 returns all rows. No maximum limit on rows returned.
3	String	True	Name of column used to sort resulting row set. Add a **ASC** or **DESC** suffix to specify the sort order. **ASC** is the default.

Example

```
%%[

var @rows, @row, @rowCount, @numRowsToReturn, @i

set @numRowsToReturn = 2 /* 0 means return all rows, no
limit */
set @rows = ExecuteFilterOrderedRows("DataExtension _Test
_Example _Emails",@numRowsToReturn,"emailAddress desc")
```

```
set @rowCount = rowcount(@rows)

if @rowCount > 0 then

  output(concat("rowCount: ", @rowCount))

  for @i = 1 to @rowCount do

    var @emailAddress
    set @row = row(@rows, @i) /* get row based on counter */
    set @emailAddress = field(@row,"emailAddress")

    ]%%

    <br>Row %%=v(@i)=%%, emailAddress is
%%=v(@emailAddress)=%%

    %%[

  next @i ]%%

%%[ else ]%%

No rows found

%%[ endif ]%%
```

Output

```
rowCount: 2
Row 1, emailAddress is dale@limedash.com
Row 2, emailAddress is suzy@limedash.com
```

Field

This function returns the value of a field from a row set or the value of an application programming interface (API) object property.

Arguments

`Field(1,2,3)`

Ordinal	Type	Required	Description
1	String	True	Row set or API object from which to return the value or property
2	String	True	Name of the row set field or API object property to retrieve
3	Boolean	False	Indicates whether to return an empty string value or an error if the specified field or property does not exist. Specifying `0` will return a null value, while `1` will result in a runtime error. The default value is `1`.

Example 1

Data Extension: *LoyaltyMembers*

Name	Data Type	Length	Primary Key	Nullable	Default Value
EmailAddress	EmailAddress	254	N	N	
SubscriberKey	Text	254	Y	N	
FirstName	Text	50	N	Y	
LastName	Text	50	N	Y	
Created	Date		N	Y	Current Date

The *LoyaltyMembers* Data Extension includes these rows:

EmailAddress	SubscriberKey	FirstName	LastName	Created
doug@limedash.com	8473	Doug	Smith	2017-10-21 12:01
suzy@limedash.com	5497	Suzy	Jackson	2017-10-20 11:01
dale@limedash.com	7114	Dale	Cameron	2017-10-19 10:01

If the target field does not exist and **0** is specified as the third parameter, an empty string is returned. Otherwise a runtime error occurs.

```
%%[

var @rows, @row, @rowCount
var @emailAddress
set @emailAddress = "dale@limedash.com"

set @rows = LookupRows("LoyaltyMembers","emailAddress",
@emailAddress)
set @rowCount = rowcount(@rows)

if @rowCount > 0 then

  var @firstName, @favoriteColor
  set @row = row(@rows,1) /* get row #1 */
  set @firstName = field(@row,"FirstName")
  set @favoriteColor = field(@row,"FavoriteColor",0)

]%%

FirstName: %%=v(@firstName)=%%
<br>FavoriteColor: %%=v(@favoriteColor)=%%

%%[ else ]%%

No rows found

%%[ endif ]%%
```

Output

```
FirstName: Doug
FavoriteColor:
```

Example 2
Data Extension: *LoyaltyMembers*

Name	Data Type	Length	Primary Key	Nullable	Default Value
EmailAddress	EmailAddress	254	N	N	
SubscriberKey	Text	254	Y	N	
FirstName	Text	50	N	Y	
LastName	Text	50	N	Y	
Created	Date		N	Y	Current Date

The *LoyaltyMembers* Data Extension includes these rows:

EmailAddress	SubscriberKey	FirstName	LastName	Created
doug@limedash.com	8473	Doug	Smith	2017-10-21 12:01
suzy@limedash.com	5497	Suzy	Jackson	2017-10-20 11:01
dale@limedash.com	7114	Dale	Cameron	2017-10-19 10:01

In addition to using the Field function to return a field from a row set, it can also be used to retrieve the value of an API property.

> **NOTE:** You can only utilize the Field function on API Objects in a landing or microsite page.

```
%%[

var @rr, @rowCount, @emailAddress
set @emailAddress = "dale@limedash.com"

set @rr = CreateObject("RetrieveRequest")
SetObjectProperty(@rr,"ObjectType","DataExtensionObject
[LoyaltyMembers]")
AddObjectArrayItem(@rr,"Properties","FirstName")

set @sfp = CreateObject("SimpleFilterPart")
SetObjectProperty(@sfp,"Property","EmailAddress")
SetObjectProperty(@sfp,"SimpleOperator","equals")
```

```
AddObjectArrayItem(@sfp,"Value", @emailAddress)

SetObjectProperty(@rr,"Filter", @sfp)

set @rows = InvokeRetrieve(@rr)
set @rowCount = rowcount(@rows)

if @rowCount > 0 then

  var @properties
  set @row = row(@rows, 1)
  set @properties = field(@row,"Properties")
  set @rowCountProperties = rowCount(@properties)

  if @rowCountProperties > 0 then

    var @firstName
    set @property = row(@properties, 1)
    set @name = field(@property, "Name")
    set @value = field(@property ,"Value")

    set @firstName = @value

  endif

]%%

FirstName: %%=v(@firstName)=%%

%%[ else ]%%

No rows found

%%[ endif ]%%
```

Output

```
FirstName: Doug
```

InsertData

This function inserts a row in a Data Extension with the specified column name and value pairs. It returns the number of rows inserted by the operation.

> **NOTE:** This function only works in a landing page, microsite page or CloudPage, or in an SMS message in MobileConnect. Use the InsertDE function if you need to insert rows into a Data Extension in an email.

Arguments

`InsertData(1,2,3,[4a,4b]...)`

Ordinal	Type	Required	Description
1	String	True	Name of the Data Extension receiving the new row
2	String	True	Name of the column receiving the value
3	String	True	Value to insert into the column
4a	String	False	Additional column name receiving the value (see note)
4b	String	False	Additional value to insert into the column (see note)

> **NOTE:** Additional pairs of columns and values can be appended as arguments.

Example 1

The following illustrates the use of this function with the minimum number of arguments.

Data Extension: *LoyaltyMembers*

Name	Data Type	Length	Primary Key	Nullable	Default Value
EmailAddress	EmailAddress	254	N	N	
SubscriberKey	Text	254	Y	N	
FirstName	Text	50	N	Y	
LastName	Text	50	N	Y	
Created	Date		N	Y	Current Date

The *LoyaltyMembers* Data Extension includes these rows:

EmailAddress	SubscriberKey	FirstName	LastName	Created
doug@limedash.com	8473	Doug	Smith	2017-10-21 12:01
suzy@limedash.com	5497	Suzy	Jackson	2017-10-20 11:01
dale@limedash.com	7114	Dale	Cameron	2017-10-19 10:01

Here is an example utilizing the preceding context:

```
%%[

var @insertCount, @emailAddress, @subscriberKey

set @emailAddress = "barb@limedash.com"
set @subscriberKey = "5767"

set @insertCount =
insertData("LoyaltyMembers","EmailAddress",
@emailAddress,"SubscriberKey", @subscriberKey)

]%%
insertCount: %%=v(@insertCount)=%%
```

Output

```
insertCount: 1
```

After the operation, the *LoyaltyMembers* Data Extension includes these rows:

EmailAddress	SubscriberKey	FirstName	LastName	Created
doug@limedash.com	8473	Doug	Smith	2017-10-21 12:01
suzy@limedash.com	5497	Suzy	Jackson	2017-10-20 11:01
dale@limedash.com	7114	Dale	Cameron	2017-10-19 10:01
barb@limedash.com	5767			2017-10-22 13:01

Example 2

The following illustrates the use of this function with additional arguments.

Data Extension: *LoyaltyMembers*

Name	Data Type	Length	Primary Key	Nullable	Default Value
EmailAddress	EmailAddress	254	N	N	
SubscriberKey	Text	254	Y	N	
FirstName	Text	50	N	Y	
LastName	Text	50	N	Y	
Created	Date		N	Y	Current Date

The *LoyaltyMembers* Data Extension includes these rows:

EmailAddress	SubscriberKey	FirstName	LastName	Created
doug@limedash.com	8473	Doug	Smith	2017-10-21 12:01
suzy@limedash.com	5497	Suzy	Jackson	2017-10-20 11:01
dale@limedash.com	7114	Dale	Cameron	2017-10-19 10:01

Here is an example utilizing the preceding context:

```
%%[

var @insertCount, @emailAddress, @subscriberKey, @firstName,
@lastName

set @emailAddress = "barb@limedash.com"
set @subscriberKey = "5767"
set @firstName = "Barb"
set @lastName = "Brown"

set @insertCount =
insertData("LoyaltyMembers","EmailAddress",
@emailAddress,"SubscriberKey", @subscriberKey,"FirstName",
@firstName,"LastName", @lastName)

]%%
insertCount: %%=v(@insertCount)=%%
```

Output

```
insertCount: 1
```

After the operation, the *LoyaltyMembers* Data Extension includes these rows:

EmailAddress	SubscriberKey	FirstName	LastName	Created
doug@limedash.com	8473	Doug	Smith	2017-10-21 12:01
suzy@limedash.com	5497	Suzy	Jackson	2017-10-20 11:01
dale@limedash.com	7114	Dale	Cameron	2017-10-19 10:01
barb@limedash.com	5767	Barb	Brown	2017-10-22 13:01

InsertDE

This function inserts a row in a Data Extension with the specified column name and value pairs. No output is returned from this function.

> **NOTE:** This function only works in an email. Use InsertData if you need to insert rows into a Data Extension in a landing page, microsite page or CloudPage, or in an SMS message.

Arguments

`InsertDE(1,2,3,[4a,4b]...)`

Ordinal	Type	Required	Description
1	String	True	Name of the Data Extension receiving the new row
2	String	True	Name of the column receiving the value
3	String	True	Value to insert into the column
4a	String	False	Additional column name receiving the value (see note)
4b	String	False	Additional value to insert into the column (see note)

> **NOTE:** Additional pairs of columns and values can be appended as arguments.

Example 1
The following illustrates the use of this function with the minimum number of arguments.

Data Extension: *LoyaltyMembers*

Name	Data Type	Length	Primary Key	Nullable	Default Value
EmailAddress	EmailAddress	254	N	N	
SubscriberKey	Text	254	Y	N	
FirstName	Text	50	N	Y	
LastName	Text	50	N	Y	
Created	Date		N	Y	Current Date

The *LoyaltyMembers* Data Extension includes these rows:

EmailAddress	SubscriberKey	FirstName	LastName	Created
doug@limedash.com	8473	Doug	Smith	2017-10-21 12:01
suzy@limedash.com	5497	Suzy	Jackson	2017-10-20 11:01
dale@limedash.com	7114	Dale	Cameron	2017-10-19 10:01

Here is an example utilizing the preceding context:

```
%%[

var @insertCount, @emailAddress, @subscriberKey

set @emailAddress = "barb@limedash.com"
set @subscriberKey = "5767"

InsertDE("LoyaltyMembers","EmailAddress",
@emailAddress,"SubscriberKey", @subscriberKey)

]%%
```

Output

```
insertCount: 1
```

After the operation, the *LoyaltyMembers* Data Extension includes these rows:

EmailAddress	SubscriberKey	FirstName	LastName	Created
doug@limedash.com	8473	Doug	Smith	2017-10-21 12:01
suzy@limedash.com	5497	Suzy	Jackson	2017-10-20 11:01
dale@limedash.com	7114	Dale	Cameron	2017-10-19 10:01
barb@limedash.com	5767			2017-10-22 13:01

Example 2

The following illustrates the use of this function with additional arguments.

Data Extension: *LoyaltyMembers*

Name	Data Type	Length	Primary Key	Nullable	Default Value
EmailAddress	EmailAddress	254	N	N	
SubscriberKey	Text	254	Y	N	
FirstName	Text	50	N	Y	
LastName	Text	50	N	Y	
Created	Date		N	Y	Current Date

The *LoyaltyMembers* Data Extension includes these rows:

EmailAddress	SubscriberKey	FirstName	LastName	Created
doug@limedash.com	8473	Doug	Smith	2017-10-21 12:01
suzy@limedash.com	5497	Suzy	Jackson	2017-10-20 11:01
dale@limedash.com	7114	Dale	Cameron	2017-10-19 10:01

Here is an example utilizing the preceding context:

```
%%[

var @insertCount, @emailAddress, @subscriberKey, @firstName,
@lastName

set @emailAddress = "barb@limedash.com"
set @subscriberKey = "5767"
set @firstName = "Barb"
set @lastName = "Brown"

InsertDE("LoyaltyMembers","EmailAddress",
@emailAddress,"SubscriberKey", @subscriberKey,"FirstName",
@firstName,"LastName", @lastName)

]%%
```

Output

```
insertCount: 1
```

After the operation, the *LoyaltyMembers* Data Extension includes these rows:

EmailAddress	SubscriberKey	FirstName	LastName	Created
doug@limedash.com	8473	Doug	Smith	2017-10-21 12:01
suzy@limedash.com	5497	Suzy	Jackson	2017-10-20 11:01
dale@limedash.com	7114	Dale	Cameron	2017-10-19 10:01
barb@limedash.com	5767	Barb	Brown	2017-10-22 13:01

Lookup

This function returns the value of a single column from a Data Extension.

Arguments

`Lookup(1,2,3,4,[5a,5b]...)`

Ordinal	Type	Required	Description
1	String	True	Name of the Data Extension from which to return a value
2	String	True	Name of the column from which to return a value
3	String	True	Name of the column that identifies the row to retrieve
4	String	True	Value that identifies the row to retrieve
5a	String	False	Additional column name that identifies the row to retrieve (see note)
5b	String	False	Additional value that identifies the row to retrieve (see note)

> **NOTE:** Additional pairs of columns and values can be appended as arguments.

Example 1

The following illustrates the use of this function with the minimum number of arguments.

Data Extension: *LoyaltyMembers*

Name	Data Type	Length	Primary Key	Nullable	Default Value
EmailAddress	EmailAddress	254	N	N	
SubscriberKey	Text	254	Y	N	
FirstName	Text	50	N	Y	
LastName	Text	50	N	Y	
Created	Date		N	Y	Current Date

The *LoyaltyMembers* Data Extension includes these rows:

EmailAddress	SubscriberKey	FirstName	LastName	Created
doug@limedash.com	8473	Doug	Smith	2017-10-21 12:01
suzy@limedash.com	5497	Suzy	Jackson	2017-10-20 11:01
dale@limedash.com	7114	Dale	Cameron	2017-10-19 10:01

Here is an example utilizing the preceding context:

```
%%[

var @EmailAddress, @lookupValue

set @lookupValue = AttributeValue("_subscriberkey") /* value
from attribute or DE column in send context */
set @lookupValue = "5497" /* or a literal value */

set @EmailAddress =
Lookup("LoyaltyMembers","EmailAddress","SubscriberKey",
@lookupValue)

]%%
EmailAddress: %%=v(@EmailAddress)=%%
```

Output

```
EmailAddress: suzy@limedash.com
```

Example 2

The following illustrates the use of this function with additional arguments.

Data Extension: *LoyaltyMembers*

Name	Data Type	Length	Primary Key	Nullable	Default Value
EmailAddress	EmailAddress	254	N	N	
SubscriberKey	Text	254	Y	N	
FirstName	Text	50	N	Y	
LastName	Text	50	N	Y	
Created	Date		N	Y	Current Date

The *LoyaltyMembers* Data Extension includes these rows:

EmailAddress	SubscriberKey	FirstName	LastName	Created
doug@limedash.com	8473	Doug	Smith	2017-10-21 12:01
suzy@limedash.com	5497	Suzy	Jackson	2017-10-20 11:01
dale@limedash.com	7114	Dale	Cameron	2017-10-19 10:01

Here is an example utilizing the preceding context:

```
%%[

var @EmailAddress, @lookupValue1, @lookupValue2

set @lookupValue1 = AttributeValue("_subscriberkey") /*
value from attribute or DE column in send context */
set @lookupValue1 = "5497" /* or a literal value */

set @lookupValue2 = AttributeValue("FirstName") /* value from
attribute or DE column in send context */
set @lookupValue2 = "Suzy" /* or a literal value */

set @EmailAddress =
Lookup("LoyaltyMembers","EmailAddress","SubscriberKey",
@lookupValue1, "FirstName", @lookupValue2)

]%%
EmailAddress: %%=v(@EmailAddress)=%%
```

Output

```
EmailAddress: suzy@limedash.com
```

LookupOrderedRows

This function returns a set of ordered rows from a Data Extension.

Arguments

`LookupOrderedRows(1,2,3,4,5,[6a,6b]...)`

Ordinal	Type	Required	Description
1	String	True	Name of the Data Extension from which to return rows
2	Number	True	Number of rows to return. Specifying 0 returns all matching rows. Maximum rows returned is 2,000.
3	String	True	Order-by clause that determines the order of the rows returned. Include a suffix of **ASC** (default) or **DESC** to specify the sort order of the rows.
4	String	True	Name of the column that identifies the rows to retrieve
5	String	True	Value that identifies the rows to retrieve
6a	String	False	Additional column name that identifies the rows to retrieve (see note)
6b	String	False	Additional value that identifies the rows to retrieve (see note)

> **NOTE:** Additional pairs of columns and values can be appended as arguments.

Example 1

The following illustrates the use of this function with the minimum number of arguments.

Data Extension: *LoyaltyMembers*

Name	Data Type	Length	Primary Key	Nullable	Default Value
EmailAddress	EmailAddress	254	N	N	
SubscriberKey	Text	254	Y	N	
FirstName	Text	50	N	Y	
Region	Text	50	N	Y	
Rank	Number		N	Y	

The *LoyaltyMembers* Data Extension includes these rows:

EmailAddress	SubscriberKey	FirstName	Region	Rank
doug@limedash.com	8473	Doug	north	1
suzy@limedash.com	5497	Suzy	North	3
dale@limedash.com	7114	Dale	West	2
barb@limedash.com	5767	Barb	North	1
curt@limedash.com	5152	Curt	north	2
nora@limedash.com	7014	Nora	South	1
leon@limedash.com	8225	Leon	East	3
lily@limedash.com	9496	Lily	East	1

Here is an example utilizing the preceding context:

```
%%[
var @rows, @row, @rowCount, @numRowsToReturn, @region, @i

set @region = AttributeValue("Region") /* value from
attribute or DE column in send context */
set @region = "North" /* or a literal value */
set @numRowsToReturn = 0 /* 0 means all, max 2000 */
set @rows = LookupOrderedRows("LoyaltyMembers",
@numRowsToReturn, "rank desc, firstName asc", "region",
@region)
set @rowCount = rowcount(@rows)

output(concat("region: ", @region))

if @rowCount > 0 then

  for @i = 1 to @rowCount do

    var @firstName, @emailAddress, @rank
    set @row = row(@rows, @i) /* get row based on counter */
    set @rank = field(@row,"rank")
    set @firstName = field(@row,"firstName")
    set @emailAddress = field(@row,"emailAddress")

    ]%%
```

```
    <br>Row %%=v(@i)=%%, rank: %%=v(@rank)=%%, firstName:
%%=v(@firstName)=%%, emailAddress: %%=v(@emailAddress)=%%

    %%[

  next @i ]%%

%%[ else ]%%

No rows found

%%[ endif ]%%
```

Output

```
region: North
Row 1, rank: 3, firstName: Suzy, emailAddress:
suzy@limedash.com
Row 2, rank: 2, firstName: Curt, emailAddress:
curt@limedash.com
Row 3, rank: 1, firstName: Doug, emailAddress:
doug@limedash.com
Row 4, rank: 1, firstName: Barb, emailAddress:
barb@limedash.com
```

Example 2

The following illustrates the use of this function with additional arguments.

Data Extension: *LoyaltyMembers*

Name	Data Type	Length	Primary Key	Nullable	Default Value
EmailAddress	EmailAddress	254	N	N	
SubscriberKey	Text	254	Y	N	
FirstName	Text	50	N	Y	
Region	Text	50	N	Y	
Rank	Number		N	Y	

The *LoyaltyMembers* Data Extension includes these rows:

EmailAddress	SubscriberKey	FirstName	Region	Rank
doug@limedash.com	8473	Doug	north	1
suzy@limedash.com	5497	Suzy	North	3
dale@limedash.com	7114	Dale	West	2
barb@limedash.com	5767	Barb	North	1
curt@limedash.com	5152	Curt	north	2
nora@limedash.com	7014	Nora	South	1
leon@limedash.com	8225	Leon	East	3
lily@limedash.com	9496	Lily	East	1

Here is an example utilizing the preceding context:

```
%%[
var @rows, @row, @rowCount, @numRowsToReturn, @region, @i,
@rank

set @region = AttributeValue("Region") /* value from
attribute or DE column in send context */
set @region = "North" /* or a literal value */

set @rank = AttributeValue("Rank") /* value from attribute
or DE column in send context */
set @rank = "1" /* or a literal value */

set @numRowsToReturn = 0 /* 0 means all, max 2000 */
set @rows = LookupOrderedRows("LoyaltyMembers",
@numRowsToReturn, "rank desc, firstName asc", "region",
@region, "rank", @rank)
set @rowCount = rowcount(@rows)

output(concat("region: ", @region))
output(concat("<br>rank: ", @rank))

if @rowCount > 0 then

  for @i = 1 to @rowCount do

    var @firstName, @emailAddress
```

```
    set @row = row(@rows, @i) /* get row based on counter */
    set @firstName = field(@row,"firstName")
    set @emailAddress = field(@row,"emailAddress")

    ]%%

    <br>Row %%=v(@i)=%%, firstName: %%=v(@firstName)=%%,
emailAddress: %%=v(@emailAddress)=%%

    %%[

  next @i ]%%

%%[ else ]%%

No rows found

%%[ endif ]%%
```

Output

```
region: North
rank: 1
Row 1, firstName: Doug, emailAddress: doug@limedash.com
Row 2, firstName: Barb, emailAddress: barb@limedash.com
```

LookupOrderedRowsCS

This function returns a set of ordered rows from a Data Extension. This variation of the LookupOrderedRows function treats selection values as case-sensitive.

Arguments

`LookupOrderedRowsCS(1,2,3,4,5,[6a,6b]...)`

Ordinal	Type	Required	Description
1	String	True	Name of the Data Extension from which to return rows
2	Number	True	Number of rows to return. Specifying 0 returns all matching rows. Maximum rows returned is 2,000.
3	String	True	Comma-separated list of fields that determine the order of the rows returned. Optionally, each column can be followed by **ASC** (default) or **DESC** to specify the sort order.
4	String	True	Name of the column that identifies the rows to retrieve
5	String	True	Value that identifies the rows to retrieve
6a	String	False	Additional column name that identifies the rows to re-trieve (see note)
6b	String	False	Additional value that identifies the rows to retrieve (see note)

NOTE: Additional pairs of columns and values can be appended as arguments.

Example 1

The following illustrates the use of this function with the minimum number of arguments.

Data Extension: *LoyaltyMembers*

Name	Data Type	Length	Primary Key	Nullable	Default Value
EmailAddress	EmailAddress	254	N	N	
SubscriberKey	Text	254	Y	N	
FirstName	Text	50	N	Y	
Region	Text	50	N	Y	
Rank	Number		N	Y	

The *LoyaltyMembers* Data Extension includes these rows:

EmailAddress	SubscriberKey	FirstName	Region	Rank
doug@limedash.com	8473	Doug	north	1
suzy@limedash.com	5497	Suzy	North	3
dale@limedash.com	7114	Dale	West	2
barb@limedash.com	5767	Barb	North	1
curt@limedash.com	5152	Curt	north	2
nora@limedash.com	7014	Nora	South	1
leon@limedash.com	8225	Leon	East	3
lily@limedash.com	9496	Lily	East	1

Here is an example utilizing the preceding context:

```
%%[
var @rows, @row, @rowCount, @numRowsToReturn, @region, @i

set @region = AttributeValue("Region") /* value from
attribute or DE column in send context */
set @region = "north" /* or a literal value */
set @numRowsToReturn = 0 /* 0 means all, max 2000 */
set @rows = LookupOrderedRowsCS("LoyaltyMembers",
@numRowsToReturn,"rank desc, firstName asc","region",
@region)
set @rowCount = rowcount(@rows)

output(concat("region: ", @region))

if @rowCount > 0 then

  for @i = 1 to @rowCount do

    var @emailAddress, @firstName, @rank
    set @row = row(@rows, @i) /* get row based on counter */
    set @rank = field(@row,"rank")
    set @firstName = field(@row,"firstName")
    set @emailAddress = field(@row,"emailAddress")

    ]%%
```

```
    <br>Row %%=v(@i)=%%, rank: %%=v(@rank)=%%, firstName:
%%=v(@firstName)=%%, emailAddress: %%=v(@emailAddress)=%%

    %%[

  next @i ]%%

%%[ else ]%%

No rows found

%%[ endif ]%%
```

Output

```
region: north
Row 1, rank: 2, firstName: Curt, emailAddress:
curt@limedash.com
Row 2, rank: 1, firstName: Doug, emailAddress:
doug@limedash.com
```

Example 2
The following illustrates the use of this function with additional arguments.

Data Extension: *LoyaltyMembers*

Name	Data Type	Length	Primary Key	Nullable	Default Value
EmailAddress	EmailAddress	254	N	N	
SubscriberKey	Text	254	Y	N	
FirstName	Text	50	N	Y	
Region	Text	50	N	Y	
Rank	Number		N	Y	

The *LoyaltyMembers* Data Extension includes these rows:

EmailAddress	SubscriberKey	FirstName	Region	Rank
doug@limedash.com	8473	Doug	north	1
suzy@limedash.com	5497	Suzy	North	3
dale@limedash.com	7114	Dale	West	2
barb@limedash.com	5767	Barb	North	1
curt@limedash.com	5152	Curt	north	2
nora@limedash.com	7014	Nora	South	1
leon@limedash.com	8225	Leon	East	3
lily@limedash.com	9496	Lily	East	1

Here is an example utilizing the preceding context:

```
%%[
var @rows, @row, @rowCount, @numRowsToReturn, @region, @i

set @region = AttributeValue("Region") /* value from
attribute or DE column in send context */
set @region = "north" /* or a literal value */

set @rank = AttributeValue("Rank") /* value from attribute
or DE column in send context */
set @rank = "1" /* or a literal value */

set @numRowsToReturn = 0 /* 0 means all, max 2000 */
set @rows = LookupOrderedRowsCS("LoyaltyMembers",
@numRowsToReturn, "rank desc, firstName asc", "region",
@region, "rank", @rank)
set @rowCount = rowcount(@rows)

output(concat("region: ", @region))
output(concat("<br>rank: ", @rank))

if @rowCount > 0 then

  for @i = 1 to @rowCount do

    var @firstName, @emailAddress
    set @row = row(@rows, @i) /* get row based on counter */
```

```
    set @firstName = field(@row,"firstName")
    set @emailAddress = field(@row,"emailAddress")

    ]%%

    <br>Row %%=v(@i)=%%, firstName: %%=v(@firstName)=%%,
emailAddress: %%=v(@emailAddress)=%%

    %%[

  next @i ]%%

%%[ else ]%%

No rows found

%%[ endif ]%%
```

Output

```
region: north
rank: 1
Row 1, firstName: Doug, emailAddress: doug@limedash.com
```

LookupRows

This function returns a set of unordered rows from a Data Extension.

Arguments

`LookupRows(1,2,3,[4a,4b]...)`

Ordinal	Type	Required	Description
1	String	True	Name of the Data Extension from which to return rows
2	String	True	Name of the column that identifies the rows to retrieve
3	String	True	Value that identifies the rows to retrieve
4a	String	False	Additional column name that identifies the rows to retrieve (see note)
4b	String	False	Additional value that identifies the rows to retrieve (see note)

> **NOTE:** Additional pairs of columns and values can be appended as arguments.

Example 1

The following illustrates the use of this function with the minimum number of arguments.

Data Extension: *LoyaltyMembers*

Name	Data Type	Length	Primary Key	Nullable	Default Value
EmailAddress	EmailAddress	254	N	N	
SubscriberKey	Text	254	Y	N	
FirstName	Text	50	N	Y	
Region	Text	50	N	Y	
Rank	Number		N	Y	

The *LoyaltyMembers* Data Extension includes these rows:

EmailAddress	SubscriberKey	FirstName	Region	Rank
doug@limedash.com	8473	Doug	north	1
suzy@limedash.com	5497	Suzy	North	3
dale@limedash.com	7114	Dale	West	2
barb@limedash.com	5767	Barb	North	1
curt@limedash.com	5152	Curt	north	2
nora@limedash.com	7014	Nora	South	1
leon@limedash.com	8225	Leon	East	3
lily@limedash.com	9496	Lily	East	1

Here is an example utilizing the preceding context:

```
%%[
var @rows, @row, @rowCount, @numRowsToReturn, @region, @i

set @region = AttributeValue("Region") /* value from
attribute or DE column in send context */
set @region = "North" /* or a literal value */
set @rows = LookupRows("LoyaltyMembers","region", @region)
set @rowCount = rowcount(@rows)

output(concat("region: ", @region))

if @rowCount > 0 then

  for @i = 1 to @rowCount do

    var @emailAddress, @firstName, @rank
    set @row = row(@rows, @i) /* get row based on counter */
    set @firstName = field(@row,"firstName")
    set @emailAddress = field(@row,"emailAddress")

    ]%%

    <br>Row %%=v(@i)=%%, firstName: %%=v(@firstName)=%%,
emailAddress: %%=v(@emailAddress)=%%
```

```
    %%[

  next @i ]%%

%%[ else ]%%

No rows found

%%[ endif ]%%
```

Output

```
region: North
Row 1, firstName: Doug, emailAddress: doug@limedash.com
Row 2, firstName: Suzy, emailAddress: suzy@limedash.com
Row 3, firstName: Barb, emailAddress: barb@limedash.com
Row 4, firstName: Curt, emailAddress: curt@limedash.com
```

Example 2
The following illustrates the use of this function with additional arguments.

Data Extension: *LoyaltyMembers*

Name	Data Type	Length	Primary Key	Nullable	Default Value
EmailAddress	EmailAddress	254	N	N	
SubscriberKey	Text	254	Y	N	
FirstName	Text	50	N	Y	
Region	Text	50	N	Y	
Rank	Number		N	Y	

The *LoyaltyMembers* Data Extension includes these rows:

EmailAddress	SubscriberKey	FirstName	Region	Rank
doug@limedash.com	8473	Doug	north	1
suzy@limedash.com	5497	Suzy	North	3
dale@limedash.com	7114	Dale	West	2
barb@limedash.com	5767	Barb	North	1
curt@limedash.com	5152	Curt	north	2
nora@limedash.com	7014	Nora	South	1
leon@limedash.com	8225	Leon	East	3
lily@limedash.com	9496	Lily	East	1

Here is an example utilizing the preceding context:

```
%%[
var @rows, @row, @rowCount, @numRowsToReturn, @region, @i

set @region = AttributeValue("Region") /* value from
attribute or DE column in send context */
set @region = "North" /* or a literal value */

set @rank = AttributeValue("Rank") /* value from attribute
or DE column in send context */
set @rank = "1" /* or a literal value */

set @rows = LookupRows("LoyaltyMembers","region", @region,
"rank", @rank)
set @rowCount = rowcount(@rows)

output(concat("region: ", @region))
output(concat("<br>rank ", @rank))

if @rowCount > 0 then

  for @i = 1 to @rowCount do

    var @emailAddress, @firstName, @rank
    set @row = row(@rows, @i) /* get row based on counter */
    set @firstName = field(@row,"firstName")
    set @emailAddress = field(@row,"emailAddress")
```

```
    ]%%

    <br>Row %%=v(@i)=%%, firstName: %%=v(@firstName)=%%,
emailAddress: %%=v(@emailAddress)=%%

    %%[

  next @i ]%%

%%[ else ]%%

No rows found

%%[ endif ]%%
```

Output

```
region: North
rank: 1
Row 1, firstName: Doug, emailAddress: doug@limedash.com
Row 2, firstName: Barb, emailAddress: barb@limedash.com
```

LookupRowsCS

This function returns a set of unordered rows from a Data Extension. This variation of the LookupRows function treats selection values as case-sensitive.

Arguments

`LookupRowsCS(1,2,3,[4a,4b]...)`

Ordinal	Type	Required	Description
1	String	True	Name of the Data Extension from which to return rows
2	String	True	Name of the column that identifies the rows to retrieve
3	String	True	Value that identifies the rows to retrieve
4a	String	False	Additional column name that identifies the rows to retrieve (see note)
4b	String	False	Additional value that identifies the rows to re-trieve (see note)

> **NOTE:** Additional pairs of columns and values can be appended as arguments.

Example 1

Data Extension: *LoyaltyMembers*

Name	Data Type	Length	Primary Key	Nullable	Default Value
EmailAddress	EmailAddress	254	N	N	
SubscriberKey	Text	254	Y	N	
FirstName	Text	50	N	Y	
Region	Text	50	N	Y	
Rank	Number		N	Y	

The *LoyaltyMembers* Data Extension includes these rows:

EmailAddress	SubscriberKey	FirstName	Region	Rank
doug@limedash.com	8473	Doug	north	1
suzy@limedash.com	5497	Suzy	North	3
dale@limedash.com	7114	Dale	West	2
barb@limedash.com	5767	Barb	North	1
curt@limedash.com	5152	Curt	north	2
nora@limedash.com	7014	Nora	South	1
leon@limedash.com	8225	Leon	East	3
lily@limedash.com	9496	Lily	East	1

Here is an example utilizing the preceding context:

```
%%[
var @rows, @row, @rowCount, @numRowsToReturn, @region, @i

set @region = AttributeValue("Region") /* value from
attribute or DE column in send context */
set @region = "north" /* or a literal value */
set @rows = LookupRowsCS("LoyaltyMembers","region", @region)
set @rowCount = rowcount(@rows)

output(concat("region: ", @region))

if @rowCount > 0 then

  for @i = 1 to @rowCount do

    var @emailAddress, @firstName, @rank
    set @row = row(@rows, @i) /* get row based on counter */
    set @firstName = field(@row,"firstName")
    set @emailAddress = field(@row,"emailAddress")

    ]%%

    <br>Row %%=v(@i)=%%, firstName: %%=v(@firstName)=%%,
emailAddress: %%=v(@emailAddress)=%%
```

```
    %%[

  next @i ]%%

%%[ else ]%%

No rows found

%%[ endif ]%%
```

Output

```
region: north
Row 1, firstName: Doug, emailAddress: doug@limedash.com
Row 2, firstName: Curt, emailAddress: curt@limedash.com
```

Example 2
Data Extension: *LoyaltyMembers*

Name	Data Type	Length	Primary Key	Nullable	Default Value
EmailAddress	EmailAddress	254	N	N	
SubscriberKey	Text	254	Y	N	
FirstName	Text	50	N	Y	
Region	Text	50	N	Y	
Rank	Number		N	Y	

The *LoyaltyMembers* Data Extension includes these rows:

EmailAddress	SubscriberKey	FirstName	Region	Rank
doug@limedash.com	8473	Doug	north	1
suzy@limedash.com	5497	Suzy	North	3
dale@limedash.com	7114	Dale	West	2
barb@limedash.com	5767	Barb	North	1
curt@limedash.com	5152	Curt	north	2
nora@limedash.com	7014	Nora	South	1
leon@limedash.com	8225	Leon	East	3
lily@limedash.com	9496	Lily	East	1

Here is an example utilizing the preceding context:

```
%%[
var @rows, @row, @rowCount, @numRowsToReturn, @region, @i

set @region = AttributeValue("Region") /* value from
attribute or DE column in send context */
set @region = "north" /* or a literal value */

set @rank = AttributeValue("Rank") /* value from attribute
or DE column in send context */
set @rank = "1" /* or a literal value */

set @rows = LookupRowsCS("LoyaltyMembers","region", @region)
set @rowCount = rowcount(@rows)

output(concat("region: ", @region))
output(concat("<br>region: ", @rank))

if @rowCount > 0 then

  for @i = 1 to @rowCount do

    var @emailAddress, @firstName, @rank
    set @row = row(@rows, @i) /* get row based on counter */
    set @firstName = field(@row,"firstName")
    set @emailAddress = field(@row,"emailAddress")

    ]%%

    <br>Row %%=v(@i)=%%, firstName: %%=v(@firstName)=%%,
emailAddress: %%=v(@emailAddress)=%%

    %%[

  next @i ]%%

%%[ else ]%%

No rows found

%%[ endif ]%%
```

Output

```
region: north
rank: 1
Row 1, firstName: Doug, emailAddress: doug@limedash.com
```

Row

This function returns a specific row from a row set.

Arguments

`Row(1,2)`

Ordinal	Type	Required	Description
1	String	Y	Row set from which to return the row
2	Number	Y	Position of element to retrieve from the row set

Example

Data Extension: *LoyaltyMembers*

Name	Data Type	Length	Primary Key	Nullable	Default Value
EmailAddress	EmailAddress	254	N	N	
SubscriberKey	Text	254	Y	N	
FirstName	Text	50	N	Y	
LastName	Text	50	N	Y	
Created	Date		N	Y	Current Date

The *LoyaltyMembers* Data Extension includes these rows:

EmailAddress	SubscriberKey	FirstName	LastName	Created
doug@limedash.com	8473	Doug	Smith	2017-10-21 12:01
suzy@limedash.com	5497	Suzy	Jackson	2017-10-20 11:01
dale@limedash.com	7114	Dale	Cameron	2017-10-19 10:01

Here is an example utilizing the preceding context:

```
%%[
var @rows, @row, @rowCount
var @emailAddress
set @emailAddress = AttributeValue("emailaddr") /* value
from attribute or DE column in send context */
set @emailAddress = "dale@limedash.com" /* or a literal
value */

set @rows = LookupRows("LoyaltyMembers","EmailAddress",
@emailAddress)
set @rowCount = rowcount(@rows)

if @rowCount > 0 then

  var @firstName, @lastName
  set @row = row(@rows,1) /* get row #1 */
  set @firstName = field(@row,"firstName")
  set @lastName = field(@row,"lastName")

]%%

firstName: %%=v(@firstName)=%%, lastName: %%=v(@lastName)=%%

%%[ else ]%%

No rows found

%%[ endif ]%%
```

Output

```
firstName: Dale, lastName: Cameron
```

RowCount

This function returns the number of rows in a row set.

Argument

`RowCount(1)`

Ordinal	Type	Required	Description
1	String	Y	Row set from which to return the count

Example

Data Extension: *LoyaltyMembers*

Name	Data Type	Length	Primary Key	Nullable	Default Value
EmailAddress	EmailAddress	254	N	N	
SubscriberKey	Text	254	Y	N	
FirstName	Text	50	N	Y	
Region	Text	50	N	Y	
Rank	Number		N	Y	

The *LoyaltyMembers* Data Extension includes these rows:

EmailAddress	SubscriberKey	FirstName	Region	Rank
doug@limedash.com	8473	Doug	north	1
suzy@limedash.com	5497	Suzy	North	3
dale@limedash.com	7114	Dale	West	2
barb@limedash.com	5767	Barb	North	1
curt@limedash.com	5152	Curt	north	2
nora@limedash.com	7014	Nora	South	1
leon@limedash.com	8225	Leon	East	3
lily@limedash.com	9496	Lily	East	1

Here is an example utilizing the preceding context:

```
%%[
var @rows, @row, @rowCount
var @region
set @region = "North"

set @rows = LookupRows("LoyaltyMembers","Region", @region)
set @rowCount = rowcount(@rows)

]%%
rowCount: %%=v(@rowCount)=%%
```

Output

```
rowCount: 4
```

UpdateData

This function updates the Data Extension row referenced in the column and value arguments. Values updated are specified with column name and value pairs. It returns the number of rows updated by the operation.

> **NOTE:** This function only works in a landing page, microsite page or CloudPage, or in an SMS message in MobileConnect. Use the UpdateDE function if you need to update rows in a Data Extension in an email.

Arguments

```
UpdateData(1,2,3,4,[5a,5b],6,7,[8a,8b]...)
```

Ordinal	Type	Required	Description
1	String	True	Name of the Data Extension containing the rows to update
2	Number	True	Number of column and value pairs in the preceding selection arguments
3	String	True	Column name used for selecting rows to update
4	String	True	Column value for selecting rows to update
5a	String	False	Additional column name used for selecting rows to update (see note)
5b	String	False	Additional column value for selecting rows to update (see note)
6	String	True	Column name to update
7	String	True	Column value to update
8a	String	False	Additional column name to update (see note)
8b	String	False	Additional column value to update (see note)

> **NOTE:** Additional pairs of columns and values can be appended as arguments for selecting and updating rows. Refer to Example 2.

Example 1
Data Extension: *LoyaltyMembers*

Name	Data Type	Length	Primary Key	Nullable	Default Value
EmailAddress	EmailAddress	254	N	N	
SubscriberKey	Text	254	Y	N	
FirstName	Text	50	N	Y	
LastName	Text	50	N	Y	
Created	Date		N	Y	Current Date
Updated	Date		N	Y	

The *LoyaltyMembers* Data Extension includes these rows:

EmailAddress	SubscriberKey	First Name	Last Name	Created	Updated
doug@limedash.com	8473	Doug	Smith	2017-10-21 12:01	
suzy@limedash.com	5497	Suzy	Jackson	2017-10-20 11:01	
dale@limedash.com	7114	Dale	Cameron	2017-10-19 10:01	

Here is an example utilizing the preceding context:

```
%%[

var @emailAddress, @newFirstName, @rowsUpdated

set @emailAddress = AttributeValue("emailaddr") /* value
from attribute or DE column in send context */
set @emailAddress = "dale@limedash.com" /* or a literal
value */

set @newFirstName = "Douglas"

set @rowsUpdated  =
UpdateData("LoyaltyMembers",1,"EmailAddress", @emailAddress,
"FirstName", @newFirstName)
```

```
]%%
rowsUpdated: %%=v(@rowsUpdated)=%%
```

Output

```
updateCount : 1
```

After the operation, the *LoyaltyMembers* Data Extension includes these row values:

EmailAddress	SubscriberKey	First Name	Last Name	Created	Updated
doug@limedash.com	8473	Douglas	Smith	2017-10-21 12:01	2017-10-22 14:01
suzy@limedash.com	5497	Suzy	Jackson	2017-10-20 11:01	
dale@limedash.com	7114	Dale	Cameron	2017-10-19 10:01	

Example 2

Using the same context as the previous example, this second example uses additional pairs of column names values to select and update rows:

```
%%[

var @emailAddress, @currFirstName, @newFirstName,
@rowsUpdated, @updatedDate

set @emailAddress = AttributeValue("emailaddr") /* value
from attribute or DE column in send context */
set @emailAddress = "dale@limedash.com" /* or a literal
value */

set @currFirstName = AttributeValue("firstName") /* value
from attribute or DE column in send context */
set @currFirstName = "Doug" /* or a literal value */

set @newFirstName = "Douglas"
set @updatedDate = Now(1)
```

```
set @rowsUpdated  =
UpdateData("LoyaltyMembers",2,"EmailAddress", @emailAddress,
"FirstName", @currFirstName, "FirstName", @newFirstName,
"Updated", @updatedDate)

]%%
rowsUpdated: %%=v(@rowsUpdated)=%%
```

Output

```
updateCount : 1
```

UpdateDE

This function updates the Data Extension row referenced in the column and value arguments. Values updated are specified with column name and value pairs. This function does not return a value.

> **NOTE:** This function only works in an email send. It will not execute in a Send Preview. Use the UpdateData function if you need update rows in a Data Extension in a landing page, microsite page or CloudPage, or in an SMS message in MobileConnect.

Arguments

`UpdateDE(1,2,3,4,[5a,5b],6,7,[8a,8b]...)`

Ordinal	Type	Required	Description
1	String	True	Name of the Data Extension containing the rows to update
2	Number	True	Number of column and value pairs in the preceding selection arguments
3	String	True	Column name used for selecting rows to update
4	String	True	Column value for selecting rows to update
5a	String	False	Additional column name used for selecting rows to update (see note)
5b	String	False	Additional column value for selecting rows to update (see note)
6	String	True	Column name to update
7	String	True	Column value to update

Ordinal	Type	Required	Description
8a	String	False	Additional column name to update (see note)
8b	String	False	Additional column value to update (see note)

NOTE: Additional pairs of columns and values can be appended as arguments for selecting and updating rows.

Example 1

The following illustrates the use of this function with the minimum number of arguments.

Data Extension: *LoyaltyMembers*

Name	Data Type	Length	Primary Key	Nullable	Default Value
EmailAddress	EmailAddress	254	N	N	
SubscriberKey	Text	254	Y	N	
FirstName	Text	50	N	Y	
LastName	Text	50	N	Y	
Created	Date		N	Y	Current Date
Updated	Date		N	Y	

The *LoyaltyMembers* Data Extension includes these rows:

EmailAddress	SubscriberKey	First Name	Last Name	Created	Updated
doug@limedash.com	8473	Doug	Smith	2017-10-21 12:01	
suzy@limedash.com	5497	Suzy	Jackson	2017-10-20 11:01	
dale@limedash.com	7114	Dale	Cameron	2017-10-19 10:01	

Here is an example utilizing the preceding context:

```
%%[

var @emailAddress, @newFirstName, @rowsUpdated,
@updatedDate

set @emailAddress = AttributeValue("emailaddr") /* value
from attribute or DE column in send context */
set @emailAddress = "dale@limedash.com" /* or a literal
value */

set @newFirstName = "Douglas"
set @updatedDate = Now(1)

UpdateDE("LoyaltyMembers",1,"EmailAddress", @emailAddress,
"FirstName", @newFirstName, "Updated", @updatedDate)

]%%
```

Output
After the operation, the *LoyaltyMembers* Data Extension includes these row values:

EmailAddress	SubscriberKey	First Name	Last Name	Created	Updated
doug@limedash.com	8473	Douglas	Smith	2017-10-21 12:01	2017-10-22 14:01
suzy@limedash.com	5497	Suzy	Jackson	2017-10-20 11:01	
dale@limedash.com	7114	Dale	Cameron	2017-10-19 10:01	

Example 2
The following illustrates the use of this function with additional arguments.

Data Extension: *LoyaltyMembers*

Name	Data Type	Length	Primary Key	Nullable	Default Value
EmailAddress	EmailAddress	254	N	N	
SubscriberKey	Text	254	Y	N	
FirstName	Text	50	N	Y	
LastName	Text	50	N	Y	
Created	Date		N	Y	Current Date
Updated	Date		N	Y	

The *LoyaltyMembers* Data Extension includes these rows:

EmailAddress	SubscriberKey	First Name	Last Name	Created	Updated
doug@limedash.com	8473	Doug	Smith	2017-10-21 12:01	
suzy@limedash.com	5497	Suzy	Jackson	2017-10-20 11:01	
dale@limedash.com	7114	Dale	Cameron	2017-10-19 10:01	

Here is an example utilizing the preceding context:

```
%%[

var @emailAddress, @currFirstName, @newFirstName,
@rowsUpdated, @updatedDate

set @emailAddress = AttributeValue("emailaddr") /* value
from attribute or DE column in send context */
set @emailAddress = "dale@limedash.com" /* or a literal
value */

set @currFirstName = AttributeValue("firstName") /* value
from attribute or DE column in send context */
set @currFirstName = "Doug" /* or a literal value */

set @newFirstName = "Douglas"
```

```
set @updatedDate = Now(1)

UpdateDE("LoyaltyMembers",2,"EmailAddress", @emailAddress,
"FirstName", @currFirstName, "FirstName", @newFirstName,
"Updated", @updatedDate)

]%%
```

Output
After the operation, the *LoyaltyMembers* Data Extension includes these row values:

EmailAddress	SubscriberKey	First Name	Last Name	Created	Updated
doug@limedash.com	8473	Douglas	Smith	2017-10-21 12:01	2017-10-22 14:01
suzy@limedash.com	5497	Suzy	Jackson	2017-10-20 11:01	
dale@limedash.com	7114	Dale	Cameron	2017-10-19 10:01	

UpsertData

This function adds or updates the Data Extension row referenced in the column and value arguments. Values updated are specified with column name and value pairs. If no record matches the values specified, a new row is added. It returns the number of rows added or updated by the operation.

> **NOTE:** This function only works in a landing page, microsite page or CloudPage, or in an SMS message in MobileConnect. Use the UpsertDE function if you need to add or insert rows into a Data Extension in an email.

Arguments

`UpsertData(1,2,3,4,[5a,5b],6,7,[8a,8b]...)`

Ordinal	Type	Required	Description
1	String	True	Name of the Data Extension containing the rows to add or update
2	Number	True	Number of column and value pairs in the proceeding selection arguments
3	String	True	Column name used for selecting rows to add or update
4	String	True	Column value for selecting rows to add or update
5a	String	False	Additional column name used for selecting rows to add or update (see note)
5b	String	False	Additional column value for selecting rows to add or update (see note)
6	String	True	Column name to add or update
7	String	True	Column value to add or update
8a	String	False	Additional column name to add or update (see note)
8b	String	False	Additional column value to add or update (see note)

> **NOTE:** Additional pairs of columns and values can be appended as arguments for selecting and upserting rows.

Example 1

The following illustrates the use of this function with the minimum number of arguments.

Data Extension: *LoyaltyMembers*

Name	Data Type	Length	Primary Key	Nullable	Default Value
EmailAddress	EmailAddress	254	N	N	
SubscriberKey	Text	254	Y	N	
FirstName	Text	50	N	Y	
LastName	Text	50	N	Y	
Created	Date		N	Y	Current Date
Updated	Date		N	Y	

The *LoyaltyMembers* Data Extension includes these rows:

EmailAddress	Subscriber-Key	First Name	Last Name	Created	Updated
doug@limedash.com	8473	Doug	Smith	2017-10-21 12:01	
suzy@limedash.com	5497	Suzy	Jackson	2017-10-20 11:01	
dale@limedash.com	7114	Dale	Cameron	2017-10-19 10:01	

Here is an example utilizing the preceding context:

```
%%[

var @emailAddress, @newFirstName, @rowsUpdated,
@updatedDate

set @emailAddress = AttributeValue("emailaddr") /* value
from attribute or DE column in send context */
set @emailAddress = "dale@limedash.com" /* or a literal
value */

set @newFirstName = "Douglas"
set @updatedDate = Now(1)

set @upsertCount =
upsertData("LoyaltyMembers",1,"EmailAddress", @emailAddress,
"FirstName", @newFirstName, "Updated", @updatedDate)

]%%
UpsertCount: %%=v(@upsertCount)=%%
```

Output

```
UpsertCount: 1
```

After the operation, the *LoyaltyMembers* Data Extension includes these row values:

EmailAddress	SubscriberKey	First Name	Last Name	Created	Updated
doug@limedash.com	8473	Douglas	Smith	2017-10-21 12:01	2017-10-22 14:01
suzy@limedash.com	5497	Suzy	Jackson	2017-10-20 11:01	
dale@limedash.com	7114	Dale	Cameron	2017-10-19 10:01	

Example 2

The following illustrates the use of this function with additional arguments.

Data Extension: *LoyaltyMembers*

Name	Data Type	Length	Primary Key	Nullable	Default Value
EmailAddress	EmailAddress	254	N	N	
SubscriberKey	Text	254	Y	N	
FirstName	Text	50	N	Y	
LastName	Text	50	N	Y	
Created	Date		N	Y	Current Date
Updated	Date		N	Y	

The *LoyaltyMembers* Data Extension includes these rows:

EmailAddress	Subscriber-Key	First Name	Last Name	Created	Updated
doug@limedash.com	8473	Doug	Smith	2017-10-21 12:01	
suzy@limedash.com	5497	Suzy	Jackson	2017-10-20 11:01	
dale@limedash.com	7114	Dale	Cameron	2017-10-19 10:01	

Here is an example utilizing the preceding context:

```
%%[

var @emailAddress, @currFirstName, @newFirstName,
@rowsUpdated, @updatedDate

set @emailAddress = AttributeValue("emailaddr") /* value
from attribute or DE column in send context */
set @emailAddress = "dale@limedash.com" /* or a literal
value */

set @currFirstName = AttributeValue("firstName") /* value
from attribute or DE column in send context */
set @currFirstName = "Doug" /* or a literal value */

set @newFirstName = "Douglas"
set @updatedDate = Now(1)

set @upsertCount =
upsertData("LoyaltyMembers",2,"EmailAddress", @emailAddress,
"FirstName", @currFirstName, "FirstName", @newFirstName,
"Updated", @updatedDate)

]%%
UpsertCount: %%=v(@upsertCount)=%%
```

Output

```
UpsertCount: 1
```

After the operation, the *LoyaltyMembers* Data Extension includes these row values:

EmailAddress	SubscriberKey	First Name	Last Name	Created	Updated
doug@limedash.com	8473	Doug	Smith	2017-10-21 12:01	
suzy@limedash.com	5497	Suzy	Jackson	2017-10-20 11:01	
dale@limedash.com	7114	Dale	Cameron	2017-10-19 10:01	
barb@limedash.com	5767	Barbara	Brown	2017-10-22 14:01	2017-10-22 14:01

UpsertDE

This function adds or updates the Data Extension row referenced in the column and value arguments. Values updated are specified with column name and value pairs. If no record matches the values specified, a new row is added. This function does not return a value.

> **NOTE:** This function only works in an email. Use the UpsertData function if you need to add or insert rows into a Data Extension in a landing page, microsite page or CloudPage, or in an SMS message in MobileConnect.

Arguments

```
UpsertDE(1,2,3,4,[5a,5b],6,7,[8a,8b]...)
```

Ordinal	Type	Required	Description
1	String	True	Name of the Data Extension containing the rows to add or update
2	Number	True	Number of column and value pairs in the preceding selection arguments
3	String	True	Column name used for selecting rows to add or update
4	String	True	Column value for selecting rows to add or update
5a	String	False	Additional column name used for selecting rows to add or update (see note)

Ordinal	Type	Required	Description
5b	String	False	Additional column value for selecting rows to add or update (see note)
6	String	True	Column name to add or update
7	String	True	Column value to add or update
8a	String	False	Additional column name to add or update (see note)
8b	String	False	Additional column value to add or update (see note)

> **NOTE:** Additional pairs of columns and values can be appended as arguments for selecting and upserting rows.

Example 1

The following illustrates the use of this function with the minimum number of arguments.

Data Extension: *LoyaltyMembers*

Name	Data Type	Length	Primary Key	Nullable	Default Value
EmailAddress	EmailAddress	254	N	N	
SubscriberKey	Text	254	Y	N	
FirstName	Text	50	N	Y	
LastName	Text	50	N	Y	
Created	Date		N	Y	Current Date
Updated	Date		N	Y	

The *LoyaltyMembers* Data Extension includes these rows:

EmailAddress	SubscriberKey	First Name	Last Name	Created	Updated
doug@limedash.com	8473	Doug	Smith	2017-10-21 12:01	
suzy@limedash.com	5497	Suzy	Jackson	2017-10-20 11:01	
dale@limedash.com	7114	Dale	Cameron	2017-10-19 10:01	

Here is an example utilizing the preceding context:

```
%%[

var @emailAddress, @currFirstName, @newFirstName,
@rowsUpdated, @updatedDate

set @emailAddress = AttributeValue("emailaddr") /* value
from attribute or DE column in send context */
set @emailAddress = "dale@limedash.com" /* or a literal
value */

set @newFirstName = "Douglas"
set @updatedDate = Now(1)

UpsertDE("LoyaltyMembers",1,"EmailAddress", @emailAddress,
"FirstName", @newFirstName, "Updated", @updatedDate)

]%%
```

Output
After the operation, the *LoyaltyMembers* Data Extension includes these row values:

EmailAddress	SubscriberKey	First Name	Last Name	Created	Updated
doug@limedash.com	8473	Douglas	Smith	2017-10-21 12:01	2017-10-22 14:01
suzy@limedash.com	5497	Suzy	Jackson	2017-10-20 11:01	
dale@limedash.com	7114	Dale	Cameron	2017-10-19 10:01	

Example 2

The following illustrates the use of this function with additional arguments.

Data Extension: *LoyaltyMembers*

Name	Data Type	Length	Primary Key	Nullable	Default Value
EmailAddress	EmailAddress	254	N	N	
SubscriberKey	Text	254	Y	N	
FirstName	Text	50	N	Y	
LastName	Text	50	N	Y	
Created	Date		N	Y	Current Date
Updated	Date		N	Y	

The *LoyaltyMembers* Data Extension includes these rows:

EmailAddress	SubscriberKey	First Name	Last Name	Created	Updated
doug@limedash.com	8473	Doug	Smith	2017-10-21 12:01	
suzy@limedash.com	5497	Suzy	Jackson	2017-10-20 11:01	
dale@limedash.com	7114	Dale	Cameron	2017-10-19 10:01	

Here is an example utilizing the preceding context:

```
%%[

var @emailAddress, @currFirstName, @newFirstName,
@rowsUpdated, @updatedDate

set @emailAddress = AttributeValue("emailaddr") /* value
from attribute or DE column in send context */
set @emailAddress = "dale@limedash.com" /* or a literal
value */

set @currFirstName = AttributeValue("firstName") /* value
from attribute or DE column in send context */
```

```
set @currFirstName = "Doug" /* or a literal value */

set @newFirstName = "Douglas"
set @updatedDate = Now(1)

UpsertDE("LoyaltyMembers",2,"EmailAddress", @emailAddress,
"FirstName", @currFirstName, "FirstName", @newFirstName,
"Updated", @updatedDate)

]%%
```

Output

After the operation, the *LoyaltyMembers* Data Extension includes these row values:

EmailAddress	SubscriberKey	First Name	Last Name	Created	Updated
doug@limedash.com	8473	Douglas	Smith	2017-10-21 12:01	2017-10-22 14:01
suzy@limedash.com	5497	Suzy	Jackson	2017-10-20 11:01	
dale@limedash.com	7114	Dale	Cameron	2017-10-19 10:01	

Example 3

The following illustrates the use of this function with additional arguments that adds a new row.

Data Extension: *LoyaltyMembers*

Name	Data Type	Length	Primary Key	Nullable	Default Value
EmailAddress	EmailAddress	254	N	N	
SubscriberKey	Text	254	Y	N	
FirstName	Text	50	N	Y	
LastName	Text	50	N	Y	
Created	Date		N	Y	Current Date
Updated	Date		N	Y	

The *LoyaltyMembers* Data Extension includes these rows:

EmailAddress	SubscriberKey	First Name	Last Name	Created	Updated
doug@limedash.com	8473	Doug	Smith	2017-10-21 12:01	
suzy@limedash.com	5497	Suzy	Jackson	2017-10-20 11:01	
dale@limedash.com	7114	Dale	Cameron	2017-10-19 10:01	

Here is an example utilizing the preceding context:

```
%%[

var @emailAddress, @currFirstName, @newFirstName,
@rowsUpdated, @updatedDate

set @emailAddress = AttributeValue("emailaddr") /* value
from attribute or DE column in send context */
set @emailAddress = "barb@limedash.com" /* or a literal
value */

set @currFirstName = AttributeValue("firstName") /* value
from attribute or DE column in send context */
set @currFirstName = "Barb" /* or a literal value */

set @newFirstName = "Barbara"
set @updatedDate = Now(1)

UpsertDE("LoyaltyMembers",2,"EmailAddress", @emailAddress,
"FirstName", @currFirstName, "FirstName", @newFirstName,
"Updated", @updatedDate)

]%%
```

Output

After the operation, the *LoyaltyMembers* Data Extension includes these row values:

EmailAddress	SubscriberKey	First Name	Last Name	Created	Updated
doug@limedash.com	8473	Doug	Smith	2017-10-21 12:01	
suzy@limedash.com	5497	Suzy	Jackson	2017-10-20 11:01	
dale@limedash.com	7114	Dale	Cameron	2017-10-19 10:01	
barb@limedash.com	5767	Barbara	Brown	2017-10-22 14:01	2017-10-22 14:01

Date & Time Functions

Overview

The date and time AMPscript functions are used to return, convert and adjust date and time values.

For functions with date-input arguments, those arguments must take one of the following forms:

- Includes a date only
- Includes both a date and time
- Includes a time only; in this case, the current date is assumed.
- Includes the GMT qualifier and conforms to the RFC 1123 time format
- Includes the date, time and a timezone offset. These must conform to the ISO 8601 format.

DateAdd

This function returns a date with the specified number interval added to the specified part of the date.

Arguments

`DateAdd(1,2,3)`

Ordinal	Type	Required	Description
1	Date	True	The date to adjust
2	Number	True	The interval to add
3	String	True	The part of the date to adjust by the preceding interval. Valid values include **`Y`**, **`M`**, **`D`**, **`H`**, and **`MI`**

Example

```
%%[

var @today, @plusOneYear, @minusOneYear, @plusOneMonth,
@minusOneMonth, @plusOneDay, @minusOneDay, @plusOneHour,
@minusOneHour, @plusOneMinute, @minusOneMinute
set @today = Now(1) /* valid */
set @today = "15/10/2017" /* invalid */
set @today = "15-OCT-2017" /* valid */
set @today = "2017-10-15" /* valid */
set @today = "October 15, 2017" /* valid */
set @today = "10/15/2017" /* valid */
set @today = "10/15/2017 6:30 am" /* valid */
set @plusOneYear = DateAdd(@today, 1, "Y")
set @minusOneYear = DateAdd(@today, -1, "Y")
set @plusOneMonth = DateAdd(@today, 1, "M")
set @minusOneMonth = DateAdd(@today, -1, "M")
set @plusOneDay = DateAdd(@today, 1, "D")
set @minusOneDay = DateAdd(@today, -1, "D")
set @plusOneHour = DateAdd(@today, 1, "H")
set @minusOneHour = DateAdd(@today, -1, "H")
set @plusOneMinute = DateAdd(@today, 1, "MI")
set @minusOneMinute = DateAdd(@today, -1, "MI")

]%%
today: %%=v(@today)=%%
<br>plusOneYear: %%=v(@plusOneYear)=%%
<br>minusOneYear: %%=v(@minusOneYear)=%%
<br>plusOneMonth: %%=v(@plusOneMonth)=%%
<br>minusOneMonth: %%=v(@minusOneMonth)=%%
<br>plusOneDay: %%=v(@plusOneDay)=%%
<br>minusOneDay: %%=v(@minusOneDay)=%%
<br>plusOneHour: %%=v(@plusOneHour)=%%
<br>minusOneHour: %%=v(@minusOneHour)=%%
<br>plusOneMinute: %%=v(@plusOneMinute)=%%
<br>minusOneMinute: %%=v(@minusOneMinute)=%%
```

Output

```
today: 10/15/2017 6:30 am
plusOneYear: 10/15/2018 6:30:00 AM
```

```
minusOneYear: 10/15/2016 6:30:00 AM
plusOneMonth: 11/15/2017 6:30:00 AM
minusOneMonth: 9/15/2017 6:30:00 AM
plusOneDay: 10/16/2017 6:30:00 AM
minusOneDay: 10/14/2017 6:30:00 AM
plusOneHour: 10/15/2017 7:30:00 AM
minusOneHour: 10/15/2017 5:30:00 AM
plusOneMinute: 10/15/2017 6:31:00 AM
minusOneMinute: 10/15/2017 6:29:00 AM
```

DateDiff

This function returns the difference between two dates based on the specified date part.

Arguments

`DateDiff(1,2,3)`

Ordinal	Type	Required	Description
1	Date	True	The start date from which to subtract
2	Date	True	The date to subtract from the start date
3	String	True	The part of the date to adjust. Valid values include **Y**, **M**, **D**, **H**, and **MI**

Example

```
%%[

var @startDate, @endDate, @diffYear, @diffMonth, @diffDay,
@diffHours, @diffMinutes
set @startDate = '2016-08-15 6:30 AM'
set @endDate = '2017-10-16 8:31 AM'
set @diffYear = dateDiff(@startDate, @endDate,"Y")
set @diffMonth = dateDiff(@startDate, @endDate,"M")
set @diffDay = dateDiff(@startDate, @endDate,"D")
set @diffHours = dateDiff(@startDate, @endDate,"H")
set @diffMinutes = dateDiff(@startDate, @endDate,"MI")

]%%
startDate: %%=v(@startDate)=%%
<br>endDate: %%=v(@endDate)=%%
<br>diffYear: %%=v(@diffYear)=%%
```

```
<br>diffMonth: %%=v(@diffMonth)=%%
<br>diffDay: %%=v(@diffDay)=%%
<br>diffHours: %%=v(@diffHours)=%%
<br>diffMinutes: %%=v(@diffMinutes)=%%
```

Output

```
startDate: 2016-08-15 6:30 AM
endDate: 2017-10-16 8:31 AM
diffYear: 1
diffMonth: 14
diffDay: 427
diffHours: 10250
diffMinutes: 615001
```

DateParse

This function converts the string representation of a date and time into its DateTime equivalent.

Arguments

`DateParse(1,2)`

Ordinal	Type	Required	Description
1	Date	True	The date string to parse
2	Boolean	False	A **`True`** value returns the date in UTC format

Example

```
%%[

var @dateString1
var @date1
var @dateString2
var @date2
var @dateString3
var @date3
var @dateString4
var @date4
var @dateString5
var @date5
```

```
set @dateString1 = "2017-10-15"
set @date1 = DateParse(@dateString1,0)

set @dateString2 = "02/29/2016 05:42:00"
set @date2 = DateParse(@dateString2,0)

set @dateString3 = "6:00 AM"
set @date3 = DateParse(@dateString3,1)

set @dateString4 = "Sun, 15 Oct 2017 19:35:00 GMT"
set @date4 = DateParse(@dateString4,0)

set @dateString5 = "2017-10-15T19:35:00.0000000-06:00"
set @date5 = DateParse(@dateString5,0)

]%%
dateString1: %%=v(@dateString1)=%%
<br>date1: %%=v(@date1)=%%
<br><br>dateString2: %%=v(@dateString2)=%%
<br>date2: %%=v(@date2)=%%
<br><br>dateString3: %%=v(@dateString3)=%%
<br>date3: %%=v(@date3)=%%
<br><br>dateString4: %%=v(@dateString4)=%%
<br>date4: %%=v(@date4)=%%
<br><br>dateString5: %%=v(@dateString5)=%%
<br>date5: %%=v(@date5)=%%
```

Output

```
dateString1: 2017-10-15
date1: 10/15/2017 12:00:00 AM

dateString2: 02/29/2016 05:42:00
date2: 2/29/2016 5:42:00 AM

dateString3: 6:00 AM
date3: 10/15/2017 12:00:00 PM

dateString4: Sun, 15 Oct 2017 19:35:00 GMT
date4: 10/15/2017 1:35:00 PM

dateString5: 2017-10-15T19:35:00.0000000-06:00
date5: 10/15/2017 7:35:00 PM
```

DatePart

This function returns the specified part of a date string.

Arguments

`DatePart(1,2)`

Ordinal	Type	Required	Description
1	String	True	The date string from which to extract a part
2	String	True	The part of the date to retrieve. Valid values include **`year`**, **`Y`**, **`month`**, **`M`**, **`monthName`**, **`day`**, **`D`**, **`hour`**, **`H`**, **`minute`** and **`MI`**

Example

```
%%[

var @dateString, @year, @month, @monthName, @day, @hour,
@minute

set @dateString = "Sun, 15 Oct 2017 19:35:00"
set @year = datePart(@dateString, "Y")
set @month = datePart(@dateString, "M")
set @monthName = datePart(@dateString, "monthName")
set @day = datePart(@dateString, "D")
set @hour = datePart(@dateString, "H")
set @minute = datePart(@dateString, "minute")

]%%
<br>dateString: %%=v(@dateString)=%%
<br>year: %%=v(@year)=%%
<br>month: %%=v(@month)=%%
<br>monthName: %%=v(@monthName)=%%
<br>day: %%=v(@day)=%%
<br>hour: %%=v(@hour)=%%
<br>minute: %%=v(@minute)=%%
```

Output

```
dateString: Sun, 15 Oct 2017 19:35:00
year: 2017
month: 10
monthName: October
day: 15
hour: 7
minute: 35
```

FormatDate

This function formats a date/time string in the specified format pattern and locale.

Arguments
`FormatDate(1,2,3,4)`

Ordinal	Type	Required	Description
1	String	True	The date string to format
2	String	True	The output date format pattern (see table below for valid values)
3	String	False	The output time format pattern (see table below for valid values)
4	String	False	The ISO locale code for the output

These are the valid format patterns, given a date of **`2017-09-15T06:07:08.1230000-06:00`**:

Element	Format Pattern	Output
Long	l	Friday, September 15, 2017
Short	s	9/15/2017
Month, Year	Y	September, 2017
Year	YY	17
Year	YYYY	2017
Month	M	September 15
Month	MM	09
Month	MMM	Sep
Month	MMMM	September

Element	Format Pattern	Output
Day	dd	15
Day	dddd	Fri
Day	ddddd	Friday
Hour	hh	06
Minutes	mm	07
Seconds	ss	08
Milliseconds (time only)	MM	123
AM/PM	tt	AM
Timezone offset	zz	-06
Timezone offset	zzz	-06:00

NOTE: Format patterns are not case-sensitive, but they must be used in the correct pattern argument (for example, both **mm** and **MM** are date *and* time formats).

NOTE: This function returns lowercase month and day names for non-US culture codes by default.

Example

```
%%[

var @dateString, @timeString, @dateISO, @dateRFC,
@dateLong, @dateShort, @frFRDate, @monthYear, @yearShort,
@yearFull, @monthNameDay, @monthNumber, @monthShortName,
@monthFullName, @dayNumber, @dayShortName, @dayFullName,
@hour, @minute, @seconds, @milliseconds, @AMPM,
@offsetHours, @offsetHoursMinutes

set @dateString = "2017-09-15T06:07:08.1230000-06:00"
set @timeString = "06:08:07.123 AM"

set @dateISO   = FormatDate(@dateString,"iso")
set @dateRFC   = FormatDate(@dateString,"rfc")
set @dateLong   = FormatDate(@dateString,"l")
set @dateShort   = FormatDate(@dateString,"s")
```

```
set @frFRDate = properCase(FormatDate(@dateString,"l","","fr-
FR"))

set @monthYear = FormatDate(@dateString,"Y")
set @yearShort = FormatDate(@dateString,"YY")
set @yearFull = FormatDate(@dateString,"YYYY")
set @monthNameDay = FormatDate(@dateString,"M")
set @monthNumber = FormatDate(@dateString,"MM")
set @monthShortName = FormatDate(@dateString,"MMM")
set @monthFullName = FormatDate(@dateString,"MMMM")
set @dayNumber = FormatDate(@dateString,"dd")
set @dayShortName = FormatDate(@dateString,"dddd")
set @dayFullName = FormatDate(@dateString,"ddddd")

set @hour = FormatDate(@timeString,"","hh")
set @minute = FormatDate(@timeString,"","mm")
set @seconds = FormatDate(@timeString,"","ss")
set @milliseconds = FormatDate(@timeString,"","MMM")
set @AMPM = FormatDate(@timeString,"","tt")
set @offsetHours = FormatDate(@dateString,"zz")
set @offsetHoursMinutes = FormatDate(@dateString,"zzz")

]%%
dateString: %%=v(@dateString)=%%
<br>dateISO: %%=v(@dateISO)=%%
<br>dateRFC: %%=v(@dateRFC)=%%
<br>dateLong: %%=v(@dateLong)=%%
<br>dateShort: %%=v(@dateShort)=%%
<br>frFRDate: %%=v(@frFRDate)=%%
<br><br>monthYear: %%=v(@monthYear)=%%
<br>yearShort: %%=v(@yearShort)=%%
<br>yearFull: %%=v(@yearFull)=%%
<br>monthNameDay: %%=v(@monthNameDay)=%%
<br>monthNumber: %%=v(@monthNumber)=%%
<br>monthShortName: %%=v(@monthShortName)=%%
<br>monthFullName: %%=v(@monthFullName)=%%
<br>dayNumber: %%=v(@dayNumber)=%%
<br>dayShortName: %%=v(@dayShortName)=%%
<br>dayFullName: %%=v(@dayFullName)=%%
<br><br>timeString: %%=v(@timeString)=%%
<br>hour: %%=v(@hour)=%%
<br>minute: %%=v(@minute)=%%
```

```
<br>seconds: %%=v(@seconds)=%%
<br>milliseconds: %%=v(@milliseconds)=%%
<br>AMPM: %%=v(@AMPM)=%%
<br>offsetHours: %%=v(@offsetHours)=%%
<br>offsetHoursMinutes: %%=v(@offsetHoursMinutes)=%%
```

Output

```
dateString: 2017-09-15T06:07:08.1230000-06:00
dateISO: 2017-09-15T06:07:08.1230000-06:00
dateRFC: Fri, 15 Sep 2017 06:07:08 GMT
dateLong: Friday, September 15, 2017
dateShort: 9/15/2017
frFRDate: Vendredi 15 Septembre 2017

monthYear: September, 2017
yearShort: 17
yearFull: 2017
monthNameDay: September 15
monthNumber: 09
monthShortName: Sep
monthFullName: September
dayNumber: 15
dayShortName: Fri
dayFullName: Friday

timeString: 06:07:08.123 AM
hour: 06
minute: 07
seconds: 08
milliseconds: 123
AMPM: AM
offsetHours: -06
offsetHoursMinutes: -06:00
```

LocalDateToSystemDate

This function converts the specified date/time into system time. The system date and time is based on the data center location of your Marketing Cloud account.

Arguments

`LocalDateToSystemDate(1)`

Ordinal	Type	Required	Description
1	String	True	The date to convert

Example

```
%%[

var @localDate, @systemDate
set @localDate = Now(1)
set @systemDate  = LocalDateToSystemDate(@localDate)

]%%
localDate: %%=v(@localDate)=%%
<br>systemDate: %%=v(@systemDate)=%%
```

Output

```
localDate: 10/15/2017 1:42:35 PM
systemDate: 10/15/2017 3:42:35 PM
```

Now

This function returns the current system date and time. The system date and time is based on the data center location of your Marketing Cloud account.

Arguments

`Now(1)`

Ordinal	Type	Required	Description
1	Boolean	False	Preserve the send time value. A value of **`true`** will preserve it. The default value is **`false`** if no value is specified.

Example

```
%%[

var @currentSystemDateTime
set @currentSystemDateTime   = Now(1)

]%%
currentSystemDateTime: %%=v(@currentSystemDateTime)=%%
```

Output

```
10/15/2017 3:44:04 PM
```

SystemDateToLocalDate

This function converts the specified system date/time into the local date/time.

Arguments

`SystemDateToLocalDate(1)`

Ordinal	Type	Required	Description
1	String	True	The date to convert

Example

```
%%[

var @systemDate, @localDate
```

```
set @systemDate  = Now(1)
set @localDate =  SystemDateToLocalDate(@systemDate)

]%%
systemDate: %%=v(@systemDate)=%%
<br>localDate: %%=v(@localDate)=%%
```

Output

```
systemDate: 10/15/2017 3:45:35 PM
localDate: 10/15/2017 1:45:35 PM
```

Einstein Email Recommendation Functions

Overview

In addition to the set of personalization strings available for Einstein Email Recommendations, Marketing Cloud also includes one AMPscript function for working with Einstein Email Recommendations Content.

> **NOTE:** When using Einstein Email Recommendations in AMPscript statements to compare a constant, product, or catalog attribute, use `||` for an **`or`** logical operator and **`&&`** for an **`and`** logical operator.

RatingStars

This function generates a rating star image, based on a rating attribute of the recommended product.

Arguments

`RatingStars(1,2,3)`

Ordinal	Type	Required	Description
1	Number	True	The highest ranking to display
2	String	True	Star color as html hex code or color name
3	Number	True	Size and width of star in pixels

Example

When used in conjunction with Einstein Email Recommendations Code, the following example will generate a rating star image in the context of the recommended product.

```
%%=RatingStars(5, "yellow", 25)=%%
```

Output

This function will return an **img** element with a **src** attribute set as the URL of the generated image.

Encryption & Encoding Functions

Overview

Integrations with Marketing Cloud often necessitate a secure or obfuscated exchange of personal data. This chapter outlines the functions available in Marketing Cloud for encoding, encrypting, decoding and decrypting data elements that relate to messages and CloudPages.

Base64Decode

This function decodes a Base64 encoded string.

Arguments

`Base64Decode(1,2,3)`

Ordinal	Type	Required	Description
1	String	True	String value to decode
2	String	False	Optional .NET-supported character-encoding type to utilize in decoding (**`ASCII`**, **`UTF-7`**, **`UTF-8`**, **`UTF-16`**, and **`UTF-32`**)
3	Number	False	When utilized in an email message, a value of **`1`** will abort the send if the specified string cannot be successfully decoded. A value of **`0`** will allow the send to continue. The default value is **`1`**.

Example

```
%%[

var @str
var @enc
```

```
var @encASCII
var @encUTF7
var @encUTF8
var @encUTF16
var @encUTF32
var @dec
var @decASCII
var @decUTF7
var @decUTF8
var @decUTF16
var @decUTF32

set @enc  = "ZG91Z0BsaW1lZGFzaC5jb20="
set @encASCII = "ZG91Z0BsaW1lZGFzaC5jb20="
set @encUTF7 = "ZG91ZytBRUEtbGltZWRhc2guY29t"
set @encUTF8 = "ZG91Z0BsaW1lZGFzaC5jb20="
set @encUTF16 =
"ZABvAHUAZwBAAGwAaQBtAGUAZABhAHMAaAAuAGMAbwBtAA=="
set @encUTF32 = "ZAAAAG8AAAB1AAAAZwAAAEAAAABsAAAAaQAAAG0A
AABlAAAAZAAAAGEAAABzAAAAaAAAAC4AAABjAAAAbwAAAG0AAAA="

set @dec = Base64Decode(@enc)
set @decASCII = Base64Decode(@encASCII, "ASCII")
set @decUTF7 = Base64Decode(@encUTF7, "UTF-7")
set @decUTF8 = Base64Decode(@encUTF8, "UTF-8")
set @decUTF16 = Base64Decode(@encUTF16, "UTF-16")
set @decUTF32 = Base64Decode(@encUTF32, "UTF-32")

]%%
enc: %%=v(@enc)=%%
<br>encASCII: %%=v(@encASCII)=%%
<br>encUTF7: %%=v(@encUTF7)=%%
<br>encUTF8: %%=v(@encUTF8)=%%
<br>encUTF16: %%=v(@encUTF16)=%%
<br>encUTF32: %%=v(@encUTF32)=%%
<br>dec: %%=v(@dec)=%%
<br>decASCII: %%=v(@decASCII)=%%
<br>decUTF7: %%=v(@decUTF7)=%%
<br>decUTF8: %%=v(@decUTF8)=%%
<br>decUTF16: %%=v(@decUTF16)=%%
<br>decUTF32: %%=v(@decUTF32)=%%
```

Output

```
enc: ZG91Z0BsaW1lZGFzaC5jb20=
encASCII: ZG91Z0BsaW1lZGFzaC5jb20=
encUTF7: ZG91ZytBRUEtbGltZWRhc2guY29t
encUTF8: ZG91Z0BsaW1lZGFzaC5jb20=
encUTF16: ZABvAHUAZwBAAGwAaQBtAGUAZABhAHMAaAAuAGMAbwBtAA==
encUTF32: ZAAAAG8AAAB1AAAAZwAAAEAAAABsAAAAaQAAAG0AAABlAAA
AZAAAAGEAAABzAAAAaAAAAC4AAABjAAAAbwAAAG0AAAA=
dec: doug@limedash.com
decASCII: doug@limedash.com
decUTF7: doug@limedash.com
decUTF8: doug@limedash.com
decUTF16: doug@limedash.com
decUTF32: doug@limedash.com
```

Base64Encode

This function Base64 encodes a string.

Arguments

`Base64Encode(1,2)`

Ordinal	Type	Required	Description
1	String	True	String value to encode
2	String	False	Optional .NET character-encoding type to utilize in encoding. Valid values are **`ASCII`**, **`UTF-7`**, **`UTF-8`**, **`UTF-16`**, and **`UTF-32`**.

Example 1

```
%%[

var @str
var @enc
var @encASCII
var @encUTF7
var @encUTF8
var @encUTF16
var @encUTF32
```

```
set @str = "doug@limedash.com"

set @enc = Base64Encode(@str)
set @encASCII = Base64Encode(@str, "ASCII")
set @encUTF7 = Base64Encode(@str, "UTF-7")
set @encUTF8 = Base64Encode(@str, "UTF-8")
set @encUTF16 = Base64Encode(@str, "UTF-16")
set @encUTF32 = Base64Encode(@str, "UTF-32")

]%%
str: %%=v(@str)=%%
<br>enc: %%=v(@enc)=%%
<br>encASCII: %%=v(@encASCII)=%%
<br>encUTF7: %%=v(@encUTF7)=%%
<br>encUTF8: %%=v(@encUTF8)=%%
<br>encUTF16: %%=v(@encUTF16)=%%
<br>encUTF32: %%=v(@encUTF32)=%%
```

Output

```
str: doug@limedash.com
enc: ZG91Z0BsaW1lZGFzaC5jb20=
encASCII: ZG91Z0BsaW1lZGFzaC5jb20=
encUTF7: ZG91ZytBRUEtbGltZWRhc2guY29t
encUTF8: ZG91Z0BsaW1lZGFzaC5jb20=
encUTF16: ZABvAHUAZwBAAGwAaQBtAGUAZABhAHMAaAAuAGMAbwBtAA==
encUTF32: ZAAAAG8AAAB1AAAAZwAAAEAAAABsAAAAaQAAAG0AAABlAAA
AZAAAAGEAAABzAAAAaAAAAC4AAABjAAAAbwAAAG0AAAA=
```

DecryptSymmetric

This function decrypts a string with the specified algorithm and qualifiers.

Arguments

`DecryptSymmetric(1,2,3,4,5,6,7,8)`

Ordinal	Type	Required	Description
1	String	True	String to decrypt
2	String	True	Algorithm used to decrypt the string. Valid values are **`aes`**, **`des`**, and **`tripledes`**. Optional cipher modes for **`des`** and **`tripledes`** include: ▪ **`cbc`** (Cipher Block Chaining, *default*) ▪ **`cfb`** (Cipher Feedback) ▪ **`ecb`** (Electronic Codebook) Optional padding codes for **`des`** and **`tripledes`** include: ▪ **`ansix923`** (sequence of bytes filled with zeros before the length) ▪ **`iso10126`** (random data before the length) ▪ **`none`** ▪ **`pkcs7`** (sequence of bytes, each of which is equal to the total number of padding bytes added , *default*) ▪ **`zeros`** Modes and padding are specified after the algorithm and are delimited by semicolons: **`des;mode=ecb;padding=zeros`**.
3	String	True	Password External Key for retrieval from Key Management
4	String	True	Password value
5	String	True	Salt External Key for retrieval from Key Management
6	String	True	Salt value as an 8-byte hex string
7	String	True	Initialization vector External Key for retrieval from Key Management
8	String	True	Initialization vector value as a 16-byte hex string

Example

```
%%[

var @password
var @salt
var @initVector

var @encAES
var @encDES01
var @encDES02
var @encDES03
var @encDES04
var @encDES05
var @encDES06
var @encDES07
var @encDES08
var @encDES09
var @encDES10
var @encDES11
var @encDES12
var @encDES13
var @encDES14
var @encDES15
var @encDES16
var @encDES17
var @encDES18
var @encTripleDES01
var @encTripleDES02
var @encTripleDES03
var @encTripleDES04
var @encTripleDES05
var @encTripleDES06
var @encTripleDES07
var @encTripleDES08
var @encTripleDES09
var @encTripleDES10
var @encTripleDES11
var @encTripleDES12
var @encTripleDES13
var @encTripleDES14
var @encTripleDES15
```

```
var @encTripleDES16
var @encTripleDES17
var @encTripleDES18

set @password = "fresh"
set @salt = "e0cf1267f564b362"
set @initVector = "4963b7334a46352623252955df21d7f3"

set @encAES = "4fKWdv7fJRkFsYO6RRtrMg=="
set @encDES01 = "Qs+p/Gw8hughK4EbaPxFLg=="
set @encDES02 = "Qs+p/Gw8hug5Q04gtQQ3Jw=="
set @encDES03 = "Qs+p/Gw8hujEN7j5qYz8/A=="
set @encDES04 = "Qs+p/Gw8hug="
set @encDES05 = "Qs+p/Gw8hughK4EbaPxFLg=="
set @encDES06 = "Qs+p/Gw8hug="
set @encDES07 = "OjFSuxhf85augugb0wUaLg=="
set @encDES08 = "OjFSuxhf85amqnIztzgoIg=="
set @encDES09 = "OjFSuxhf85ZHduos1dQyeg=="
set @encDES10 = "OjFSuxhf85Y="
set @encDES11 = "OjFSuxhf85augugb0wUaLg=="
set @encDES12 = "OjFSuxhf85Y="
set @encDES13 = "Qs+p/Gw8huiQqlLLjpNC5g=="
set @encDES14 = "Qs+p/Gw8huhz0yIqcW8eDQ=="
set @encDES15 = "Qs+p/Gw8hugteYp97SZQJA=="
set @encDES16 = "Qs+p/Gw8hug="
set @encDES17 = "Qs+p/Gw8huiQqlLLjpNC5g=="
set @encDES18 = "Qs+p/Gw8hug="
set @encTripleDES01 = "5Zwb4S0ylZsfF+KHXpd17A=="
set @encTripleDES02 = "5Zwb4S0ylZuUQ3v4JsD4uA=="
set @encTripleDES03 = "5Zwb4S0ylZssnYGXucyn2A=="
set @encTripleDES04 = "5Zwb4S0ylZs="
set @encTripleDES05 = "5Zwb4S0ylZsfF+KHXpd17A=="
set @encTripleDES06 = "5Zwb4S0ylZs="
set @encTripleDES07 = "gnpVkeFLdtpJO1d6cmlWxA=="
set @encTripleDES08 = "gnpVkeFLdtpBsFpJx+kqCw=="
set @encTripleDES09 = "gnpVkeFLdtr/hikI5d8kUg=="
set @encTripleDES10 = "gnpVkeFLdto="
set @encTripleDES11 = "gnpVkeFLdtpJO1d6cmlWxA=="
set @encTripleDES12 = "gnpVkeFLdto="
set @encTripleDES13 = "5Zwb4S0ylZvWK0u1DJNlYQ=="
set @encTripleDES14 = "5Zwb4S0ylZtOKfaL4b4xvQ=="
set @encTripleDES15 = "5Zwb4S0ylZv5vh3YpVg5ZQ=="
```

```
set @encTripleDES16 = "5Zwb4S0ylZs="
set @encTripleDES17 = "5Zwb4S0ylZvWK0u1DJNlYQ=="
set @encTripleDES18 = "5Zwb4S0ylZs= "

set @decAES = DecryptSymmetric(@encAES, "aes", @null,
@password, @null, @salt, @null, @initVector)
set @decDES01 = DecryptSymmetric(@encDES01, "des;mode=cbc",
@null, @password, @null, @salt, @null, @initVector)
set @decDES02 = DecryptSymmetric(@encDES02,
"des;mode=cbc;padding=ansix923", @null, @password, @null,
@salt, @null, @initVector)
set @decDES03 = DecryptSymmetric(@encDES03,
"des;mode=cbc;padding=iso10126", @null, @password, @null,
@salt, @null, @initVector)
set @decDES04 = DecryptSymmetric(@encDES04,
"des;mode=cbc;padding=none", @null, @password, @null, @salt,
@null, @initVector)
set @decDES05 = DecryptSymmetric(@encDES05,
"des;mode=cbc;padding=pkcs7", @null, @password, @null, @salt,
@null, @initVector)
set @decDES06 = DecryptSymmetric(@encDES06,
"des;mode=cbc;padding=zeros", @null, @password, @null,
@salt, @null, @initVector)
set @decDES07 = DecryptSymmetric(@encDES07, "des;mode=cfb",
@null, @password, @null, @salt, @null, @initVector)
set @decDES08 = DecryptSymmetric(@encDES08,
"des;mode=cfb;padding=ansix923", @null, @password, @null,
@salt, @null, @initVector)
set @decDES09 = DecryptSymmetric(@encDES09,
"des;mode=cfb;padding=iso10126", @null, @password, @null,
@salt, @null, @initVector)
set @decDES10 = DecryptSymmetric(@encDES10,
"des;mode=cfb;padding=none", @null, @password, @null, @salt,
@null, @initVector)
set @decDES11 = DecryptSymmetric(@encDES11,
"des;mode=cfb;padding=pkcs7", @null, @password, @null, @salt,
@null, @initVector)
set @decDES12 = DecryptSymmetric(@encDES12,
"des;mode=cfb;padding=zeros", @null, @password, @null,
@salt, @null, @initVector)
set @decDES13 = DecryptSymmetric(@encDES13, "des;mode=ecb",
@null, @password, @null, @salt, @null, @initVector)
```

```
set @decDES14 = DecryptSymmetric(@encDES14,
"des;mode=ecb;padding=ansix923", @null, @password, @null,
@salt, @null, @initVector)
set @decDES15 = DecryptSymmetric(@encDES15,
"des;mode=ecb;padding=iso10126", @null, @password, @null,
@salt, @null, @initVector)
set @decDES16 = DecryptSymmetric(@encDES16,
"des;mode=ecb;padding=none", @null, @password, @null, @salt,
@null, @initVector)
set @decDES17 = DecryptSymmetric(@encDES17,
"des;mode=ecb;padding=pkcs7", @null, @password, @null, @salt,
@null, @initVector)
set @decDES18 = DecryptSymmetric(@encDES18,
"des;mode=ecb;padding=zeros", @null, @password, @null,
@salt, @null, @initVector)
set @decTripleDES01 = DecryptSymmetric(@encTripleDES01,
"tripledes;mode=cbc", @null, @password, @null, @salt, @null,
@initVector)
set @decTripleDES02 = DecryptSymmetric(@encTripleDES02,
"tripledes;mode=cbc;padding=ansix923", @null, @password,
@null, @salt, @null, @initVector)
set @decTripleDES03 = DecryptSymmetric(@encTripleDES03,
"tripledes;mode=cbc;padding=iso10126", @null, @password,
@null, @salt, @null, @initVector)
set @decTripleDES04 = DecryptSymmetric(@encTripleDES04,
"tripledes;mode=cbc;padding=none", @null, @password, @null,
@salt, @null, @initVector)
set @decTripleDES05 = DecryptSymmetric(@encTripleDES05,
"tripledes;mode=cbc;padding=pkcs7", @null, @password, @null,
@salt, @null, @initVector)
set @decTripleDES06 = DecryptSymmetric(@encTripleDES06,
"tripledes;mode=cbc;padding=zeros", @null, @password, @null,
@salt, @null, @initVector)
set @decTripleDES07 = DecryptSymmetric(@encTripleDES07,
"tripledes;mode=cfb", @null, @password, @null, @salt, @null,
@initVector)
set @decTripleDES08 = DecryptSymmetric(@encTripleDES08,
"tripledes;mode=cfb;padding=ansix923", @null, @password,
@null, @salt, @null, @initVector)
set @decTripleDES09 = DecryptSymmetric(@encTripleDES09,
"tripledes;mode=cfb;padding=iso10126", @null, @password,
@null, @salt, @null, @initVector)
```

```
set @decTripleDES10 = DecryptSymmetric(@encTripleDES10,
"tripledes;mode=cfb;padding=none", @null, @password, @null,
@salt, @null, @initVector)
set @decTripleDES11 = DecryptSymmetric(@encTripleDES11,
"tripledes;mode=cfb;padding=pkcs7", @null, @password, @null,
@salt, @null, @initVector)
set @decTripleDES12 = DecryptSymmetric(@encTripleDES12,
"tripledes;mode=cfb;padding=zeros", @null, @password, @null,
@salt, @null, @initVector)
set @decTripleDES13 = DecryptSymmetric(@encTripleDES13,
"tripledes;mode=ecb", @null, @password, @null, @salt, @null,
@initVector)
set @decTripleDES14 = DecryptSymmetric(@encTripleDES14,
"tripledes;mode=ecb;padding=ansix923", @null, @password,
@null, @salt, @null, @initVector)
set @decTripleDES15 = DecryptSymmetric(@encTripleDES15,
"tripledes;mode=ecb;padding=iso10126", @null, @password,
@null, @salt, @null, @initVector)
set @decTripleDES16 = DecryptSymmetric(@encTripleDES16,
"tripledes;mode=ecb;padding=none", @null, @password, @null,
@salt, @null, @initVector)
set @decTripleDES17 = DecryptSymmetric(@encTripleDES17,
"tripledes;mode=ecb;padding=pkcs7", @null, @password, @null,
@salt, @null, @initVector)
set @decTripleDES18 = DecryptSymmetric(@encTripleDES18,
"tripledes;mode=ecb;padding=zeros", @null, @password, @null,
@salt, @null, @initVector)

]%%
password: %%=v(@password)=%%
<br>salt: %%=v(@salt)=%%
<br>initVector: %%=v(@initVector)=%%
<br><br>encAES: %%=v(@encAES)=%%
<br>encDES01: %%=v(@encDES01)=%%
<br>encDES02: %%=v(@encDES02)=%%
<br>encDES03: %%=v(@encDES03)=%%
<br>encDES04: %%=v(@encDES04)=%%
<br>encDES05: %%=v(@encDES05)=%%
<br>encDES06: %%=v(@encDES06)=%%
<br>encDES07: %%=v(@encDES07)=%%
<br>encDES08: %%=v(@encDES08)=%%
<br>encDES09: %%=v(@encDES09)=%%
```

```
<br>encDES10: %%=v(@encDES10)=%%
<br>encDES11: %%=v(@encDES11)=%%
<br>encDES12: %%=v(@encDES12)=%%
<br>encDES13: %%=v(@encDES13)=%%
<br>encDES14: %%=v(@encDES14)=%%
<br>encDES15: %%=v(@encDES15)=%%
<br>encDES16: %%=v(@encDES16)=%%
<br>encDES17: %%=v(@encDES17)=%%
<br>encDES18: %%=v(@encDES18)=%%
<br>encTripleDES01: %%=v(@encTripleDES01)=%%
<br>encTripleDES02: %%=v(@encTripleDES02)=%%
<br>encTripleDES03: %%=v(@encTripleDES03)=%%
<br>encTripleDES04: %%=v(@encTripleDES04)=%%
<br>encTripleDES05: %%=v(@encTripleDES05)=%%
<br>encTripleDES06: %%=v(@encTripleDES06)=%%
<br>encTripleDES07: %%=v(@encTripleDES07)=%%
<br>encTripleDES08: %%=v(@encTripleDES08)=%%
<br>encTripleDES09: %%=v(@encTripleDES09)=%%
<br>encTripleDES10: %%=v(@encTripleDES10)=%%
<br>encTripleDES11: %%=v(@encTripleDES11)=%%
<br>encTripleDES12: %%=v(@encTripleDES12)=%%
<br>encTripleDES13: %%=v(@encTripleDES13)=%%
<br>encTripleDES14: %%=v(@encTripleDES14)=%%
<br>encTripleDES15: %%=v(@encTripleDES15)=%%
<br>encTripleDES16: %%=v(@encTripleDES16)=%%
<br>encTripleDES17: %%=v(@encTripleDES17)=%%
<br>encTripleDES18: %%=v(@encTripleDES18)=%%
<br><br>decAES: %%=v(@decAES)=%%
<br>decDES01: %%=v(@decDES01)=%%
<br>decDES02: %%=v(@decDES02)=%%
<br>decDES03: %%=v(@decDES03)=%%
<br>decDES04: %%=v(@decDES04)=%%
<br>decDES05: %%=v(@decDES05)=%%
<br>decDES06: %%=v(@decDES06)=%%
<br>decDES07: %%=v(@decDES07)=%%
<br>decDES08: %%=v(@decDES08)=%%
<br>decDES09: %%=v(@decDES09)=%%
<br>decDES10: %%=v(@decDES10)=%%
<br>decDES11: %%=v(@decDES11)=%%
<br>decDES12: %%=v(@decDES12)=%%
<br>decDES13: %%=v(@decDES13)=%%
<br>decDES14: %%=v(@decDES14)=%%
```

```
<br>decDES15: %%=v(@decDES15)=%%
<br>decDES16: %%=v(@decDES16)=%%
<br>decDES17: %%=v(@decDES17)=%%
<br>decDES18: %%=v(@decDES18)=%%
<br>decTripleDES01: %%=v(@decTripleDES01)=%%
<br>decTripleDES02: %%=v(@decTripleDES02)=%%
<br>decTripleDES03: %%=v(@decTripleDES03)=%%
<br>decTripleDES04: %%=v(@decTripleDES04)=%%
<br>decTripleDES05: %%=v(@decTripleDES05)=%%
<br>decTripleDES06: %%=v(@decTripleDES06)=%%
<br>decTripleDES07: %%=v(@decTripleDES07)=%%
<br>decTripleDES08: %%=v(@decTripleDES08)=%%
<br>decTripleDES09: %%=v(@decTripleDES09)=%%
<br>decTripleDES10: %%=v(@decTripleDES10)=%%
<br>decTripleDES11: %%=v(@decTripleDES11)=%%
<br>decTripleDES12: %%=v(@decTripleDES12)=%%
<br>decTripleDES13: %%=v(@decTripleDES13)=%%
<br>decTripleDES14: %%=v(@decTripleDES14)=%%
<br>decTripleDES15: %%=v(@decTripleDES15)=%%
<br>decTripleDES16: %%=v(@decTripleDES16)=%%
<br>decTripleDES17: %%=v(@decTripleDES17)=%%
<br>decTripleDES18: %%=v(@decTripleDES18)=%%
```

Output

```
password: fresh
salt: e0cf1267f564b362
initVector: 4963b7334a46352623252955df21d7f3

encAES: 4fKWdv7fJRkFsYO6RRtrMg==
encDES01: Qs+p/Gw8hughK4EbaPxFLg==
encDES02: Qs+p/Gw8hug5Q04gtQQ3Jw==
encDES03: Qs+p/Gw8hujEN7j5qYz8/A==
encDES04: Qs+p/Gw8hug=
encDES05: Qs+p/Gw8hughK4EbaPxFLg==
encDES06: Qs+p/Gw8hug=
encDES07: OjFSuxhf85augugb0wUaLg==
encDES08: OjFSuxhf85amqnIztzgoIg==
encDES09: OjFSuxhf85ZHduos1dQyeg==
encDES10: OjFSuxhf85Y=
encDES11: OjFSuxhf85augugb0wUaLg==
encDES12: OjFSuxhf85Y=
```

```
encDES13: Qs+p/Gw8huiQqlLLjpNC5g==
encDES14: Qs+p/Gw8huhz0yIqcW8eDQ==
encDES15: Qs+p/Gw8hugteYp97SZQJA==
encDES16: Qs+p/Gw8hug=
encDES17: Qs+p/Gw8huiQqlLLjpNC5g==
encDES18: Qs+p/Gw8hug=
encTripleDES01: 5Zwb4S0ylZsfF+KHXpd17A==
encTripleDES02: 5Zwb4S0ylZuUQ3v4JsD4uA==
encTripleDES03: 5Zwb4S0ylZssnYGXucyn2A==
encTripleDES04: 5Zwb4S0ylZs=
encTripleDES05: 5Zwb4S0ylZsfF+KHXpd17A==
encTripleDES06: 5Zwb4S0ylZs=
encTripleDES07: gnpVkeFLdtpJO1d6cmlWxA==
encTripleDES08: gnpVkeFLdtpBsFpJx+kqCw==
encTripleDES09: gnpVkeFLdtr/hikI5d8kUg==
encTripleDES10: gnpVkeFLdto=
encTripleDES11: gnpVkeFLdtpJO1d6cmlWxA==
encTripleDES12: gnpVkeFLdto=
encTripleDES13: 5Zwb4S0ylZvWK0u1DJNlYQ==
encTripleDES14: 5Zwb4S0ylZtOKfaL4b4xvQ==
encTripleDES15: 5Zwb4S0ylZv5vh3YpVg5ZQ==
encTripleDES16: 5Zwb4S0ylZs=
encTripleDES17: 5Zwb4S0ylZvWK0u1DJNlYQ==
encTripleDES18: 5Zwb4S0ylZs=

decAES: limedash
decDES01: limedash
decDES02: limedash
decDES03: limedash
decDES04: limedash
decDES05: limedash
decDES06: limedash
decDES07: limedash
decDES08: limedash
decDES09: limedash
decDES10: limedash
decDES11: limedash
decDES12: limedash
decDES13: limedash
decDES14: limedash
decDES15: limedash
decDES16: limedash
```

```
decDES17: limedash
decDES18: limedash
decTripleDES01: limedash
decTripleDES02: limedash
decTripleDES03: limedash
decTripleDES04: limedash
decTripleDES05: limedash
decTripleDES06: limedash
decTripleDES07: limedash
decTripleDES08: limedash
decTripleDES09: limedash
decTripleDES10: limedash
decTripleDES11: limedash
decTripleDES12: limedash
decTripleDES13: limedash
decTripleDES14: limedash
decTripleDES15: limedash
decTripleDES16: limedash
decTripleDES17: limedash
decTripleDES18: limedash
```

EncryptSymmetric

This function encrypts a string with the specified algorithm and qualifiers. Outputs a Base64 encoded value.

Arguments

`EncryptSymmetric(1,2,3,4,5,6,7,8)`

Ordinal	Type	Required	Description
1	String	True	String to encrypt
2	String	True	Algorithm used to encrypt the string. Valid values are **`aes`**, **`des`**, and **`tripledes`**. Optional cipher modes for **`des`** and **`tripledes`** include: ▪ **`cbc`** (Cipher Block Chaining, *default*) ▪ **`cfb`** (Cipher Feedback) ▪ **`ecb`** (Electronic Codebook)

Ordinal	Type	Required	Description
			Optional padding codes for **des** and **tripledes** include: ▪ **ansix923** (sequence of bytes filled with zeros before the length) ▪ **iso10126** (random data before the length) ▪ **none** ▪ **pkcs7** (sequence of bytes, each of which is equal to the total number of padding bytes added , *default*) ▪ **zeros** Modes and padding are specified after the algorithm and are delimited by semicolons: **des;mode=ecb;padding=zeros**.
3	String	True	Password External Key for retrieval from Key Management
4	String	True	Password value
5	String	True	Salt External Key for retrieval from Key Management
6	String	True	Salt value as an 8-byte hex string
7	String	True	Initialization vector External Key for retrieval from Key Management
8	String	True	Initialization vector value as a 16-byte hex string

NOTE: You can specify a Password, Salt and Initialization External Key or value, but not both. If the External Key is specified, the value will be retrieved from Key Management. If you specify values, the External Keys are ignored. Unspecified values should be represented by an undeclared AMPscript variable like **@null**.

NOTE: The **des** and **tripledes** algorithm modes and padding are optional but can be specified following the algorithm value, delimited by semicolons: **des;mode=ecb;padding=zeros**

NOTE: The **cts** and **ofb** modes for the **des** and **tripledes** algorithms are not supported in the current version of Marketing Cloud.

Example

```
%%[

var @str
var @password
var @salt
var @initVector

var @encAES
var @encDES01
var @encDES02
var @encDES03
var @encDES04
var @encDES05
var @encDES06
var @encDES07
var @encDES08
var @encDES09
var @encDES10
var @encDES11
var @encDES12
var @encDES13
var @encDES14
var @encDES15
var @encDES16
var @encDES17
var @encDES18
var @encTripleDES01
var @encTripleDES02
var @encTripleDES03
var @encTripleDES04
var @encTripleDES05
var @encTripleDES06
var @encTripleDES07
var @encTripleDES08
var @encTripleDES09
var @encTripleDES10
var @encTripleDES11
var @encTripleDES12
var @encTripleDES13
var @encTripleDES14
```

```
var @encTripleDES15
var @encTripleDES16
var @encTripleDES17
var @encTripleDES18

set @str = "limedash"
set @password = "fresh"
set @salt = "e0cf1267f564b362"
set @initVector = "4963b7334a46352623252955df21d7f3"

set @encAES = EncryptSymmetric(@str, "aes", @null,
@password, @null, @salt, @null, @initVector)
set @encDES01 = EncryptSymmetric(@str, "des;mode=cbc",
@null, @password, @null, @salt, @null, @initVector)
set @encDES02 = EncryptSymmetric(@str,
"des;mode=cbc;padding=ansix923", @null, @password, @null,
@salt, @null, @initVector)
set @encDES03 = EncryptSymmetric(@str,
"des;mode=cbc;padding=iso10126", @null, @password, @null,
@salt, @null, @initVector)
set @encDES04 = EncryptSymmetric(@str,
"des;mode=cbc;padding=none", @null, @password, @null, @salt,
@null, @initVector)
set @encDES05 = EncryptSymmetric(@str,
"des;mode=cbc;padding=pkcs7", @null, @password, @null, @salt,
@null, @initVector)
set @encDES06 = EncryptSymmetric(@str,
"des;mode=cbc;padding=zeros", @null, @password, @null, @salt,
@null, @initVector)
set @encDES07 = EncryptSymmetric(@str, "des;mode=cfb",
@null, @password, @null, @salt, @null, @initVector)
set @encDES08 = EncryptSymmetric(@str,
"des;mode=cfb;padding=ansix923", @null, @password, @null,
@salt, @null, @initVector)
set @encDES09 = EncryptSymmetric(@str,
"des;mode=cfb;padding=iso10126", @null, @password, @null,
@salt, @null, @initVector)
set @encDES10 = EncryptSymmetric(@str,
"des;mode=cfb;padding=none", @null, @password, @null, @salt,
@null, @initVector)
```

```
set @encDES11 = EncryptSymmetric(@str,
"des;mode=cfb;padding=pkcs7", @null, @password, @null, @salt,
@null, @initVector)
set @encDES12 = EncryptSymmetric(@str,
"des;mode=cfb;padding=zeros", @null, @password, @null, @salt,
@null, @initVector)
set @encDES13 = EncryptSymmetric(@str, "des;mode=ecb",
@null, @password, @null, @salt, @null, @initVector)
set @encDES14 = EncryptSymmetric(@str,
"des;mode=ecb;padding=ansix923", @null, @password, @null,
@salt, @null, @initVector)
set @encDES15 = EncryptSymmetric(@str,
"des;mode=ecb;padding=iso10126", @null, @password, @null,
@salt, @null, @initVector)
set @encDES16 = EncryptSymmetric(@str,
"des;mode=ecb;padding=none", @null, @password, @null, @salt,
@null, @initVector)
set @encDES17 = EncryptSymmetric(@str,
"des;mode=ecb;padding=pkcs7", @null, @password, @null, @salt,
@null, @initVector)
set @encDES18 = EncryptSymmetric(@str,
"des;mode=ecb;padding=zeros", @null, @password, @null, @salt,
@null, @initVector)
set @encTripleDES01 = EncryptSymmetric(@str,
"tripledes;mode=cbc", @null, @password, @null, @salt, @null,
@initVector)
set @encTripleDES02 = EncryptSymmetric(@str,
"tripledes;mode=cbc;padding=ansix923", @null, @password,
@null, @salt, @null, @initVector)
set @encTripleDES03 = EncryptSymmetric(@str,
"tripledes;mode=cbc;padding=iso10126", @null, @password,
@null, @salt, @null, @initVector)
set @encTripleDES04 = EncryptSymmetric(@str,
"tripledes;mode=cbc;padding=none", @null, @password, @null,
@salt, @null, @initVector)
set @encTripleDES05 = EncryptSymmetric(@str,
"tripledes;mode=cbc;padding=pkcs7", @null, @password, @null,
@salt, @null, @initVector)
set @encTripleDES06 = EncryptSymmetric(@str,
"tripledes;mode=cbc;padding=zeros", @null, @password, @null,
@salt, @null, @initVector)
```

```
set @encTripleDES07 = EncryptSymmetric(@str,
"tripledes;mode=cfb", @null, @password, @null, @salt, @null,
@initVector)
set @encTripleDES08 = EncryptSymmetric(@str,
"tripledes;mode=cfb;padding=ansix923", @null, @password,
@null, @salt, @null, @initVector)
set @encTripleDES09 = EncryptSymmetric(@str,
"tripledes;mode=cfb;padding=iso10126", @null, @password,
@null, @salt, @null, @initVector)
set @encTripleDES10 = EncryptSymmetric(@str,
"tripledes;mode=cfb;padding=none", @null, @password, @null,
@salt, @null, @initVector)
set @encTripleDES11 = EncryptSymmetric(@str,
"tripledes;mode=cfb;padding=pkcs7", @null, @password, @null,
@salt, @null, @initVector)
set @encTripleDES12 = EncryptSymmetric(@str,
"tripledes;mode=cfb;padding=zeros", @null, @password, @null,
@salt, @null, @initVector)
set @encTripleDES13 = EncryptSymmetric(@str,
"tripledes;mode=ecb", @null, @password, @null, @salt, @null,
@initVector)
set @encTripleDES14 = EncryptSymmetric(@str,
"tripledes;mode=ecb;padding=ansix923", @null, @password,
@null, @salt, @null, @initVector)
set @encTripleDES15 = EncryptSymmetric(@str,
"tripledes;mode=ecb;padding=iso10126", @null, @password,
@null, @salt, @null, @initVector)
set @encTripleDES16 = EncryptSymmetric(@str,
"tripledes;mode=ecb;padding=none", @null, @password, @null,
@salt, @null, @initVector)
set @encTripleDES17 = EncryptSymmetric(@str,
"tripledes;mode=ecb;padding=pkcs7", @null, @password, @null,
@salt, @null, @initVector)
set @encTripleDES18 = EncryptSymmetric(@str,
"tripledes;mode=ecb;padding=zeros", @null, @password, @null,
@salt, @null, @initVector)

]%%
str: %%=v(@str)=%%
<br>password: %%=v(@password)=%%
<br>salt: %%=v(@salt)=%%
<br>initVector: %%=v(@initVector)=%%
```

```
<br><br>encAES: %%=v(@encAES)=%%
<br>encDES01: %%=v(@encDES01)=%%
<br>encDES02: %%=v(@encDES02)=%%
<br>encDES03: %%=v(@encDES03)=%%
<br>encDES04: %%=v(@encDES04)=%%
<br>encDES05: %%=v(@encDES05)=%%
<br>encDES06: %%=v(@encDES06)=%%
<br>encDES07: %%=v(@encDES07)=%%
<br>encDES08: %%=v(@encDES08)=%%
<br>encDES09: %%=v(@encDES09)=%%
<br>encDES10: %%=v(@encDES10)=%%
<br>encDES11: %%=v(@encDES11)=%%
<br>encDES12: %%=v(@encDES12)=%%
<br>encDES13: %%=v(@encDES13)=%%
<br>encDES14: %%=v(@encDES14)=%%
<br>encDES15: %%=v(@encDES15)=%%
<br>encDES16: %%=v(@encDES16)=%%
<br>encDES17: %%=v(@encDES17)=%%
<br>encDES18: %%=v(@encDES18)=%%
<br>encTripleDES01: %%=v(@encTripleDES01)=%%
<br>encTripleDES02: %%=v(@encTripleDES02)=%%
<br>encTripleDES03: %%=v(@encTripleDES03)=%%
<br>encTripleDES04: %%=v(@encTripleDES04)=%%
<br>encTripleDES05: %%=v(@encTripleDES05)=%%
<br>encTripleDES06: %%=v(@encTripleDES06)=%%
<br>encTripleDES07: %%=v(@encTripleDES07)=%%
<br>encTripleDES08: %%=v(@encTripleDES08)=%%
<br>encTripleDES09: %%=v(@encTripleDES09)=%%
<br>encTripleDES10: %%=v(@encTripleDES10)=%%
<br>encTripleDES11: %%=v(@encTripleDES11)=%%
<br>encTripleDES12: %%=v(@encTripleDES12)=%%
<br>encTripleDES13: %%=v(@encTripleDES13)=%%
<br>encTripleDES14: %%=v(@encTripleDES14)=%%
<br>encTripleDES15: %%=v(@encTripleDES15)=%%
<br>encTripleDES16: %%=v(@encTripleDES16)=%%
<br>encTripleDES17: %%=v(@encTripleDES17)=%%
<br>encTripleDES18: %%=v(@encTripleDES18)=%%
```

Output

```
str: limedash
password: fresh
```

```
salt: e0cf1267f564b362
initVector: 4963b7334a46352623252955df21d7f3

encAES: 4fKWdv7fJRkFsYO6RRtrMg==
encDES01: Qs+p/Gw8hughK4EbaPxFLg==
encDES02: Qs+p/Gw8hug5Q04gtQQ3Jw==
encDES03: Qs+p/Gw8hujEN7j5qYz8/A==
encDES04: Qs+p/Gw8hug=
encDES05: Qs+p/Gw8hughK4EbaPxFLg==
encDES06: Qs+p/Gw8hug=
encDES07: OjFSuxhf85augugb0wUaLg==
encDES08: OjFSuxhf85amqnIztzgoIg==
encDES09: OjFSuxhf85ZHduos1dQyeg==
encDES10: OjFSuxhf85Y=
encDES11: OjFSuxhf85augugb0wUaLg==
encDES12: OjFSuxhf85Y=
encDES13: Qs+p/Gw8huiQqlLLjpNC5g==
encDES14: Qs+p/Gw8huhz0yIqcW8eDQ==
encDES15: Qs+p/Gw8hugteYp97SZQJA==
encDES16: Qs+p/Gw8hug=
encDES17: Qs+p/Gw8huiQqlLLjpNC5g==
encDES18: Qs+p/Gw8hug=
encTripleDES01: 5Zwb4S0ylZsfF+KHXpd17A==
encTripleDES02: 5Zwb4S0ylZuUQ3v4JsD4uA==
encTripleDES03: 5Zwb4S0ylZssnYGXucyn2A==
encTripleDES04: 5Zwb4S0ylZs=
encTripleDES05: 5Zwb4S0ylZsfF+KHXpd17A==
encTripleDES06: 5Zwb4S0ylZs=
encTripleDES07: gnpVkeFLdtpJO1d6cmlWxA==
encTripleDES08: gnpVkeFLdtpBsFpJx+kqCw==
encTripleDES09: gnpVkeFLdtr/hikI5d8kUg==
encTripleDES10: gnpVkeFLdto=
encTripleDES11: gnpVkeFLdtpJO1d6cmlWxA==
encTripleDES12: gnpVkeFLdto=
encTripleDES13: 5Zwb4S0ylZvWK0u1DJNlYQ==
encTripleDES14: 5Zwb4S0ylZtOKfaL4b4xvQ==
encTripleDES15: 5Zwb4S0ylZv5vh3YpVg5ZQ==
encTripleDES16: 5Zwb4S0ylZs=
encTripleDES17: 5Zwb4S0ylZvWK0u1DJNlYQ==
encTripleDES18: 5Zwb4S0ylZs=
```

MD5

This function converts the specified string into a 16-byte MD5 hash hex value.

Arguments

MD5(1,2)

Ordinal	Type	Required	Description
1	String	True	String to convert
2	String	False	Character set to use for character-encoding. Valid values are **UTF-8** (default) and **UTF-16**

> **NOTE:** The results of the MD5 hash are considered one-way, meaning they cannot be decrypted.

Example

```
%%[

var @emailAddress
var @MD5EmailAddressUTF8
var @MD5EmailAddressUTF16

set @emailAddress = AttributeValue("emailAddr") /* value
from attribute or DE column in send context */
set @emailAddress = "leon@limedash.com" /* or a literal
value */
set @MD5EmailAddressUTF8   = MD5(@emailAddress)
set @MD5EmailAddressUTF16   = MD5(@emailAddress, "UTF-16")

]%%
emailAddress: %%=v(@emailAddress)=%%
<br>MD5EmailAddressUTF8: %%=v(@MD5EmailAddressUTF8)=%%
<br>MD5EmailAddressUTF16: %%=v(@MD5EmailAddressUTF16)=%%
```

Output

```
emailAddress: leon@limedash.com
MD5EmailAddressUTF8: fc46f8458a322e7fc807a340e622557c
MD5EmailAddressUTF16: b568f29e9315771e2c06bd435cc7b2e6
```

SHA1

This function converts the specified string into a SHA1 hex value hash.

Arguments

SHA1(1,2)

Ordinal	Type	Required	Description
1	String	True	String to convert
2	String	False	Character set to use for character-encoding. Valid values are **UTF-8** (default) and **UTF-16**

> **NOTE:** The results of the SHA1 hash are considered one-way, meaning they cannot be decrypted.

Example

```
%%[

var @emailAddress
var @SHA1EmailAddressUTF8
var @SHA1EmailAddressUTF16

set @emailAddress = AttributeValue("emailAddr") /* value
from attribute or DE column in send context */
set @emailAddress = "curt@limedash.com" /* or a literal
value */
set @SHA1EmailAddressUTF8  = SHA1(@emailAddress)
set @SHA1EmailAddressUTF16  = SHA1(@emailAddress, "UTF-16")

]%%
emailAddress: %%=v(@emailAddress)=%%
<br>SHA1EmailAddressUTF8: %%=v(@SHA1EmailAddressUTF8)=%%
<br>SHA1EmailAddressUTF16: %%=v(@SHA1EmailAddressUTF16)=%%
```

Output

```
emailAddress: curt@limedash.com
SHA1EmailAddressUTF8: 349601423ece6853014397f3b5fe44ce8ddd9358
SHA1EmailAddressUTF16:
2eb6923a3078e9cfa0632461098720a99100bcdc
```

SHA256

This function converts the specified string into a SHA256 hex value hash.

Arguments

`SHA256(1,2)`

Ordinal	Type	Required	Description
1	String	True	String to convert
2	String	False	Character set to use for character-encoding. Valid values are **`UTF-8`** (default) and **`UTF-16`**

> **NOTE:** The results of the SHA256 hash are considered one-way, meaning they cannot be decrypted.

Example

```
%%[

var @emailAddress
var @SHA256EmailAddressUTF8
var @SHA256EmailAddressUTF16

set @emailAddress = AttributeValue("emailAddr") /* value
from attribute or DE column in send context */
set @emailAddress = "lily@limedash.com" /* or a literal
value */
set @SHA256EmailAddressUTF8  = SHA256(@emailAddress)
set @SHA256EmailAddressUTF16  = SHA256(@emailAddress, "UTF-
16")

]%%
emailAddress: %%=v(@emailAddress)=%%
<br>SHA256EmailAddressUTF8: %%=v(@SHA256EmailAddressUTF8)=%%
<br>SHA256EmailAddressUTF16:
%%=v(@SHA256EmailAddressUTF16)=%%
```

Output

```
emailAddress: lily@limedash.com
SHA256EmailAddressUTF8: 0dfe4d756c779f86e80e43cb3efc4d75758b9
00d8a4837cf979a0e0cd295ead1
```

```
SHA256EmailAddressUTF16: 5a643ce463059ca33d1b0c31dc8669f247344
44ace3cd5c4c74170dedec00b78
```

SHA512

This function converts the specified string into a SHA512 hex value hash.

Arguments

`SHA512(1,2)`

Ordinal	Type	Required	Description
1	String	True	String to convert
2	String	False	Character set to use for character-encoding. Valid values are **`UTF-8`** (default) and **`UTF-16`**

> **NOTE:** The results of thc SHA512 hash are considered one-way, meaning they cannot be decrypted.

Example

```
%%[

var @emailAddress
var @SHA512EmailAddressUTF8
var @SHA512EmailAddressUTF16

set @emailAddress = AttributeValue("emailAddr") /* value
from attribute or DE column in send context */
set @emailAddress = "barb@limedash.com" /* or a literal
value */
set @SHA512EmailAddressUTF8  = SHA512(@emailAddress)
set @SHA512EmailAddressUTF16  = SHA512(@emailAddress, "UTF-
16")

]%%
```

```
emailAddress: %%=v(@emailAddress)=%%
<br>SHA512EmailAddressUTF8: %%=v(@SHA512EmailAddressUTF8)=%%
<br>SHA512EmailAddressUTF16:
%%=v(@SHA512EmailAddressUTF16)=%%
```

Output

```
emailAddress: barb@limedash.com
SHA512EmailAddressUTF8: 98c111950453023a32b030cef11c1137c10ccc
fd2d33246c5c897a9c64e3dc34936e57cf74365ad9534fdf983fc81e841d782
e87e8fec46f5d640677d0374750
SHA512EmailAddressUTF16: 573d3e3b13c82436a3570cf39a37bbba08a52
7273cb330f36da6947536985d99ddcbbf15d2c164f7be64fe028baa2301a28
5ff7c782ad277a7e8c4ce89afebe6
```

URLEncode

This function returns a string in which all non-alphanumeric characters except **-**, _ and **.** have been replaced with a percent sign (**%**) followed by the equivalent hex value. Spaces are encoded as plus (**+**) signs. The string is encoded in the same way that the posted data from an HTML form is encoded or an **application/x-www-form-urlencoded** media type.

Arguments

URLEncode(1,2,3)

Ordinal	Type	Required	Description
1	String	True	String to encode
2	Boolean	False	A value of **0** (default) replaces illegal URL characters with **%20** (space). A value of **1** encodes all illegal characters.
3	Boolean	False	A value of **0** (default) encodes only characters following the **?** in the specified string. A value of **1** encodes the entire string.

Example

```
%%[

var @str
var @encStr1
var @encStr2
var @encStr3

set @str = AttributeValue("CTAURL") /* value from attribute
or DE column in send context */
set @str = "https://limedash.com/?surveyTitle=Become a
Loyalty Member Now!" /* or a literal value */

set @encStr1  = URLEncode(@str)
set @encStr2  = URLEncode(@str, 1, 0)
set @encStr3  = URLEncode(@str, 1, 1)

]%%
str: %%=v(@str)=%%
<br>encStr1: %%=v(@encStr1)=%%
<br>encStr2: %%=v(@encStr2)=%%
<br>encStr3: %%=v(@encStr3)=%%
```

Output

```
str: https://limedash.com/?surveyTitle=Become a Loyalty
Member Now!
encStr1: https://limedash.com/?surveyTitle=Become%20a%20
Loyalt
y%20Member%20Now!
encStr2: https://limedash.
com/?surveyTitle%3dBecome+a+Loyalty+
Member+Now!
encStr3: https%3a%2f%2flimedash.
com%2f%3fsurveyTitle%3dBecome+
a+Loyalty+Member+Now!
```

HTTP Functions

Overview

These functions give you the ability to interact with third-party APIs, feeds and HTTP-accessible content, while also retrieving information related to web browsers that are used to access Marketing Cloud-hosted web content.

Many online services available today provide integration capabilities through REST or SOAP Application Programming Interfaces (APIs). The HTTP functions in Marketing Cloud effectively provide an API client interface where data can be retrieved from, or sent to third-party platforms.

Applications include:

- harvesting content from external URLs (for example, product data)
- including social media or news feeds on web pages and in emails
- displaying weather information based on a Subscriber's geographic location
- adding data-driven personalized maps and charts to marketing content
- shortening personalized URL links in SMS messages.

HTTP functions respect the character set from the Content-Type HTTP header, returned in the request. For example:

Content-Type	Encoding
`text/html; charset=utf-8`	UTF-8
`text/json; charset=utf-16`	UTF-16
`text/plain; charset=us-ascii`	US-ASCII
`text/plain; charset=iso-8859-5`	ISO 8859-5

If the character set encoding is not specified in the HTTP header, Marketing Cloud interprets the content using 'WindowsCodePage 1252' character-encoding. However, this default encoding can be changed by contacting your Marketing Cloud Support Representative.

> **TIP:** HTTP testing services including httpbin, RequestBin and Hurl.it provide convenient endpoints and utilities for testing AMPscript HTTP functions.

HTTPGet

This function retrieves, or 'gets' content from a defined publicly accessible URL.

> **NOTE:** The function only works with HTTP content on TCP/IP port 80 and HTTPS on port 443. Basic access authentication in URLs is not supported (for example, `https://username:password@https://domain.com`).

Arguments

`HTTPGet(1,2,3,4)`

Ordinal	Type	Required	Description
1	String	True	URL used to retrieve content
2	String	False	Whether the process continues on an error. A value of `true` ignores errors in the process. It defaults to `false` if not specified.
3	String	False	Defines whether the function allows empty content. A value of **0** permits empty content. A value of `1` returns an error. A value of **2** skips sending an email to the Subscriber (if the function is used in an email).
4	String	False	Outputs the function status. A value of **0** indicates the status is successful, `-1` indicates a 404 error (URL not found), **-2** indicates an HTTP request error (the server did not return a 2xx status code) and **-3** indicates empty content.

Example 1

The following example retrieves HTML content from an external URL and displays it in an email, web page or message.

```
%%[

var @getRequest
set @getRequest = TreatAsContent(HTTPGet("https://httpbin.
org/html"))

]%%
%%=v(@getRequest)=%%
```

Output

The request will return HTML content from the source URL.

```
<!DOCTYPE html>
<html>
  <head>
  </head>
  <body>
      <h1>Herman Melville - Moby-Dick</h1>
      <div>
        <p>
          Availing himself of the mild, summer-cool weather
that now reigned in these latitudes, and in preparation for
the peculiarly active pursuits shortly to be anticipated,
Perth, the begrimed, blistered old blacksmith, had not
removed his portable forge to the hold again, after
concluding his contributory work for Ahab's leg...
        </p>
      </div>
  </body>
</html>
```

Example 2

The following example indicates the behavior when an external URL returns a 500 HTTP status code (Internal Server Error) and the function is set to ignore errors.

```
%%[

var @getRequest
set @getRequest = TreatAsContent(HTTPGet("https://httpbin.
org/status/500",true))

]%%
%%=v(@getRequest)=%%
```

Output

The **@getRequest** variable will be empty.

> **NOTE:** If the function is set to not ignore errors, the following error will be returned: "An exception occurred when attempting to retrieve content by a HttpGet call."

Example 3

The following example indicates the behavior when an external URL returns a 404 HTTP status code (Page Not Found) and the function is set to ignore errors.

```
%%[

var @getRequest
set @getRequest = TreatAsContent(HTTPGet("https://httpbin.
org/status/404",true,0,@status))

]%%
%%=v(@status)=%%
```

Output

The **v** function outputs the **status** variable, indicating that the server did not return a successful status code.

```
-2
```

HTTPPost

This function posts content to a defined, publicly accessible URL.

> **NOTE:** The function only works with HTTP content on TCP/IP port 80 and HTTPS on port 443. Basic access authentication in URLs is not supported (for example, `https://username:password@https://domain.com`).

Arguments

`HTTPPost(1,2,3,4,5,6,[7a,7b]...)`

Ordinal	Type	Required	Description
1	String	True	URL endpoint used to post content
2	String	True	Content-Type header value
3	String	True	Content to include in POST request
4	String	False	Variable used to return response
5	String	False	Name of additional header to include in POST request
6	String	False	Value of additional header to include in POST request
7a	String	False	Name of additional header to include in POST request (see note)
7b	String	False	Value of additional header to include in POST request (see note)

> **NOTE:** Additional header name and value pairs can be appended as arguments.

> **TIP:** If the HTTPPost function is set as a variable, the HTTP status code from the request will be set as the variable value.

Example 1

The following example makes an HTTP POST request with a JSON payload to an external endpoint.

```
%%[

var @payload, @response

set @payload = '{
    "Order Number":10110113,
    "First Name":"Nora",
    "Last Name":"Taylor",
    "Amount":{
        "Order Subtotal":120,
        "VAT":20,
        "Shipping":0,
        "Order Total":120
    }
}'

set @request = HTTPPost("https://httpbin.org/
post","application/json", @payload, @response)

]%%

status code: %%=v(@request)=%%

response: %%=v(@response)=%%
```

Output

The request returns the response body.

```
status code: 200

response: {"args":{}, "data":"{...}", "files":{}, "form":{  },
"headers":{...}, "json":{"Amount":{"Order Subtotal":120, "Order
Total":120, "Shipping":0, "VAT":20 }, "First Name":"Nora",
"Last Name":"Taylor", "Order Number":10110113 } }
```

Example 2

The following example includes additional name and value pairs in the HTTP header of the POST request. Additionally, the function has been set as a variable to return the HTTP status code from the request.

```
%%[

var @payload, @response

set @payload = '{
    "Order Number":10110113,
    "First Name":"Nora",
    "Last Name":"Taylor",
    "Amount":{
        "Order Subtotal":120,
        "VAT":20,
        "Shipping":0,
        "Order Total":120
    }
}'

set @request = HTTPPost("https://httpbin.org/
post","application/json", @payload, @response,
"Authorization", "Bearer fd5ddads6Ka1987Cfp1", "Accept-
Charset", "utf-8")

]%%

status code: %%=v(@request)=%%

response: %%=v(@response)=%%
```

Output

The request returns the status code and response payload. The following response has been abbreviated for display purposes.

```
status code: 200

response: {"args":{}, "data":"{...}", "files":{}, "form":{  },
"headers":{...}, "json":{"Amount":{"Order Subtotal":120, "Order
Total":120, "Shipping":0, "VAT":20 }, "First Name":"Nora",
"Last Name":"Taylor", "Order Number":10110113 } }
```

HTTPPost2

Similar to the HTTPPost function, this posts content to a defined, publicly accessible URL, but it also provides exception handling if an error is returned from the request.

> **NOTE:** The function only works with HTTP content on TCP/IP port 80 and HTTPS on port 443. Basic access authentication in URLs is not supported (for example, `https://username:password@https://domain.com`).

Arguments

`HTTPPost2(1,2,3,4,5,6,7,8,[9a,9b]...)`

Ordinal	Type	Required	Description
1	String	True	URL endpoint used to post content
2	String	True	Content-Type header value
3	String	True	Content to include in POST request
4	String	False	Whether the process continues on an error. A value of `true` returns an exception.
5	String	False	Variable used to return status response string
6	String	False	Variable used to return response row set (see note)
7	String	False	Name of additional header to include in POST request
8	String	False	Value of additional header to include in POST request
9a	String	False	Name of additional header to include in POST request (see note)
9b	String	False	Value of additional header to include in POST request (see note)

> **NOTE:** Ordinal 6 returns a row set (the number of rows varies depending on the URL). This is an internal row set and the fields are not available for use. Arguments 9a and 9b allow additional header name and value pairs to be appended as arguments — repeat these pairs as required.

> **TIP:** If the HTTPPost function is set as a variable, the HTTP status code from the request will be set as the variable value.

Example

The following example makes an HTTP POST request with a JSON payload to an external endpoint.

```
%%[

var @payload, @postRequest, @response, @responseRows

set @payload = '{
   "Order Number":10110113,
   "First Name":"Curt",
   "Last Name":"Harris",
   "Amount":{
      "Order Subtotal":120,
      "VAT":20,
      "Shipping":0,
      "Order Total":120
   }
}'

set @postrequest = HTTPPost2("https://httpbin.org/
post","application/json", @payload, true, @response,
@responseRows)

]%%

status code: %%=v(@postrequest)=%%

response: %%=v(@response)=%%

responseRows: %%=v(@responseRows)=%%

responseRowCount: %%=RowCount(@responseRows)=%%
```

Output

The request returns the status code, response payload and row set. The following response has been abbreviated for display purposes.

```
status code: 200

response: {"args":{}, "data":"{...}", "files":{}, "form":{  },
"headers":{...}, "json":{"Amount":{"Order Subtotal":120, "Order
Total":120, "Shipping":0, "VAT":20 }, "First Name":"Curt",
"Last Name":"Harris", "Order Number":10110113 } }

responseRows: System.Data.DataRow[]

responseRowCount: 10
```

HTTPRequestHeader

This function returns a specified header from an HTTP request. This function is only available in landing pages, microsites and CloudPages. It cannot be used in other Marketing Cloud applications.

Argument

`HTTPRequestHeader(1)`

Ordinal	Type	Required	Description
1	String	True	An HTTP header as defined in RFC 7231

> **NOTE:** Only headers that are available in the page request return a value. For example, if a user pastes a URL into a web browser instead of clicking on a page hyperlink (from another web page), the **`Referer`** header value will be empty.

Example

The following example retrieves HTTP headers from a web page session.

```
%%[

var @referrer, @userAgent, @host
set @referrer = HTTPRequestHeader("Referer")
set @userAgent = HTTPRequestHeader("User-Agent")
set @host = HTTPRequestHeader("Host")
```

```
]%%

<p>Referrer is %%=v(@referer)=%%</p>

<p>User Agent is %%=v(@userAgent)=%%</p>

<p>Host is %%=v(@host)=%%</p>
```

Output

The request will return HTML content from the source URL.

```
<p>Referrer is https://mystore.com/offers/?pageid=123</p>

<p>User Agent is Mozilla/5.0 (Macintosh; Intel Mac
OS X 10_13_3) AppleWebKit/537.36 (KHTML, like Gecko)
Chrome/64.0.3282.140 Safari/537.36</p>

<p>Host is pub.s1.exacttarget.com</p>
```

IsCHTMLBrowser

This function checks whether a given user agent value is a C-HTML browser.

C-HTML, or Compact HTML, is a subset of the HTML markup language that was developed for small information devices, such as first-generation smart phones and PDAs. The language does not support tables, image maps, multiple fonts or styling of fonts, background colors or images, frames, or style sheets, and is limited to a monochromatic display. This standard was superseded in early 2000 by other markup languages, due to advancements in mobile technology.

This function is only available in landing pages, microsites and CloudPages. It cannot be used in other Marketing Cloud applications.

Argument

`IsCHTMLBrowser(1)`

Ordinal	Type	Required	Description
1	String	True	HTTP user-agent header

The function will return a Boolean value, either `true` or `false`.

Example

The following example uses the **`HTTPRequestHeader`** function to retrieve the **`user-agent`** HTTP header as an argument to the IsCHTMLBrowser function.

```
%%[

var @chtmlBrowser

if IsCHTMLBrowser(HTTPRequestHeader("user-agent")) then
   set @chtmlBrowser = true
endif

]%%

<p>You %%=Iif(@chtmlBrowser==true,"are","are not")=%% using a
C-HTML browser</p>
```

Output

The following output will be returned when viewing the web page on an Android or iOS device.

```
<p>You are not using a C-HTML browser</p>
```

RedirectTo

This function is required when using the **`<a>`** HTML hyperlink tag in emails when the hypertext reference (**`href`**) attribute is either an attribute or a variable and the hyperlink is a tracked email link.

If link tracking in an email is not enabled when the email is sent, the RedirectTo function is not required.

If the RedirectTo function is not used in the **`href`** attribute when an attribute or variable is used, the hyperlink will not be resolved with the attribute or variable, for example it will appear as, **`https://click.email.com/%%=v(@url)=%%`**.

> **NOTE:** HTML bookmarks are not supported by the RedirectTo function; for example, a link value that resolves to **`https://limedash.com/page#bookmark1`**.

Argument

`RedirectTo(1)`

Ordinal	Type	Required	Description
1	String	True	Attribute or variable containing the URL to redirect to

Example

In the following example, an email is sent from a Sendable Data Extension containing a field named 'store'.

```
%%[

var @link
set @link = concat("https://limedash.com/offers/",store)

]%%

<p>Sign up <a href="%%=RedirectTo(@link)=%%">here</a> to
receive special offers.</p>
```

Output

For a Subscriber with a store value of 'Melbourne', the following tracked **`href`** hyperlink attribute will be resolved when the email link is clicked.

```
https://limedash.com/offers/melbourne
```

URLEncode

This function converts non-alphanumeric characters into a defined string with URL encoding (or percent encoding). This function is useful when including values as URL parameters in hyperlinks to ensure the string encoding is preserved.

Arguments

`URLEncode(1,2,3)`

Ordinal	Type	Required	Description
1	String	True	String containing the URL or value
2	Integer	False	Defines whether to convert all non-alphanumeric characters as URL parameters (`0`) or only as space characters (`1`). The default value is `0`.
3	Integer	False	Defines whether to only encode characters in a string prefixed by a URL (`0`) or all characters (`1`). The default value is `0`.

> **NOTE:** Only URL parameters where the URL is suffixed by a **`?`** character will be encoded.

Supported non-alphanumeric characters and their respective encoded values are provided below.

Character	Encoded Character	Character	Encoded Character
newline	**`%0a`**	space	**`%20`** or + (see note)
~	**`%7e`**	#	**`%23`**
"	**`%22`**	&	**`%26`**
%	**`%25`**	'	**`%27`**
,	**`%2c`**	+	**`%2b`**
<	**`%3c`**	/	**`%2f`**
>	**`%3e`**	:	**`%3a`**
\	**`%5c`**	;	**`%3b`**
^	**`%5e`**	=	**`%3d`**
_	**`%5f`**	?	**`%3f`**
`	**`%60`**	@	**`%40`**

Character	Encoded Character	Character	Encoded Character
{	%7b	[	%5b
|	%7c	]	%5d
}	%7d	$	%24

> **NOTE:** When parameter 2 is set to an argument value of **1**, the space character will be converted to **+**. When the parameter is set to an argument value of **1**, the space character will be converted to **%20** and all other characters will not be converted.

Example 1

```
%%[

var @offer
set @offer = "summer offer"

]%%

%%=URLEncode(@offer)=%%
```

Output

No conversion takes place, as there is no URL included.

```
summer offer
```

Example 2

```
%%[

var @offer
set @offer = "https://limedash.com?offer=summer offer"

]%%

%%=URLEncode(@offer)=%%
```

Output

```
https://limedash.com?offer=summer%20offer
```

Example 3

```
%%[

var @offer
set @offer = "summer offer"

]%%

%%=URLEncode(@offer,0,1)=%%
```

Output

```
summer%20offer
```

Example 4

```
%%[

var @preferences, @offer, @url, @link
set @preferences = "red,green,blue"
set @offer = "summer offer"
set @url = Concat("https://limedash.com/store?offer=", @offer,
"&preferences=", @preferences)
set @link = URLEncode(@url,1,0)

]%%

<a href="%%=RedirectTo(@link)=%%">click here</a>
```

Output

The **`href`** attribute resolves to the following URL.

```
https://limedash.com/
store?offer%3dsummer+offer%26preferences%3dred%2cgreen%2cblue
```

WrapLongURL

This function shortens URLs longer than 975 characters to mitigate broken email hyperlinks in Microsoft Outlook, where lengths of URL hyperlinks are limited to the following number of characters:

- Outlook 2007: 975 characters
- Outlook 2010: 1033 characters
- Outlook 2013: 2048 characters

The function shortens a URL by substituting the original URL with a shorter platform URL. The platform URL redirects requests to the original URL when requested by the user agent.

> **NOTE:** This function does not shorten URLs less than 975 characters in length.

> **NOTE:** URLs will only be shortened when the email is sent.

Argument

`WrapLongURL(1)`

Ordinal	Type	Required	Description
1	String	True	URL to be shortened

Example

```
%%[

var @icon
set @icon = "https://limedash.com/images/
rRprc5xG8vP0crpSqWLScVu6yKLTm...lKJK9m1napRdf6b+DAy/ixM.jpg"
/* abbreviated for display purposes */

]%%

<img src="%%=WrapLongURL(@icon)=%%" width="50" height="50"
alt="icon" />
```

Output

The value of the **src** attribute will be shortened to a URL which redirects to the original URL.

```
http://cl.exct.net/ResolveURL.
aspx?qs=faebf571997acc80ec99646da21ae0ab
```

Math Functions

Overview

In contrast to many other scripting languages that use operators like `+`, `-`,`*`, and `\`, AMPscript uses a set of functions for addition, subtraction, multiplication and division. AMPscript also includes specific math functions for performing modulo operations and generating random numbers.

> **TIP:** All math functions require numbers or decimals for parameters. Using any other data type will cause an exception.

Add

This function returns the sum of two numbers.

Arguments

`Add(1,2)`

Ordinal	Type	Required	Description
1	Number	True	First value
2	Number	True	Second value

Example 1

```
%%[

var @sum, @num1, @num2

set @num1 = 5
set @num2 = 42

set @sum  = Add(@num1, @num2)

]%%
%%=v(@num1)=%% + %%=v(@num2)=%% = %%=v(@sum)=%%
```

Output

```
5 + 42 = 47
```

Example 2

This function can also be used to convert a string into a number, by simply adding zero.

```
%%[

var @str, @num

set @str = "42"

set @num  = Add(@str,0)

]%%
String: %%=v(@str)=%%
<br>Number: %%=v(@num)=%%
```

Output

```
String: 42
Number: 42
```

Divide

This function returns the result (quotient) of dividing the first parameter by the second parameter.

Arguments

Divide(1,2)

Ordinal	Type	Required	Description
1	Number	True	Value to be divided (dividend)
2	Number	True	Value to divide by (divisor)

Example 1

```
%%[

var @quotient, @num1, @num2

set @num1 = 10
set @num2 = 5

set @quotient  = divide(@num1, @num2)

]%%
%%=v(@num1)=%% / %%=v(@num2)=%% = %%=v(@quotient)=%%
```

Output

```
10 / 2 = 5
```

Example 2

This function will return a decimal if the dividend cannot be divided evenly.

```
%%[

var @quotient, @num1, @num2

set @num1 = 10
set @num2 = 3

set @quotient  = divide(@num1, @num2)
```

```
]%%
%%=v(@num1)=%% / %%=v(@num2)=%% = %%=v(@quotient)=%%
```

Output

```
10 / 3 = 3.33333333333333
```

Mod

This function returns the remainder after the division of two numbers (also known as a modulo operation).

> **NOTE:** This function will return a decimal if either parameter is a decimal.

Arguments

Mod(1,2)

Ordinal	Type	Required	Description
1	Number	True	Value to be divided (dividend)
2	Number	True	Value to divide by (divisor)

Example

```
%%[

var @modulus, @num1, @num2

set @num1 = 10.23
set @num2 = 3

set @modulus  = mod(@num1, @num2)

]%%
%%=v(@num1)=%% % %%=v(@num2)=%% = %%=v(@modulus)=%%
```

Output

```
10 % 3 = 1
```

Multiply

This function returns the product of multiplying two numbers.

Arguments

`Multiply(1,2)`

Ordinal	Type	Required	Description
1	Number	True	Value to be multiplied
2	Number	True	Value to be multiplied

Example

```
%%[

var @product, @num1, @num2

set @num1 = 5
set @num2 = 4

set @product  = multiply(@num1, @num2)

]%%
%%=v(@num1)=%% * %%=v(@num2)=%% = %%=v(@product)=%%
```

Output

```
5 * 4 = 20
```

Random

This function returns a random number between two numbers. Both upper and lower bound parameters are inclusive.

Arguments

`Random(1,2)`

Ordinal	Type	Required	Description
1	Number	True	Value of lower bound
2	Number	True	Value of upper bound

Example

```
%%[

var @random, @num1, @num2

set @num1 = 1
set @num2 = 100

set @random  = random(@num1, @num2)

]%%
Lower bound: %%=v(@num1)=%%
<br>Upper bound: %%=v(@num2)=%%
<br>Random: %%=v(@random)=%%
```

Output

```
Lower bound: 1
Upper bound: 100
Random: 42
```

Subtract

This function returns the difference between two numbers.

Arguments

`Subtract(1,2)`

Ordinal	Type	Required	Description
1	Number	True	First value
2	Number	True	Second value

Example

```
%%[

var @diff, @num1, @num2

set @num1 = 42.51
set @num2 = 5

set @diff  = Subtract(@num1, @num2)

]%%
%%=v(@num1)=%% - %%=v(@num2)=%% = %%=v(@diff)=%%
```

Output

```
42.51 - 5 = 37.51
```

Microsoft Dynamics CRM Functions

Overview

The Marketing Cloud Connector for Microsoft Dynamics CRM enables the following:

- Sends to contacts, leads, accounts, marketing lists, and campaigns
- Sends to Dynamics CRM Custom Entities
- Email tracking and performance for individual sends and campaigns
- Marketing automation with Marketing Cloud emails and workflow templates
- Actions on tracking data from Dynamics CRM through Marketing Cloud Automations
- Smart Capture landing page interactions
- Custom charts and dashboards

Use of the following functions is limited to the MSCRM interactions in Smart Capture forms and other custom landing pages.

AddMSCRMListMember

This function adds a member to the specified Microsoft Dynamics CRM list. It does not return a value.

Arguments

`AddMSCRMListMember(1,2)`

Ordinal	Type	Required	Description
1	String	True	The GUID of the member to add
2	String	True	The GUID of the list receiving the member

Example

```
%%[

var @member
var @list

set @member = "43b4a7c9-7360-4753-955f-738bd89934b5"
set @list = "fdc5dfe4-e5e1-48af-87a1-4ac10433e895"

AddMscrmListMember(@member, @list)

]%%
```

CreateMSCRMRecord

This function creates a record in the specified Microsoft Dynamics CRM entity. It returns the GUID of the record created.

Arguments

`CreateMSCRMRecord(1,2,3,4,[5a,5b])`

Ordinal	Type	Required	Description
1	String	True	Name of the MSCRM entity
2	String	True	Number of attribute and value pairs in the preceding arguments
3	String	True	First attribute name for new record
4	String	True	First attribute value for new record
5a	String	False	Additional attribute name for new record (see note)
5b	String	False	Additional attribute value for new record (see note)

> **NOTE:** Additional pairs of attributes and values corresponding to the count in the second ordinal can be appended as arguments.

Example

```
%%[

var @firstName
var @lastName
var @emailAddress
var @contact_GUID

set @firstName = AttributeValue("firstName") /* value from
attribute or DE column in send context */
set @firstName = "Lily" /* or a literal value */

set @lastName = AttributeValue("lastName") /* value from
attribute or DE column in send context */
set @lastName = "Baker" /* or a literal value */

set @emailAddress = AttributeValue("emailaddr") /* value
from attribute or DE column in send context */
set @emailAddress = "lily@limedash.com" /* or a literal
value */

set @contact_GUID = CreateMSCRMRecord("Contact",
3, "firstname", @firstName, "lastname", @lastName,
"emailaddress", @emailAddress)

]%%
contact_GUID: %%=v(@contact_GUID)=%%
```

Output

```
contact_GUID: a16d424b-9f68-4297-ab4c-640c48431eaf
```

DescribeMSCRMEntities

This function returns the logical and display names for all available Microsoft Dynamics CRM entities.

Arguments

DescribeMSCRMEntities()

This function does not accept any arguments.

Example

```
%%[

var @i
var @entities
var @rowcount

set @entities = DescribeMSCRMEntities()
set @rowCount = rowcount(@entities)

for @i = 1 to @rowCount do

  var @entity
  var @entityName
  var @entityDisplayName

  set @entity = row(@entities,@i)
  set @Name = field(@entity, "Name")
  set @DisplayName = field(@entity, "DisplayName")

  output(concat("<br><br>Name: ", @Name))
  output(concat("<br>DisplayName: ", @DisplayName))

next @i

]%%
```

Output

```

Name: Account
DisplayName: account

Name: Campaign
DisplayName: campaign

Name: Case
DisplayName: case

Name: Contact
```

```
DisplayName: contact

Name: Lead
DisplayName: lead

Name: Opportunity
DisplayName: opportunity
...
```

DescribeMSCRMEntityAttributes

This function returns the logical name, display name and type of the specified Microsoft Dynamics CRM entity. If the attribute is Boolean, status, a picklist or a state, the function returns a comma-separated list of option and display values.

Argument

`DescribeMSCRMEntityAttributes(1)`

Ordinal	Type	Required	Description
1	String	True	The entity from which to retrieve attributes

Example

```
%%[

var @i
var @attributes
var @rowcount

set @attributes = DescribeMSCRMEntityAttributes("Lead")
set @rowCount = rowcount(@attributes)

for @i = 1 to @rowCount do

  var @attribute
  var @attributeName
  var @attributeDisplayName
  var @attributeType
  var @attributeRequired
  var @attributeOptions

  set @attribute = row(@attributes,@i)
```

```
  set @attributeName = field(@attribute, 'Name')
  set @attributeDisplayName = field(@attribute,
'DisplayName')

  set @Name = field(@attribute, "Name")
  set @DisplayName = field(@attribute, "DisplayName")
  set @Type = field(@attribute, "Type")
  set @Required = field(@attribute, "Required")
  set @Options = field(@attribute, "Options")

  output(concat("<br><br>Name: ", @Name))
  output(concat("<br>DisplayName: ", @DisplayName))
  output(concat("<br>Type: ", @Type))
  output(concat("<br>Required: ", @Required))
  output(concat("<br>Options: ", @Options))

next @i

]%%
```

Output

```
Name: address1_addressid
DisplayName: Address 1: ID
Type: Guid
Required: False
Options:

Name: address1_addresstypecode
DisplayName: Address 1: Address Type
Type: Int32
Required: False
Options: Default Value

Name: address1_city
DisplayName: City
Type: String
Required: False
Options:

...
```

RetrieveMSCRMRecords

This function retrieves rows from the specified Microsoft Dynamics CRM entity.

Arguments

`RetrieveMSCRMRecords(1,2,3,4,5)`

Ordinal	Type	Required	Description
1	String	True	The entity from which to retrieve attributes
2	String	True	Comma-separated list of fields to retrieve
3	String	True	Field name for filter value
4	String	True	Operator for filter value
5	String	True	Value for filter

Example

```
%%[

var @i
var @records
var @rowcount

set @records = RetrieveMSCRMrecords("Contact", "contactid,
firstname, lastname", "firstName", "=", "Doug")
set @rowCount = rowcount(@records)

for @i = 1 to @rowCount do

  var @record
  var @firstName
  var @lastName
  var @id

  set @record = row(@records,@i)
  set @firstName = field(@record, "firstName")
  set @lastName = field(@record, "lastName")
  set @id = field(@record, "id")

  output(concat("<br>firstName: ", @firstName))
  output(concat("<br>lastName: ", @lastName))
```

```
   output(concat("<br>id: ", @id))

next @i

]%%
```

Output

```
firstName: Doug
lastName: Smith
id: bcc3b7a0-3c61-4f1a-8cd3-1bada50af02d
```

RetrieveMSCRMRecordsFetchXML

This function accepts a Fetch XML string and returns the specified Microsoft Dynamics CRM entity attributes.

Argument

`RetrieveMSCRMRecordsFetchXML(1)`

Ordinal	Type	Required	Description
1	String	True	Fetch XML string

Example

```
%%[

var @i
var @XML
var @records
var @rowcount
var @subscriberKey

set @subscriberKey = AttributeValue("_subscriberkey") /*
value from attribute or DE column in send context */
set @subscriberKey = "a0e0ba6d-c4a2-4b06-b94d-1db3b5c6aec1"
/* or a literal value */

set @XML = ""
set @XML = concat(@XML, "<fetch mapping='logical' count='1'
version='1.0'>")
set @XML = concat(@XML, " <entity name='contact'>")
```

```
set @XML = concat(@XML, "    <attribute name='contactID'/>")
set @XML = concat(@XML, "    <attribute
name='emailAddressString'/>")
set @XML = concat(@XML, "    <attribute name='firstName'/>")
set @XML = concat(@XML, "    <attribute name='lastName'/>")
set @XML = concat(@XML, "    <filter>")
set @XML = concat(@XML, "      <condition
attribute='contactID' operator='eq' value='", @subscriberKey,
"'/>")
set @XML = concat(@XML, "    </filter>")
set @XML = concat(@XML, " </entity>")
set @XML = concat(@XML, "</fetch>")

set @records = RetrieveMSCRMRecordsFetchXML(@XML)
set @rowCount = rowcount(@records)

for @i = 1 to @rowCount do

  var @record
  var @contactID
  var @emailAddressString
  var @firstName
  var @lastName

  set @record = row(@records,@i)
  set @contactID = field(@record, "contactID")
  set @emailAddressString = field(@record,
"emailAddressString")
  set @firstName = field(@record, "firstName")
  set @lastName = field(@record, "lastName")

  output(concat("<br>contactID: ", @contactID))
  output(concat("<br>emailAddressString: ",
@emailAddressString))
  output(concat("<br>firstName: ", @firstName))
  output(concat("<br>lastName: ", @lastName))

next @i

]%%
```

Output

```
contactID: a0e0ba6d-c4a2-4b06-b94d-1db3b5c6aec1
emailaddresString: curt@limedash.com
firstName: Curt
lastName: Harris
```

SetStateMSCRMRecord

This function sets the state and status of the specified Microsoft Dynamics CRM entity. It does not return a value.

Arguments

`SetStateMSCRMRecord(1,2,3,4)`

Ordinal	Type	Required	Description
1	String	True	GUID of the record for which the state and status will be set
2	String	True	Name of the entity for record
3	String	True	State value to use. Valid values include **`Active`** and **`Inactive`**.
4	String	True	Status value to use. Valid values include `0`, `1` and `-1`. The value of `-1` resets to the default value.

Example

```
%%[

var @GUID
var @entity
var @status
var @state

set @GUID = "84dfdf51-4741-4e15-92b9-67cc595c22b7"
set @entity = "Contact"
set @status = "Invactive"
set @state = "0"

SetStateMscrmRecord(@GUID, @entity, @status, @state)

]%%
```

UpdateMSCRMRecords

This function updates one of more records in the specified Microsoft Dynamics CRM entity. It returns the number of records updated.

Arguments

`UpdateMSCRMRecords(1,2,3,4)`

Ordinal	Type	Required	Description
1	String	True	Name of the entity for records
2	String	True	Comma-separated list of record GUIDs to update
3	String	True	Name of attribute to update
4	String	True	Value of attribute to update

> **NOTE:** Additional pairs of columns and values can be appended as arguments.

Example

```
%%[
var @updateCount
var @entity
var @GUIDs
var @attribute
var @attributeValue

set @entity = "Contact"
set @GUIDs = "97459725-9592-4f6d-a92b-5aee4ddd5f2d,920ee53d-
a95c-4c89-b94f-6fcb7c865720"
set @attribute = "creditonhold"
set @attributeValue = "1"

set @updateCount = UpdateMSCRMRecords(@entity, @GUIDs,
@attribute, @attributeValue)

]%%
updateCount: %%=v(@updateCount)=%%
```

Output

```
updateCount: 2
```

UpsertMSCRMRecord

This function retrieves a record from Microsoft Dynamics CRM, using the name and value pairs to filter the results. The results are then sorted using the sort field and order specified. Records are updated with the name and value pairs from the eighth and ninth arguments. If the function does not return a record, it creates one with all provided name and value pairs. It returns the GUID of the updated or created record.

Arguments

`UpsertMSCRMRecord(1,2,3,4,5,6,7,8,9)`

Ordinal	Type	Required	Description
1	String	True	Entity to upsert
2	String	True	Field used to sort the rows returned
3	String	True	Order of rows returned. Valid values include **ASC** and **DESC**.
4	String	True	Number of attribute and value pairs in the preceding fields used to filter
5	String	True	Name of attribute to filter
6	String	True	Value of attribute to filter
7	String	True	Number of attribute and value pairs in the preceding fields used to update
8	String	True	Name of attribute to update
9	String	True	Value of attribute to update

Example

```
%%[

var @entity
var @sortAttribute
var @filterAttribute
var @filterValue
var @updateAttribute
var @updateValue
var @updated

set @entity = "Contact"
set @sortAttribute = "CreatedOn"
set @filterAttribute = "jobTitle"
```

```
set @filterValue = "Manager"
set @updateAttribute = "creditLimit"
set @updateValue = "5000.00"

set @updated  = UpsertMSCRMRecord(@entity, @sortAttribute,
"DESC", 1, @filterAttribute, @filterValue, 1,
@updateAttribute, @updateValue)

]%%
updated: %%=v(@updated)=%%
```

Output

```
updated: 3ee54c53-8b5c-4ed3-ba62-4c869b5d9fcb
```

MobileConnect Functions

Overview
In addition to the set of personalization strings available for MobileConnect, Marketing Cloud also includes AMPscript functions for using SMS conversations in MobileConnect.

SMS conversations enable message chains to be created. In a conversation, MobileConnect prefixes a Next Keyword to the Contact's response. In turn, a keyword prefix is not required when a Contact sends a Mobile Originated (MO) message and their response can trigger the sending of another SMS message to the Contact.

> **NOTE:** By default, a conversation remains open for 60 minutes after you send an outbound message or receive a message from a Contact. However this can be changed by opening a support case with your Marketing Cloud Support Representative.

CreateSmsConversation
While MobileConnect includes the ability to create conversations through assigning Next Keywords to message templates, this function provides the ability to conditionally create a conversation and can dynamically define the Next Keyword to use, instead of a defined value in the message template.

The function will return **`true`** if an conversation was successfully created, or **`false`** if an exception occurred. The function can only be used in MobileConnect messages and will return **`false`** if used in a different application context, for example in Email Studio or CloudPages.

> **NOTE:** This function cannot be used in conversation-based templates such as Double Opt-In, Vote/Survey or Info Capture messages.

Arguments

`CreateSmsConversation(1,2,3,4)`

Ordinal	Type	Required	Description
1	Number	True	Short code or long code used by MobileConnect
2	Number	True	Contact's mobile number with country code prefix
3	String	True	Keyword to use for Next Keyword function
4	String	True	Application used for the conversation use **MOBILECONNECT**

Example 1

An outbound message is sent to a Contact. A Lookup function returns an applicable offer for the Contact from a Data Extension based on their mobile number. If an 'Offer' field is equal to **`competition`** then a conversation will be created for the Contact with **`COMPETITION`** as the Next Keyword.

```
%%[

var @offer
set @offer = Lookup("SMS Offers", "Offer", "Mobile Number",
MOBILE_NUMBER)

if @offer == "competition" then

  CreateSMSConversation(61401123456, MOBILE_NUMBER,
"COMPETITION", "MOBILECONNECT")

]%%
You have been selected to enter a draw for a $100 voucher.
Reply with your email address to register.
%%[ else ]%%
10% discount at all NTO stores, 5 days only!
%%[ endif ]%%
```

A text response message is also created in MobileConnect with the **COMPETITION** keyword. The message template contains the following code:

```
%%[

InsertData("Competition Responses", "Mobile Number",
MOBILE_NUMBER, "Email Address", [MSG(0).NOUNS])

]%%
Thank you for providing your email address. You have been
registered for the competition.
```

Output

If the Lookup function used by the **@offer** variable returns **competition**, then the Contact will receive the following SMS message:

```
You have been selected to enter a draw for a $100 voucher.
Reply with your email address to register.
```

If the Contact replies to the SMS message with **sam@limedash.com**, their mobile number and email address (from the response message) will be inserted into a 'Competition Responses' Data Extension and they will receive the following response:

```
Thank you for providing your email address. You have been
registered for the competition.
```

Example 2

As an alternative to the first example, the Next Keyword parameter is defined as an argument, to conditionally set the next message template to use in the conversation.

```
%%[

var @offer, @nextKeyword
set @offer = Lookup("SMS Offers", "Offer", "Mobile Number",
MOBILE_NUMBER)

if @offer == "competition" then

  set @nextKeyword = "COMPETITION"

```

```
]%%
You have been selected to enter a draw for a $100 voucher.
Reply with your email address to register.
%%[ else set @nextKeyword = "DISCOUNT" ]%%
You qualify for a 10% discount. Reply with your email
address to register.
%%[
endif
 CreateSMSConversation(61401123456, MOBILE _NUMBER,
@nextKeyword, "MOBILECONNECT")
]%%
```

Output

If the Lookup function used by the **@offer** variable returns **competition**, then a conversation will be created and the Contact will receive the following SMS message:

```
You have been selected to enter a draw for a $100 voucher.
Reply with your email address to register.
```

If the **@offer** variable does not return **competition**, a conversation will be created and the Contact will receive the following SMS message:

```
You qualify for a 10% discount. Reply with your email
address to register.
```

When the Contact replies to the message, their response will be interpreted by the message template with the matching keyword that was defined as the **@ nextKeyword** variable.

EndSmsConversation

This function will end an active conversation-based on a given short or long code and a Contact's mobile number. Once a conversation ends, it will allow the Contact to send other MO messages related to the short or long code, otherwise the Contact will remain in the conversation until it ends, either by reaching a message template without a Next Keyword, or being ejected from the conversation by this function.

The function will return **true** if the conversation successfully ends, or **false** if an exception occurs. The function can only be used in MobileConnect messages and will return **false** if used in a different application context, for example in Email Studio or CloudPages.

> **NOTE:** This function cannot be used in conversation-based templates such as Double Opt-In, Vote/Survey or Info Capture messages.

Arguments

`EndSmsConversation(1,2)`

Ordinal	Type	Required	Description
1	Number	True	Short code or long code used by MobileConnect
2	Number	True	Contact's mobile number with country code prefix

Example

A conversation is created from a series of SMS messages with Next Keywords, as per the table below.

Message Name	Message Type	Keyword	Next Keyword
Outbound Offer	Outbound		`RESPONSE1`
Response 1	Text Response	`RESPONSE1`	`RESPONSE2`
Response 2	Text Response	`RESPONSE2`	`RESPONSE3`
Response 3	Text Response	`RESPONSE3`	

A Contact then responds `No` to the 'Outbound Offer' message and receives the 'Response 1' message.

This message contains the following code:

```
%%[

var @response
set @response = [MSG(0).NOUNS]

if IndexOf(@response,"no") > 0 then

  EndSMSConversation(61401123456, MOBILE_NUMBER)

]%%
Thank you for participating in this survey.
%%[ else ]%%
```

```
Please reply with your first name.
%%[ endif ]%%
```

Output

The reply is interpreted by the 'Response 1' message and as the response contains the word 'no' (which is evaluated as case-insensitive by the IndexOf function), the Contact receives the message below and they are ejected from the conversation.

```
Thank you for participating in this survey.
```

SetSmsConversationNextKeyword

This function will set the keyword for the next message in a conversation. It does not create a new conversation. Rather, it sets the next conversation path similar to CreateSmsConversation, but for an existing conversation. The Next Keyword is set once the Contact replies to the message.

The function will return **`true`** if the next keyword is successfully set, or **`false`** if an exception occurs. The function can only be used in MobileConnect messages and will return **`false`** if used in a different application context, for example in Email Studio or CloudPages.

> **NOTE:** This function cannot be used in conversation-based templates such as Double Opt-In, Vote/Survey or Info Capture messages.

Arguments

`SetSmsConversationNextKeyword(1,2,3)`

Ordinal	Type	Required	Description
1	Number	True	Short code or long code used by MobileConnect
2	Number	True	Contact's mobile number with country code prefix
3	String	True	Keyword to use for Next Keyword function

Example

A message template includes the following code that is used in a Text Response message within an existing conversation:

```
%%[

var @discountAmount, @nextKeyword
set @discountAmount = Lookup("SMS Offers", "Percent
Discount", "Mobile Number", MOBILE_NUMBER)
set @nextKeyword = Concat(@offer,"PERCENT")

SetSmsConversationNextKeyword(61401123456, MOBILE_NUMBER,
@nextKeyword)

]%%
Reply with your email address to receive
%%=v(@discountAmount)=%%% percent off your next purchase.
```

The **`@discountAmount`** variable returns a number based on a value in the Data Extension. A matching keyword has been created for each discount; for example **`10PERCENT`**, **`20PERCENT`** and **`50PERCENT`**. These keywords are assigned to other Text Response messages.

Output

For a **`@discountAmount`** value of **`20`**, a Contact will receive the message below and the Next Keyword will be set as **`20PERCENT`** when they reply to the message.

```
Reply with your email address to receive 20% off your next
purchase.
```

Sales & Service Cloud Functions

Overview

Marketing Cloud includes several AMPscript functions that enable interaction with Sales and Service Cloud object records and emails. Applications include:

- Creating or updating a record in a standard or custom Salesforce object
- Dynamically retrieving and personalizing fields from a Salesforce object in a Triggered Send email
- Creating a custom preference center to retrieve and update form fields from Sales Cloud objects
- Reviewing the status of a Salesforce Send email job (an email that is sent from Sales or Service Cloud using Marketing Cloud Connect)
- Converting the 15-digit Salesforce record identifier of a Contact to an 18-digit case-safe identifier when creating Subscriber records.

> **NOTE:** Marketing Cloud Connect needs to be configured to use these AMPscript functions.

CreateSalesforceObject

This function creates a new record in a Salesforce object. The Salesforce 18-digit object identifier is returned by the function.

> **NOTE:** This function can only be used to create records in standard or custom Salesforce objects, not other objects such as big objects or external objects.

Arguments

`CreateSalesforceObject(1,2,3,4,[5a,5b...])`

Ordinal	Type	Required	Description
1	String	True	API name of the Salesforce object
2	Integer	True	Number of fields inserted when creating the record
3	String	True	API field name
4	String, integer or Boolean	True	Value to insert
5a	String	False	Additional API field name (see note)
5b	String, integer or Boolean	False	Additional value to insert (see note)

NOTE: Additional API field name and value pairs can be appended as arguments. The quantity of pairs should match parameter 2.

Example

The following code is used on a landing page for a Lead Capture form. When the user completes the form, the **`CreateSalesforceObject`** function creates a new Lead record in Sales Cloud from the form field values and displays the 18-digit Salesforce identifier of the new record on the page.

```
%%[

if RequestParameter("submitted") == true then

  var @createLead
  set @createLead = CreateSalesforceObject(
        "Lead", 4,
        "FirstName", RequestParameter("firstname"),
        "LastName", RequestParameter("lastname"),
        "Company", RequestParameter("company"),
        "Email", RequestParameter("email")
      )

endif
```

```
]%%
<!DOCTYPE html>
<html>
   <body>
      %%[ if not empty(@createLead) then ]%%
         <p>%%=v(@createLead)=%% record created in Lead
Object</p>
      %%[ endif ]%%
      <h2>Register</h2>
      <form action="%%=RequestParameter('PAGEURL')=%%"
method="post">
         <label>First name</label>
         <input type="text" name="firstname">
         <label>Last name</label>
         <input type="text" name="lastname">
         <label>Company</label>
         <input type="text" name="company">
         <label>Email</label>
         <input type="text" name="email">
         <input name="submitted" type="hidden" value="true"
/>
         <input type="submit" value="Submit">
      </form>
   </body>
</html>
```

Output

The following element will be displayed on the page, before the form. **00Q6F00001APnymUAD** is the Salesforce identifier of the new record.

```
<p>00Q6F00001APnymUAD record created in Lead Object</p>
```

LongSFID

Sales and Service Cloud objects use a case-sensitive 15-digit character as a record identifier. Marketing Cloud Subscriber and Contact records require a case-insensitive identifier. This function converts 15-digit identifiers into 18-digit case-insensitive identifiers.

> **NOTE:** Marketing Cloud will not allow the import of a 15-digit Salesforce identifier into a Data Extension. The import will return a **`CaseSensitiveSalesforceID`** validation error. Fifteen-digit Salesforce identifiers must be converted into 18-digits before they can be stored in a Data Extension field.

Argument

`LongSFID(1)`

Ordinal	Type	Required	Description
1	String	True	15-character Salesforce record identifier

Example

The following code converts a Salesforce 15-digit identifier from a landing page URL query string into an 18-digit identifier and it retrieves the corresponding **`First Name`** field from a Data Extension with a matching identifier.

```
%%[

var @shortSFID, @longSFID, @firstName

set @shortSFID = QueryParameter("id")
set @longSFID = LongSFID(@shortSFID)
set @firstName = Lookup("Prospects", "First Name", "Id",
@longSFID)

]%%
<p>Hello %%=v(@firstName)=%%</p>
```

Output

For an **`id`** value of **`00Q6F00001APnym`**, the LongSFID function will return **`00Q6F00001APnymUAD`** and display the matching **`First Name`** value in the Data Extension.

RetrieveSalesforceJobSources

This function returns details of a Marketing Cloud send job to a Salesforce audience. It returns a row set containing the following fields:

Field	Description
`SourceID`	ID of the data source in Sales Cloud
`SourceType`	Type of source in Sales Cloud (for example, Report or Campaign)
`IsInclusionSource`	Boolean value indicating audience is an inclusion source

> **NOTE:** The function does not return the status of the job and therefore should not be used to validate that an email send has been completed.

Argument

`RetrieveSalesforceJobSources(1)`

Ordinal	Type	Required	Description
1	Number	True	JobID of the Salesforce send

Example

```
%%[

var @jobId, @rows, @row, @rowCount

set @jobId = 40029164
set @rows = RetrieveSalesforceJobSources(@jobid)
set @rowCount = rowcount(@rows)

if @rowCount > 0 then

  for @i = 1 to @rowCount do

      var @SourceID
      var @SourceType
      var @IsInclusionSource

      set @row = row(@rows, @i)
      set @SourceID = field(@row, "SourceID")
```

```
      set @SourceType = field(@row, "SourceType")
      set @IsInclusionSource = field(@row,
"IsInclusionSource")

      output(concat("SourceID: ", @SourceID))
      output(concat("<br>SourceType: ", @SourceType))
      output(concat("<br>IsInclusionSource: ",
@IsInclusionSource))

  next @i

else

  output(concat("No rows for ", @jobId, " found"))

endif

]%%
```

Output

```
SourceID: 00O50000003JaFnEAK
SourceType: Report
IsInclusionSource: True
```

RetrieveSalesforceObjects

This function retrieves fields from a record in a Sales or Service Cloud standard or custom object. The function returns a row set of fields.

> **NOTE:** This function should only be used in applications that do not require a high volume of requests or return a large number of records; for example, an email send to a small audience, a Triggered Send, or the retrieval of a single record on a landing page.
>
> The function may take several seconds to execute, impacting email send performance and may result in a timeout if the request volume is high for example; using a process loop to execute the function multiple times or returning a large number of rows. Unlike other AMPscript functions that return a row set — for example, LookupRows which limits the number of rows to 2000 — there is not the same type of limitation on the number of rows returned by this function.

Arguments

`RetrieveSalesforceObjects(1,2,3,4,5,[6a,6b,6c...])`

Ordinal	Type	Required	Description
1	String	True	API name of the Salesforce object
2	String	True	Comma-separated array of API field names to retrieve
3	String	True	API field name to match record
4	String	True	Comparison operator for matching records. Valid operators include: ▪ = equal to ▪ < less than ▪ > greater than ▪ != not equal to ▪ <= less than or equal to ▪ >= greater than or equal to
5	String	True	Value to match record using comparison operator in ordinal 4
6a	String	False	Additional API field name to match record (see note)
6b	String	False	Additional comparison operator to match record (see note)
6c	String	False	Additional value to match record (see note)

> **NOTE:** Additional API field name, comparison operator and value sets can be appended as arguments. However the function joins these additional sets using **`and`** clauses.

Example 1

The following example retrieves a record from the Sales Cloud Contact object and displays values on a page for a matching record **`Id`**.

```
%%[

var @subscriberRows

set @subscriberRows = RetrieveSalesforceObjects(
   "Contact",
   "FirstName,LastName,Email",
```

```
    "Id", "=", _subscriberKey )

if RowCount(@subscriberRows) == 1 then /* there should only
be one row */
  var @subscriberRow, @firstName, @lastName, @email
  set @subscriberRow = Row(@subscriberRows, 1)
  set @firstName = Field(@subscriberRow, "FirstName")
  set @lastName = Field(@subscriberRow, "LastName")
  set @email = Field(@subscriberRow, "Email")
endif

]%%
<!DOCTYPE html>
<html>
   <body>
      <h2>Your Details</h2>

      %%[ if RowCount(@subscriberRows) == 1 then ]%%
      <ul>
         <li><strong>First Name:</strong>
%%=v(@firsName)=%%</li>
         <li><strong>Last Name:</strong> %%=v(@lastName)=%%
</li>
         <li><strong>Email:</strong> %%=v(@email)=%%</li>
      </ul>
      %%[ else ]%%
      <p>You are not registered.</p>
      %%[ endif ]%%
   </body>
</html>
```

Output

If a matching Contact record is found, the above code will result in the following output:

```
<!DOCTYPE html>
<html>
   <body>
      <h2>Your Details</h2>
      <ul>
         <li><strong>First Name:</strong> Sam</li>
         <li><strong>Last Name:</strong> Jones</li>
```

```
        <li><strong>Email:</strong> sam@company.com</li>
      </ul>
   </body>
</html>
```

Example 2

The following example retrieves records from the Sales Cloud Contact object that match multiple conditions and displays them in a process loop.

```
<h2>Members</h2>
<ul>
%%[
var @subscriberRows, @countRows

set @subscriberRows = RetrieveSalesforceObjects(
"Contact",
"Member_Number__c",
"Member_Segment__c", ">", 10,
"Member_Segment__c", "<", 30 )

set @countRows = RowCount(@subscriberRows)

if @countRows > 0 then

  for @counter = 1 to @countRows do
    var @subscriberRow, @memberNumber
    set @subscriberRow = Row(@subscriberRows, @counter)
    set @memberNumber = Field(@subscriberRow,
"Member_Number__c")
]%%

    <li><strong>%%=v(@counter)=%%</strong> Member Number:
%%=v(@memberNumber)=%%</li>

%%[ next @counter ]%%

%%[ else ]%%

    <li>No records found</li>

%%[ endif ]%%
</ul>
```

Output

If a matching Contact record is found, the code will result in the following output:

```
<h2>Members</h2>
<ul>
   <li><strong>1</strong> Member Number: 64326</li>
   <li><strong>2</strong> Member Number: 45742</li>
   <li><strong>3</strong> Member Number: 53246</li>
   <li><strong>4</strong> Member Number: 86753</li>
   <li><strong>5</strong> Member Number: 34672</li>
   <li><strong>6</strong> Member Number: 96731</li>
   <li><strong>7</strong> Member Number: 16374</li>
</ul>
```

UpdateSingleSalesforceObject

This function updates a record in a Sales or Service Cloud standard or custom object. The function returns `1` if the record is updated successfully or `0`if it fails.

> **NOTE:** Certain Salesforce objects enforce record-locking when a record is modified, to ensure the referential integrity of data. This applies to records that have a relationship to lookup records in a different object. If the function is used to asynchronously update multiple records (for example, the function is included in an email) and the object has lock contention, the records may fail to update.

Arguments

`UpdateSingleSalesforceObject(1,2,3,4,[5a,5b]...)`

Ordinal	Type	Required	Description
1	String	True	API name of the Salesforce object
2	String	True	Record identifier to update
3	String	True	API field name to update
4	String	True	Value to update
5a	String	False	Additional API field name to update (see note)
5b	String	False	Additional value to update (see note)

> **NOTE:** Additional API field name and value pairs can be appended as arguments.

Example

The following example pre-populates a landing page form with a Contact record using the **RetrieveSalesforceObjects** function.

When the form is submitted, the UpdateSingleSalesforceObject function updates the Contact record with values from the submitted form.

```
var @Id, @firstName, @lastName, @email, @subscriberRows,
@subscriberRow
set @Id = _subscriberKey

if RequestParameter("submitted") != true then

  set @subscriberRows = RetrieveSalesforceObjects(
     "Contact",
     "FirstName,LastName,Email",
     "Id", "=", @Id )

  set @subscriberRow = Row(@subscriberRows, 1)
  set @firstName = Field(@subscriberRow, "FirstName")
  set @lastName = Field(@subscriberRow, "LastName")
  set @email = Field(@subscriberRow, "Email")

else

  var @updateRecord
  set @firstname = RequestParameter("firstname")
  set @lastName = RequestParameter("lastname")
  set @email = RequestParameter("email")
  set @updateRecord = UpdateSingleSalesforceObject(
      "Contact",@Id,
      "FirstName", @firstname,
      "LastName", @lastName,
      "Email", @email
     )

endif
]%%

<!DOCTYPE html>
<html>
   <body>
```

```
        %%[ if @updateRecord == 1 then ]%%
           <p>Record Updated</p>
        %%[ elseif @updateRecord == 0 then ]%%
          <p>Update Failed</p>
        %%[ endif ]%%
        <h2>Update Your Details</h2>
        <form action="%%=RequestParameter('PAGEURL')=%%"
method="post">
           <label>First name</label>
           <input type="text" name="firstname"
value="%%=v(@firstName)=%%">
           <label>Last name</label>
           <input type="text" name="lastname"
value="%%=v(@lastName)=%%">
           <label>Email</label>
           <input type="text" name="email"
value="%%=v(@email)=%%">
           <input name="submitted" type="hidden" value="true"
/>
           <input type="submit" value="Submit">
        </form>
     </body>
</html>
```

Output

If the record is updated successfully, a confirmation message will be displayed and the form fields will be populated with the submitted form values.

```
<!DOCTYPE html>
<html>
   <body>
      <p>Record Updated</p>
      <h2>Update Your Details</h2>
      <form action="https://pub.exacttarget.com/
lcuh4w3abcd?qs=1550dccf35ce..." method="post">
         <label>First name</label>
         <input type="text" name="firstname" value="Suzy">
         <label>Last name</label>
         <input type="text" name="lastname" value="Jackson">
         <label>Email</label>
         <input type="text" name="email"
value="suzy@limedash.com">
```

```
            <input name="submitted" type="hidden" value="true"
/>
            <input type="submit" value="Submit">
        </form>
    </body>
</html>
```

Site-Based Functions

Overview

AMPscript includes several functions for working with website or 'site-based' content in Marketing Cloud. See the table below for a few different options for creating site-based content in Marketing Cloud:

Application	Feature	Description
Email Studio	Landing Pages (Classic Content)	Stand-alone, individual web pages that can be published with static or personalized content
Email Studio	Microsites (Classic Content)	A collection of one or more landing pages
CloudPages	Landing Pages	Stand-alone, individual pages that can be published with static or personalized content with editor interface options (Classic Editor or Content Builder)
CloudPages	Code Resource	JavaScript, CSS, JSON or other supporting web page assets
CloudPages	Microsites	A collection of one or more landing pages with a graphical site map interface

Applications for AMPscript and site-based content include:

- personalized landing pages for marketing campaigns, promotions or offers
- custom preference centers
- web pages and forms that integrate with data from Sales and Service Cloud Objects

> **TIP:** AMPscript can be used in CloudPages Code Resources; for example, to conditionally change CSS styles based on the Business Unit MID, or to modify styles based on URL parameters.

AuthenticatedEmployeeID

This function returns the numeric identifier of the authenticated Marketing Cloud account user who is accessing the page. This is useful when creating customized home pages for child Business Units (a feature available in earlier Enterprise 2.0 accounts).

> **NOTE:** This function will only return the correct value when using Classic Content Microsites and where Sender Authenticated Redirection is enabled. The function should not be used with CloudPages.

Arguments

`AuthenticatedEmployeeID()`

This function does not accept any arguments.

Example

The following example uses the Lookup function on a customized home page to conditionally display content based on the Marketing Cloud account user identifier of the user accessing the page (with an active Marketing Cloud session).

```
%%[

var @employeeId, @role

set @employeeId = AuthenticatedEmployeeID()

set @role = Lookup("Employees", "Role", "ID", @employeeId)

if @role == "Manager" then

]%%
<h2>Welcome to the Management Marketing Cloud Portal</h2>
<!-- management content here -->
%%[ else ]%%
```

```
<h2>Welcome to the Saff Marketing Cloud Portal</h2>
<!-- staff content here -->
%%[ endif ]%%
```

Output

If the Lookup function returns **`Manager`** for the **`@employeeId`** variable, the following content will be displayed:

```
<h2>Welcome to the Management Marketing Cloud Portal</h2>
<!-- management content here -->
```

AuthenticatedEmployeeNotificationAddress

This function returns the notification email address of the authenticated Marketing Cloud account user who is accessing the page. This is useful when creating customized home pages for child Business Units (a feature available in earlier Enterprise 2.0 accounts).

> **NOTE:** This function will only return the correct value when using Classic Content Microsites and where Sender Authenticated Redirection is enabled. The function should not be used with CloudPages.

Arguments

`AuthenticatedEmployeeNotificationAddress()`

This function does not accept any arguments.

Example

The following example displays the notification email address of the Marketing Cloud user accessing the page (with an active Marketing Cloud session) on a customized home page.

```
<p>Your notification email address is
%%=AuthenticatedEmployeeNotificationAddress()=%%</p>.
<p>You can update your email address on the Cloud
Preferences page.</p>
```

Output

The function returns the email address associated with the Marketing Cloud user account.

```
<p>Your notification email address is sam@limedash.com</p>.
<p>You can update your email address on the Cloud
Preferences page.</p>
```

AuthenticatedEmployeeUserName

This function returns the username of the authenticated Marketing Cloud account user who is accessing the page. This is useful when creating customized home pages for child Business Units (a feature available in earlier Enterprise 2.0 accounts).

> **NOTE:** This function will only return the correct value when using Classic Content Microsites and where Sender Authenticated Redirection is enabled. The function should not be used with CloudPages.

Arguments

`AuthenticatedEmployeeUserName()`

This function does not accept any arguments.

Example

The following example displays the username of the Marketing Cloud user accessing the page (with an active Marketing Cloud session) on a customized home page.

```
<p>Hello %%=AuthenticatedEmployeeUserName()=%%,</p>
```

Output

The function returns the username associated with the Marketing Cloud user account.

```
<p>Hello Sam,</p>
```

AuthenticatedEnterpriseID

This function returns the enterprise identifier of Marketing Cloud account (the MID of the Parent Business Unit), based on the context of the authenticated user. This is useful when creating customized home pages for child Business Units (a feature available in earlier Enterprise 2.0 accounts).

> **NOTE:** This function will only return the correct value when using Classic Content Microsites and where Sender Authenticated Redirection is enabled. The function should not be used with CloudPages.

Arguments

`AuthenticatedEnterpriseID()`

This function does not accept any arguments.

Example

The following example displays the enterprise identifier of the Marketing Cloud account on a customized home page.

```
<p>The Parent MID is %%=AuthenticatedEnterpriseID()=%%.</p>
```

Output

The function returns the Parent MID of the Marketing Cloud user account.

```
<p>The Parent MID is 10987654.</p>
```

AuthenticatedMemberID

This function returns the MID of the Marketing Cloud account, based on the context of the authenticated user's session. This is useful when creating customized home pages for child Business Units (a feature available in earlier Enterprise 2.0 accounts).

> **NOTE:** This function will only return the correct value when using Classic Content Microsites and where Sender Authenticated Redirection is enabled. The function should not be used with CloudPages.

> **TIP:** You can use the **`memberid`** personalization string to display the related Business Unit MID of a published landing page or code resource.

Arguments

`AuthenticatedMemberID()`

This function does not accept any arguments.

Example

The following example displays the Business Unit MID on a customized home page, based on the context of the authenticated user.

```
<p>This Business Unit MID is %%=AuthenticatedMemberID()=%%.</
p>
```

Output

The function returns the Business Unit MID based on the context of the authenticated user's Marketing Cloud session.

```
<p>This Business Unit MID is 10987456.</p>
```

AuthenticatedMemberName

This function returns the name of the Marketing Cloud user's account, based on the context of their authenticated session. This is useful when creating customized home pages for child Business Units (a feature available in earlier Enterprise 2.0 accounts).

> **NOTE:** This function will only return the correct value when using Classic Content Microsites and where Sender Authenticated Redirection is enabled. The function should not be used with CloudPages.

Arguments

`AuthenticatedMemberName()`

This function does not accept any arguments.

Example

The following example displays the name of the Marketing Cloud user's account on a customized home page, based on the context of the authenticated user.

```
<p>Hello %%=AuthenticatedMemberName()=%%,</p>
```

Output

The function returns the name associated with the Marketing Cloud user account.

```
<p>Hello Sam,</p>
```

CloudPagesURL

This function provides a convenient method of linking to landing pages (created in CloudPages) from email messages.

When an email is sent that includes a link to a landing page with this function, a URL link is generated to the landing page and is appended with an encrypted query string.

This encrypted query string provides a reference to the email, which means that system personalization strings can be used on a landing page to retrieve values related to the sent email. And as the string is encrypted, no Subscriber information is passed in clear text.

> **TIP:** When creating hyperlinks with template-based emails in Content Builder, the Link Properties dialog enables you to select a landing page from CloudPages Collection or CloudPages Microsite. This feature will automatically build the CloudPagesURL function with the associated page identifier included as an argument.

Arguments

`CloudPagesURL(1,2,3,[4a,4b]...)`

Ordinal	Type	Required	Description
1	Number	True	Page identifier of the CloudPage landing page, available from Page Properties in the CloudPages Collection
2	String	False	Parameter name included in encrypted query string
3	String or number	False	Parameter value included in encrypted query string
4a	String	False	Additional parameter name (see note)
4b	String or number	False	Additional parameter value (see note)

> **NOTE:** Additional parameter name and value pairs can be appended as arguments.

Example 1

An email is sent that includes the following link to a landing page using the CloudPagesURL function:

```
<a href="%%=CloudPagesURL(123)=%%">click here to visit your
landing page</a>
```

The following HTML is used on the landing page. The **`_subscriberKey`** personalization string is used to retrieve a corresponding value from a Data Extension.

```
%%[

var @firstName
set @firstName = Lookup("Members", "First Name", "Subscriber
Key", _subscriberKey)

]%%

<!DOCTYPE html>
<html>
   <body>
      <h2>Hello %%=v(@firstName)=%%,</h2>
      <p>Welcome to your personalized landing page.</p>
   </body>
</html>
```

Output

The CloudPagesURL function returns the page URL of the landing page appended with an encrypted query string with Subscriber data. For example:
`https://pub.exacttarget.com/adytgmabc?qs=bfd0bc86b7b0dc08be758fc47e321b5e`

The page is personalized with a Data Extension field value, which is based on the Subscriber Key of the email sent to the Subscriber.

```
<!DOCTYPE html>
<html>
   <body>
      <h2>Hello Andrew,</h2>
      <p>Welcome to your personalized landing page.</p>
   </body>
</html>
```

Example 2

This example is a variation of the first example that includes additional URL parameters in the function, using **`First Name`** and **`Status`** fields from the Sendable Data Extension that is used to send the email. The email includes the following link to a landing page using the CloudPagesURL function.

```
<a href="%%=CloudPagesURL(123,'fname',[First Name],'status',
Status)=%%">click here to visit your landing page</a>
<!DOCTYPE html>
<html>
   <body>
      <h2>Hello %%=RequestParameter('fname')=%%,</h2>
      <p>You are a valued %%=RequestParameter('status')=%%
member.</p>
   </body>
</html>
```

Output

The CloudPagesURL function returns the page URL of the landing page appended with an encrypted query string of Subscriber data and URL parameters. For example: **`https://pub.exacttarget.com/adytgmabc?qs=fbd6b52adcf04df...`**

The page is personalized with values from the Sendable Data Extension, retrieved from the decrypted query string parameter.

```
<!DOCTYPE html>
<html>
   <body>
      <h2>Hello Andrew,</h2>
      <p>You are a valued Gold member.</p>
   </body>
</html>
```

IsNullDefault

This function is used to return a default value for empty Smart Capture form field values.

When a Smart Capture form is created with Classic Content in Email Studio, AMPscript is automatically generated by the feature to populate the form data into a List or Data Extension. This generated AMPscript can be modified from the Processing tab in the Edit Content dialog.

This function is not used by other Smart Capture form creation methods; for example, Classic Editor or Content Builder in CloudPages.

> **NOTE:** This function is only available with Smart Capture forms. It will not return a null occurrence value when used in a different context.

Arguments

`IsNullDefault(1,2)`

Ordinal	Type	Required	Description
1	String	True	Value to return for non-null occurrences
2	String	True	Value to return for null occurrences

Example

The following code is automatically generated by the Smart Capture form to populate records in a Data Extension.

```
%%[

set @de _col = CreateObject("APIProperty")
SetObjectProperty(@de _col, "Name", "level")
SetObjectProperty(@de _col, "Value",
IsNullDefault(RequestParameter("level"), "standard"))
AddObjectArrayItem(@de, "Properties", @de _col)

]%%
```

Output

If the **`level`** form field value is null or empty when the form is submitted, the field value will be added to the target Data Extension with a value of **`standard`**.

LiveContentMicrositeURL

This function enables integration with Live Content in Marketing Cloud. Live Content includes the following features:

- **Live Image**: compares the effectiveness of two images within email content
- **Live Offers**: dynamically renders coupon barcodes or text as an image on a landing page

> **NOTE:** Only Live Offers (coupons) is currently supported by this function.

While Live Offers can dynamically include a coupon image in an email, this function returns a link to view the coupon on a microsite page. This is useful when including Live Offers in SMS messages or text-only emails.

Arguments

`LiveContentMicrositeURL(1,2)`

Ordinal	Type	Required	Description
1	String	True	Content type; currently only **`coupon`** is supported as an argument value
2	String	True	External Key of the Live Content

Example

The following code is used in an SMS to generate a link for a Live Offers coupon that uses an External Key of **`50percent`**.

```
Claim your 50% off coupon at:
%%=LiveContentMicrositeURL('coupon', '50percent')=%%
```

Output

The function returns the URL of the microsite page to display the coupon.

```
Claim your 50% off coupon at: https://pub.exacttarget.com/
ux3uhhrjabc
```

MicrositeURL

This function is similar to CloudPagesURL, but it's specifically for linking to microsite pages created in Classic Content.

When an email is sent that includes a link to a microsite page with this function, a URL link is generated to the page and is appended with an encrypted query string.

This encrypted query string provides a reference to the email, which means that system personalization strings can be used on the page to retrieve values related to the sent email. And as the string is encrypted, no Subscriber information is passed in clear text.

> **NOTE:** This function only works with microsite pages created in Classic Content. It cannot be used with microsite pages created in CloudPages.

Arguments

`MicrositeURL(1,2,3,[4a,4b]...)`

Ordinal	Type	Required	Description
1	Number	True	Page ID of the microsite page, available from the Properties page
2	String	False	Parameter name included in encrypted query string
3	String or number	False	Parameter value included in encrypted query string
4a	String	False	Additional parameter name (see note)
4b	String or number	False	Additional parameter value (see note)

> **NOTE:** Additional parameter name and value pairs can be appended as arguments.

The following URL parameter names are reserved and cannot be included as arguments:

- `l`
- `v`
- `s`
- `d`
- `m`
- `n`

Example 1

An email is sent that includes the following link to a landing page using the MicrositeURL function:

```
<a href="%%=MicrositeURL(876)=%%">click here to visit your
landing page</a>
```

The following HTML is used on the microsite page. The **`_subscriberKey`** personalization string is used to retrieve a corresponding value from a Data Extension.

```
%%[

var @firstName
set @firstName = Lookup("Members", "First Name", "Subscriber
Key", _subscriberKey)

]%%

<!DOCTYPE html>
<html>
   <body>
      <h2>Hello %%=v(@firstName)=%%,</h2>
      <p>Welcome to your personalized landing page.</p>
   </body>
</html>
```

Output

The MicrositeURL function returns the page URL of the microsite page appended with an encrypted query string with Subscriber data. For example: **`https://pages.exacttarget.com/page.aspx?QS=c76003443ff9837d7d0...`**

The page is personalized with a Data Extension field value, which is based on the Subscriber Key of the email sent to the Subscriber.

```
<!DOCTYPE html>
<html>
   <body>
      <h2>Hello Andrew,</h2>
      <p>Welcome to your personalized landing page.</p>
   </body>
</html>
```

Example 2

This example is a variation of the first example, that includes additional URL parameters in the function, using **`First Name`** and **`Status`** fields from the Sendable Data Extension that is used to send the email. The email includes the following link to a microsite page using the MicrositeURL function.

```
<a href="%%=MicrositeURL(876,'fname',[First Name],'status',
Status)=%%">click here to visit your landing page</a>
<!DOCTYPE html>
<html>
   <body>
      <h2>Hello %%=RequestParameter('fname')=%%,</h2>
      <p>You are a valued %%=RequestParameter('status')=%%
member.</p>
   </body>
</html>
```

Output

The MicrositeURL function returns the page URL of the Microsite page appended with an encrypted query string of Subscriber data and URL parameters. For example: **`https://pages.exacttarget.com/page.aspx?QS=c76003443ff9837d7d0...`**

The page is personalized with values from the Sendable Data Extension, retrieved from the decrypted query string parameter.

```
<!DOCTYPE html>
<html>
   <body>
      <h2>Hello Andrew,</h2>
      <p>You are a valued Gold member.</p>
   </body>
</html>
```

QueryParameter

This function retrieves a value from a URL query string, based on a defined parameter key.

> **NOTE:** You can use this function to retrieve parameter values from encrypted query string URLs created by the CloudPagesURL or MicrositeURL functions.

Argument
QueryParameter(1)

Ordinal	Type	Required	Description
1	String	True	URL parameter key

Example
An email is sent with a link to a landing page created in CloudPages. The link uses the CloudPagesURL function to include a field as a URL parameter, based on a value in the Sendable Data Extension.

```
<a href="%%=CloudPagesURL(123,'p',Product)=%%">view your
product page</a>
```

The landing page includes the following code:

```
<!DOCTYPE html>
<html>
   <body>
      <p>Thank you for purchasing %%=QueryParameter('p')=%.
</p>
   </body>
</html>
```

Output
The CloudPagesURL function returns the page URL of the landing page appended with an encrypted query string of Subscriber data and the URL parameter.

The page is personalized with the corresponding **`Product`** value from the Sendable Data Extension which is retrieved from the decrypted **`p`** query string parameter.

```
<!DOCTYPE html>
<html>
   <body>
      <p>Thank you for purchasing blue sunglasses.</p>
   </body>
</html>
```

Redirect

This function redirects a landing page to a specified URL.

> **NOTE:** Any code that appears before the Redirect function will be interpreted, but any code that appears after the function will not.

Argument

`Redirect(1)`

Ordinal	Type	Required	Description
1	String	True	The redirect URL

Example

An email is sent with a link to a landing page created in CloudPages. The link uses the CloudPagesURL function to include a field as a URL parameter, based on a value in the Sendable Data Extension.

```
<a href="%%=CloudPagesURL(123,'src',Source)=%%">view your
product page</a>
```

The landing page includes the following code:

```
%%[

var @source
set @source = QueryParameter('src')

InsertData("Click Data", "Source", @source, "Subscriber Key",
_subscriberKey)
Redirect(concat("https://limedash.com?src=", @source))

]%%
```

Output

When the page loads, the **src** URL parameter value is retrieved from the encrypted query string and inserted into a Data Extension with the Subscriber Key.

The page then returns a 302 HTTP status code and redirects the user agent to the defined URL, passing the URL parameter value that was concatenated to the URL; for example **https://limedash.com?src=email**.

RequestParameter

This function is similar to QueryParameter, but in addition to retrieving a value from a URL query string, it can also be used to retrieve form field values.

> **NOTE:** You can use this function to retrieve parameter values from URLs in encrypted query strings created by the CloudPagesURL or MicrositeURL functions.

Argument

RequestParameter(1)

Ordinal	Type	Required	Description
1	String	True	URL parameter key or field name attribute

Example

The following code is used on a landing page for a registration form. When the user completes the form, the InsertData function creates a new Data Extension record from the form field values.

```
%%[

if RequestParameter("submitted") == true then

  InsertData(
        "Registrations",
        "FirstName", RequestParameter("firstname"),
        "LastName", RequestParameter("lastname"),
        "Company", RequestParameter("company"),
        "Email", RequestParameter("email")
      )
```

```
endif

]%%

<!DOCTYPE html>
<html>
   <body>
      %%[ if RequestParameter("submitted") == true then ]%%
         <p>Thank you for submitting your details.</p>
      %%[ else ]%%
      <h2>Register</h2>
      <form action="%%=RequestParameter('PAGEURL')=%%"
method="post">
         <label>First name</label>
         <input type="text" name="firstname">
         <label>Last name</label>
         <input type="text" name="lastname">
         <label>Company</label>
         <input type="text" name="company">
         <label>Email</label>
         <input type="text" name="email">
         <input name="submitted" type="hidden" value="true"
/>
         <input type="submit" value="Submit">
      </form>
      %%[ endif ]%%
   </body>
</html>
```

Output

When the form is submitted, a Data Extension record will be created with the form field values and the following text will be displayed on the page.

```
<p>Thank you for submitting your details.</p>
```

Social Functions

Overview

The AMPscript social functions are used for interacting with the Social Sharing features in Marketing Cloud.

GetPublishedSocialContent

This function returns previous Social Content specified by the Region ID.

> **NOTE:** This function is only for use in Microsites and Landing Pages and will only return Content Areas built in Classic Content.

Argument

`GetPublishedSocialContent(1)`

Ordinal	Type	Required	Description
1	Number	True	Region ID of the Social Content Area to return

> **NOTE:** This function is not supported in the current version of Marketing Cloud.

Example

```
%%=GetPublishedSocialContent(12345)=%%
```

GetSocialPublishURL

This function returns HTML for sharing a predefined region of content using the social network code found in the table below. When a recipient clicks on a social link defined by this function, they are directed to the social network. The default content to be shared is the Marketing Cloud landing page that contains the content defined in the predefined content region.

Arguments

```
GetSocialPublishURL(1,2,[3a,3b])
```

Ordinal	Type	Required	Description
1	Number	True	Code that represents the social network (see below)
2	String	True	Name of the predefined content region to share on the social network
3a	String	False	Optional parameter name specific to the selected social network (see note)
3b	String	False	Optional parameter value specific to the selected social network (see note)

> **NOTE:** Additional pairs of columns and values can be appended as arguments.

The social network codes are as follows:

Code	Social Network
2	Del.icio.us
3	Digg
1	Facebook
6	Google
15	Google+
9	LinkedIn
7	Microsoft
4	MySpace
10	ShareThis
5	StumbleUpon
11	Twitter
8	Yahoo

Example

In the following example, content is surrounded by a social content slot and then referenced in the function as the content to share:

```
<!-- RegionStart[contentslot:"limedash-loyalty", title:"Join
the Limedash Loyalty Program Today"] -->
Join the <a href="https://limedash.com/join">Limedash</a>
Loyalty Program Today!
<!-- RegionEnd[contentslot:"limedash-loyalty"] -->

<br><br><a href="%%=GetSocialPublishURL('1','limedash-loyalty')
=%%">Share on Facebook</a>
<br><a href="%%=GetSocialPublishURL('11','limedash-loyalty')
=%%">Share on Twitter</a>
```

Output

```
<!-- RegionStart[contentslot:"limedash-loyalty", title:"Join
the Limedash Loyalty Program Today"] -->
Join the <a href="http://cl.S7.exct.net/?qs=69824b638bd8e36e7f8
594ea85ce01efac0641753cd0b6cb51f33e9b009c6e8ec48662ad22858
410655d420eba31bbd3">Limedash</a> Loyalty Program Today!
<!-- RegionEnd[contentslot:"limedash-loyalty"] -->

<br><br><a href="http://pages.S7.exacttarget.com/Publish.aspx?
qs=71b8883ce06d4a85ee3a3b44ed76c8255d6095655ba67d40656454bab
98292855b79ce4567eb1c47b7fe3482668b1c3f3c876a93d3f53d09741fa5
c97cb7110b4fd57bdee8261b3c71f741224aeb0fd57a5ca8457f867872046
a2c87a4f844e987a19b2d74a6a712f0e5b62682e6e86fea665dfa0d2e2de7">
Share on Facebook</a>
<br><a href="http://pages.S7.exacttarget.com/Publish.aspx?qs=71
b8883ce06d4a85ee3a3b44ed76c8255d6095655ba67d40656454bab982
9285ede778d2f596ba9812d21883826ec05006a8c8824a62794e7938ee0c5e
76bdde24b8b6d61b79d6a00bacc6758e4926f1d4a534c9be67e6dfa15aa03c
e73f5fb5049e51aa521c73d7ca847372758ab27f8c62016d4998f90e">Share
on Twitter</a>
```

GetSocialPublishURLByName

This function returns HTML for sharing a predefined region of content using a social network name found in the table below. When a recipient clicks on a social link defined by this function, they are directed to the social network and the default content to be shared is the Marketing Cloud landing page that contains the content defined in the predefined content region.

Arguments

```
GetSocialPublishURLByName(1,2,[3a,3b]...)
```

Ordinal	Type	Required	Description
1	String	True	Name of the social network (see below)
2	String	True	Name of the predefined content region to share on the social network
3a	String	False	Optional parameter name specific to the selected social network (see note)
3a	String	False	Optional parameter value specific to the selected social network (see note)

> **NOTE:** Additional pairs of columns and values can be appended as arguments.

Valid social network names are as follows:

Social Network
Del.icio.us
Digg
Facebook
Google
Google+
LinkedIn
Microsoft
MySpace
ShareThis
StumbleUpon
Twitter
Yahoo

In the following example, content is surrounded by a social content slot and then referenced in the function as the content to share:

Example

```
<!-- RegionStart[contentslot:"limedash-loyalty", title:"Join
the Limedash Loyalty Program Today"] -->
Join the <a href="https://limedash.com/join">Limedash</a>
Loyalty Program Today!
<!-- RegionEnd[contentslot:"limedash-loyalty"] -->

<br><br><a href="%%=GetSocialPublishURL('Facebook','limedash-
loyalty')=%%">Share on Facebook</a>
<br><a href="%%=GetSocialPublishURL('Twitter','limedash-
loyalty')=%%">334Share on Twitter</a>
```

Output

```
<!-- RegionStart[contentslot:"limedash-loyalty", title:"Join
the Limedash Loyalty Program Today"] -->
Join the <a href="http://cl.S7.exct.net/?qs=69824b638bd8e36e7f8
594ea85ce01efac0641753cd0b6cb51f33e9b009c6e8ec48662ad228584106
55d420eba31bbd3">Limedash</a> Loyalty Program Today!
<!-- RegionEnd[contentslot:"limedash-loyalty"] -->

<br><br><a  href="http://pages.S7.exacttarget.com/Publish.aspx?
qs=71b8883ce06d4a85ee3a3b44ed76c8255d6095655ba67d40656454bab98
292855b79ce4567eb1c47b7fe3482668b1c3f3c876a93d3f53d09741fa5c97
cb7110b4fd57bdee8261b3c71f741224aeb0fd57a5ca8457f867872046a2c8
7a4f844e987a19b2d74a6a712f0e5b62682e6e86fea665dfa0d2e2de7">
Share on Facebook</a>
<br><a href="http://pages.S7.exacttarget.com/Publish.aspx?qs=71
b8883ce06d4a85ee3a3b44ed76c8255d6095655ba67d40656454bab982928
5ede778d2f596ba9812d21883826ec05006a8c8824a62794e7938ee0c5e76b
dde24b8b6d61b79d6a00bacc6758e4926f1d4a534c9be67e6dfa15aa03ce7
3f5fb5049e51aa521c73d7ca847372758ab27f8c62016d4998f90e">Share
on Twitter</a>
```

String Functions

Overview

The string AMPscript functions are generally used to perform any string operation, including parsing, converting, concatenating, trimming and matching.

Char

This function returns the ASCII character for the specified ASCII character code.

Arguments

`Char(1,2)`

Ordinal	Type	Required	Description
1	Number	True	Character code
2	Number	False	Number of times to repeat the ASCII character returned

Example

```
%%[

var @greeting
set @greeting = ""
set @greeting = concat(@greeting, "Just wanted to say ",
Char(34), "Hello", Char(34), " ")
set @greeting = concat(@greeting, "and tell you we",
Char(39) ,"re b", Char(97,4) , "ck!")

]%%
greeting: %%=v(@greeting)=%%
```

Output

```
greeting: Just wanted to say "Hello" and tell you we're
baaaack!
```

Concat

This function concatenates one or more strings.

Arguments

`Concat(1,n)`

Ordinal	Type	Required	Description
1	String	True	First string to concatenate
n	String	False	Second string to concatenate

> **NOTE:** Additional parameter values can be appended as arguments.

Example

```
%%[

var @firstName
var @lastName
var @fullName

set @firstName = AttributeValue("firstName") /* value from
attribute or DE column in send context */
set @firstName = "Suzy" /* or a literal value */

set @lastName = AttributeValue("lastName") /* value from
attribute or DE column in send context */
set @lastName = "Jackson" /* or a literal value */

set @fullName  = Concat(@firstName, " ", @lastName)

]%%
firstName: %%=v(@firstName)=%%
<br>lastName: %%=v(@lastName)=%%
<br>fullName: %%=v(@fullName)=%%
```

Output

```
firstName: Suzy
lastName: Jackson
fullName: Suzy Jackson
```

IndexOf

This function returns the position of the first occurrence of a specified value in a string. The index numbering starts at 1.

Arguments

`IndexOf(1,2)`

Ordinal	Type	Required	Description
1	String	True	String to search
2	String	True	String value to find

Example

```
%%[

var @fullName
var @firstName

set @fullName = AttributeValue("fullName") /* value from
attribute or DE column in send context */
set @fullName = "Dale Cameron" /* or a literal value */

if indexOf(@fullName, " ") > 0 then
  set @firstName = Substring(@fullName,1,
Subtract(IndexOf(@fullName," "),1))
endif

]%%
fullName: %%=v(@fullName)=%%
<br>firstName: %%=v(@firstName)=%%
```

Output

```
fullName: Dale Cameron
firstName: Dale
```

Length

This function returns the number of characters in the specified string.

Argument

Length(1)

Ordinal	Type	Required	Description
1	String	True	String to measure

Example

```
%%[

var @terms, @termsBlurb, @len, @max

set @max = 105

set @terms = AttributeValue("terms") /* value from attribute
or DE column in send context */
set @terms = "" /* or a literal value */
set @terms = concat(@terms, "The Rewards program is
intended for personal use only. ")
set @terms = concat(@terms, "Commercial use is prohibited.
This program is not targeted towards, ")
set @terms = concat(@terms, "nor intended for use by, anyone
under the age of 13. ")
set @terms = concat(@terms, "If you are between the ages of
13 and 18, you may only use Rewards ")
set @terms = concat(@terms, "under the supervision of a
parent or legal guardian who agrees to ")
set @terms = concat(@terms, "be bound by these Terms of
Use.")

set @termsBlurb = @terms

set @len = length(@terms)

if @len > @max then
  set @termsBlurb = concat(trim(substring(@terms, 1, @max)),
"...")
```

```
endif

]%%
terms: %%=v(@terms)=%%
<br>len: %%=v(@len)=%%
<br>termsBlurb: %%=v(@termsBlurb)=%%
```

Output

```
terms: The Rewards program is intended for personal use
only. Commercial use is prohibited. This program is not
targeted towards, nor intended for use by, anyone under the
age of 13. If you are between the ages of 13 and 18, you may
only use Rewards under the supervision of a parent or legal
guardian who agrees to be bound by these Terms of Use.
len: 340
termsBlurb: The Rewards program is intended for personal use
only. Commercial use is prohibited. This program is not...
```

Lowercase

This function converts all uppercase letters in the specified string into lowercase letters.

Argument

`Lowercase(1)`

Ordinal	Type	Required	Description
1	String	True	String to convert into lowercase

Example

```
%%[

var @locale, @localeLower

set @locale = AttributeValue("locale") /* value from
attribute or DE column in send context */
set @locale = "EN-US" /* or a literal value */

set @localeLower = lowercase(@locale)
```

```
]%%
locale: %%=v(@locale)=%%
<br>localeLower: %%=v(@localeLower)=%%
```

Output

```
locale: EN-US
localeLower: en-us
```

ProperCase

This function capitalizes the first letter in the specified string and any other letters in the string that follow any character other than a letter. It converts all other letters into lowercase.

Argument

ProperCase(1)

Ordinal	Type	Required	Description
1	String	True	String to convert into proper case

Example

```
%%[

var @fullName, @fullNameProperCase

set @fullName = AttributeValue("fullName") /* value from
attribute or DE column in send context */
set @fullName = "BARB BROWN" /* or a literal value */

set @fullNameProperCase = ProperCase(@fullName)

]%%
fullName: %%=v(@fullName)=%%
<br>fullNameProperCase: %%=v(@fullNameProperCase)=%%
```

Output

```
fullName: BARB BROWN
fullNameProperCase: Barb Brown
```

RegExMatch

This function searches for and returns a string for the first occurrence of the matching regular expression pattern.

Arguments

`RegExMatch(1,2,3,[n])`

Ordinal	Type	Required	Description
1	String	True	String to search for a match
2	String	True	Regular expression to use in the search
3	String	True	Name or ordinal of the matching group to return
n	String	False	Additional repeating string parameter options (see note)

> **NOTE:** Additional repeating string parameter options can be appended as arguments.

> **NOTE:** Valid repeating string parameter options include any value from the .NET RegexOptions enumeration.

Example

```
%%[

var @s
var @o
var @p
var @m

output(concat("<br>Strip leading zeroes from a string"))
set @s = "0000012345"
set @p = "^0*(\d+)$"
set @o = RegExMatch(@s, @p, 1)
output(concat("<br>string:  ", @s))
output(concat('<br>pattern: "', @p, '"'))
output(concat("<br>output: ", @o))

output(concat("<br><br>Check for all digits, no match"))
```

```
set @s = "12345x"
set @p = "^\d*$"
set @o = RegExMatch(@s, @p, 0)
output(concat("<br>string: ", @s))
output(concat('<br>pattern: "', @p, '"'))
output(concat("<br>output: ", @o))

output(concat("<br><br>Check for all digits, match"))
set @s = "12345"
set @p = "^\d*$"
set @o = RegExMatch(@s, @p, 0)
output(concat("<br>string: ", @s))
output(concat('<br>pattern: "', @p, '"'))
output(concat("<br>output: ", @o))

output(concat("<br><br>Replace parenthetical text with
space"))
set @s = "whee (whatever it is) whoop"
set @p = "\s\(.+\)\s"
set @m = RegExMatch(@s, @p, 0, "IgnoreCase")
set @o = replace(@s, @m, " ")
output(concat("<br>string:  ", @s))
output(concat('<br>pattern: "', @p, '"'))
output(concat("<br>match: ", @m))
output(concat("<br>replaced: ", @o))

output(concat("<br><br>Retrieve accessToken value from REST
response"))
set @s = '{"accessToken": "e68d15020fc64547b3de7a54bf82e40a",
"expiresIn": 3600}'
set @p = '^{"accessToken": "(.*)",.*$'
set @o = RegExMatch(@s, @p, 1)
output(concat("<br>string: ", @s))
output(concat("<br>pattern: '", @p, "'"))
output(concat("<br>output: ", @o))

]%%
```

Output

```
Strip leading zeroes from a string
string: 0000012345
pattern: "^0*(\d+)$"
output: 12345

Check for all digits, no match
string: 12345x
pattern: "^\d*$"
output:

Check for all digits, match
string: 12345
pattern: "^\d*$"
output: 12345

Replace parenthetical text with space
string: whee (whatever it is) whoop
pattern: "\s\(.+\)\s"
match: (whatever it is)
replaced: whee whoop

Retrieve accessToken value from REST response
string: {"accessToken": "e68d15020fc64547b3de7a54bf82e40a",
"expiresIn": 3600}
pattern: '^{"accessToken": "(.*)",.*$'
output: e68d15020fc64547b3de7a54bf82e40a
```

Replace

This function replaces the first string value with the second string value in the specified string.

Arguments

`Replace(1,2,3)`

Ordinal	Type	Required	Description
1	String	True	String to search
2	String	True	String to find
3	String	True	Replacement string

Example

```
%%[

var @blurb
var @blurbReplaced

set @blurb = AttributeValue("blurb") /* value from attribute
or DE column in send context */
set @blurb = "" /* or a literal value */
set @blurb = concat(@blurb, "Enjoy rewards that you choose,
like discounts on accessories<br>")
set @blurb = concat(@blurb, "and other services. The options
are only available to Members.<br><br>")
set @blurb = concat(@blurb, "Enjoy the rewards today!<br>")

set @blurbReplaced = replace(@blurb, "<br>", " ")

]%%
blurb: %%=v(@blurb)=%%
<br>blurbReplaced: %%=v(@blurbReplaced)=%%
```

Output

```
blurb: Enjoy rewards that you choose, like discounts on
accessories
and other services. The options are only available to
Members.

Enjoy the rewards today!

blurbReplaced: Enjoy rewards that you choose, like
discounts on accessories and other services. The options
are only available to Members. Enjoy the rewards today!
```

ReplaceList

This function replaces the first string value with the second string value and any subsequent values in the specified string.

Arguments

`ReplaceList(1,2,3,n)`

Ordinal	Type	Required	Description
1	String	True	String to search
2	String	True	Replacement string
3	String	True	First String to find
n	String	False	Subsequent string to find (see note)

> **NOTE:** Additional strings to find can be appended as arguments.

Example

```
%%[

var @colors
var @colorsNew

set @colors = ""
set @colors = concat(@colors, "red/orange/yellow,green/
blue,indigo/violet")
set @colorsNew  = ReplaceList(@colors, "|", "/", ",")

]%%
colors: %%=v(@colors)=%%
<br>colorsNew: %%=v(@colorsNew)=%%
```

Output

```
colors: red/orange/yellow,green/blue,indigo/violet
colorsNew: red|orange|yellow|green|blue|indigo|violet
```

StringToDate

This function parses the specified date string and returns a .NET DateTime object.

Arguments

`StringToDate(1,2)`

Ordinal	Type	Required	Description
1	String	True	Date string to parse
2	String	False	Optional .NET character-encoding type to utilize in encoding. Valid values are **`UTF-8`** (default) and **`UTF-16`**.

> **NOTE:** The second argument is not supported in the current version of Marketing Cloud.

Example

```
%%[

var @dateString1
var @date1
var @dateString2
var @date2

set @dateString1 = "2017-10-15 00:24"
set @date1 = StringToDate(@dateString1)

set @dateString2 = "2/29/2016 23:45"
set @date2 = StringToDate(@dateString2)

]%%
dateString1: %%=v(@dateString1)=%%
<br>date1: %%=v(@date1)=%%
<br><br>dateString2: %%=v(@dateString2)=%%
<br>date2: %%=v(@date2)=%%
```

Output

```
dateString1: 2017-10-15 00:24
date1: 10/15/2017 12:24:00 AM

dateString2: 2/29/2016 23:45
date2: 2/29/2016 11:45:00 PM
```

StringToHex

This function converts the specified string into its hex equivalent.

Arguments

`StringToHex(1,2)`

Ordinal	Type	Required	Description
1	String	True	String to convert
2	String	False	Optional .NET character-encoding type to utilize in conversion. Valid values are **`UTF-8`** (default) and **`UTF-16`**.

Example

```
%%[

var @string1
var @string1Hex

set @string1 = "limedash"
set @string1Hex  = StringToHex(@string1)

set @string2 = "loyalty"
set @string2Hex  = StringToHex(@string2, "UTF-16")

]%%
string1: %%=v(@string1)=%%
<br>string1Hex: %%=v(@string1Hex)=%%
<br>string2: %%=v(@string2)=%%
<br>string2Hex: %%=v(@string2Hex)=%%
```

Output

```
string1: limedash
string1Hex: 6c696d6564617368
string2: loyalty
string2Hex: 6c006f00790061006c0074007900
```

Substring

This function returns a portion of the specified string starting at a certain character position and no longer than the specified length. If the specified character position is more than the length of the specified string, the function returns an empty string.

Arguments

Substring(1,2,3)

Ordinal	Type	Required	Description
1	String	True	The string from which to extract a portion
2	Number	True	Starting position of substring
3	Number	False	Length of substring

Example

```
%%[

var @fullName
var @firstName

set @fullName = AttributeValue("fullName") /* value from
attribute or DE column in send context */
set @fullName = "Curt Harris" /* or a literal value */

if indexOf(@fullName, " ") > 0 then
  set @firstName = Substring(@fullName,1,
Subtract(IndexOf(@fullName," "),1))
endif

]%%
fullName: %%=v(@fullName)=%%
<br>firstName: %%=v(@firstName)=%%
```

Output

```
fullName: Curt Harris
firstName: Curt
```

Trim

This function removes the leading and trailing spaces from the specified string.

Argument

`Trim(1)`

Ordinal	Type	Required	Description
1	String	True	String value to trim

Example 1

```
%%[

var @firstName
var @firstNameTrimmed

set @firstName = AttributeValue("FirstName") /* value from
attribute or DE column in send context */
set @firstName = "  Dale   " /* or a literal value */
set @firstNameTrimmed = trim(@firstName)

]%%
Hello, %%=v(@firstName)=%%!
<br><br>Hello, %%=v(@firstNameTrimmed)=%%!
```

Output

```
Hello, Dale !

Hello, Dale!
```

Uppercase

This function converts all lowercase letters in the specified string to uppercase.

Argument

`Uppercase(1)`

Ordinal	Type	Required	Description
1	String	True	String to convert into uppercase

Example

```
%%[

var @locale, @localeUpper

set @locale = AttributeValue("locale") /* value from
attribute or DE column in send context */
set @locale = "en-us" /* or a literal value */

set @localeUpper = Uppercase(@locale)

]%%
locale: %%=v(@locale)=%%
<br>localeUpper: %%=v(@localeUpper)=%%
```

Output

```
locale: en-us
localeUpper: EN-US
```

Utility Functions

Overview
AMPscript includes several miscellaneous functions which provide conditional evaluation, variable output and other utilities.

AttributeValue
This function returns the value of an attribute based on the context of the Contact or Subscriber. These values are derived from a field or attribute related to the Contact or Subscriber that the message is sent to. These can include the following data sources:

- Email Subscriber Profile Attributes
- Sendable Data Extension Fields
- Journey Builder Entry Source Attributes
- MobileConnect List Attributes
- MobilePush Attributes
- Journey Builder Entry Source.

The function is similar to Attribute Personalization Strings which return a contextual value of an attribute. However, this function will return **`null`** if the attribute is not available in the data source context. This can be useful when working with data sources that use different schemas.

Argument
`AttributeValue(1)`

Ordinal	Type	Required	Description
1	String	True	The attribute name

Example 1

The following example indicates the behavior when an email is sent from a Sendable Data Extension which does not include a 'first name' field.

```
%%[

var @firstName, @displayName

set @firstName = [First Name]

if empty(@firstName) then
  set @displayName = "friend"
else
  set @displayName = @firstName
endif

]%%
<p>Hello %%=v(@displayName)=%%,</p>
```

Output

As the field is not available, an error will be generated and the email will not be sent.

```
Unable to generate preview

An unrecognized expression appears in a script block.
Script Expression: [First Name]
MemberID: 87654321
JobID: 0
```

Example 2

Similar to the first example, this example demonstrates the behavior when an email is sent from a Sendable Data Extension where the field is not available, but where the AttributeValue function is used.

```
%%[

var @firstName, @displayName

set @firstName = AttributeValue("First Name")

if empty(@firstName) then
```

```
  set @displayName = "friend"
else
  set @displayName = @firstName
endif

]%%
<p>Hello %%=v(@displayName)=%%,</p>
```

Output

The function returns **null**, and as the **@firstName** variable is empty, the **@displayName** is set to the defined string constant.

```
<p>Hello friend,</p>
```

Example 3

This example indicates the behavior when a **Customer First Name** attribute is available in the data source used in the context of the email send.

```
%%[

var @firstName, @displayName

set @firstName = AttributeValue("Customer First Name")

if empty(@firstName) then
  set @displayName = "friend"
else
  set @displayName = @firstName
endif

]%%
<p>Hello %%=v(@displayName)=%%,</p>
```

Output

As the attribute is available in the data source and the value is not empty, the **@displayName** variable is set to the attribute value.

```
<p>Hello Suzy,</p>
```

Domain

This function returns the domain of an email address.

> **NOTE:** If the argument passed to the function is not a valid email address, the function will return a **`null`** output.

Argument

`Domain(1)`

Ordinal	Type	Required	Description
1	String	True	The email address

Example

The following example displays the domain of the Subscriber's email address using the **`emailaddr`** email Subscriber data string.

```
<p>Your email domain is %%=Domain(emailaddr)=%%.</p>
```

Output

For a Subscriber with the email address **`dale@limedash.com`**, the following output will be displayed:

```
<p>Your email domain is limedash.com.</p>
```

Empty

This function provides a conditional evaluation of an expression. If the expression evaluates as **`null`** or empty, the function will output **`true`**, otherwise it will output **`false`**.

Argument

`Empty(1)`

Ordinal	Type	Required	Description
1	String	True	An attribute, variable or nested function to evaluate

Example

The following example evaluates the MemberId attribute. If the attribute field is empty, then the function will evaluate to **`true`**.

```
%%[

var @memberId, @nonMember

set @memberId = MemberId

if empty(@memberId) then
  set @displayMemberId = "You are not a member"
else
  set @displayMemberId = Concat("Your member id is
",@memberId)
endif

]%%
<p>%%=v(@displayMemberId)=%%.</p>
```

Output

For records without a MemberId attribute value, the following string will be displayed.

```
<p>You are not a member</p>
```

Format

This function formats a string in the specified format pattern and locale.

Format patterns follow the C# format types outlined in the official Microsoft documentation:

- Standard Numeric Format Strings
- Standard Date and Time Format Strings

Some of these custom formats are supported:

- Custom Numeric Format Strings
- Custom Date and Time Format Strings

Arguments

`Format(1,2,3,4)`

Ordinal	Type	Required	Description
1	String	True	The string to format
2	String	True	The output format pattern (see table below for values)
3	String	False	Data format indicator. Valid values are `Date` and `Number`
4	String	False	The ISO locale code for the output

Here are a few examples of format patterns, given a date of `2017-09-15T06:07:08.1230000-06:00`:

Element	Format Pattern	Output
Long Date	`D`	`Friday, September 15, 2017`
Short date	`d`	`9/15/2017`
Full Date, short time	`f`	`Friday, September 15, 2017 6:07 AM`
Full Date, long time	`F`	`Vendredi 15 Septembre 2017 06:07`
General Date/Time, short time	`g`	`Friday, September 15, 2017 6:07:08 AM`
General Date/Time, long time	`G`	`9/15/2017 6:07 AM`
Month, Day	`M` or `m`	`September 15`
Round Trip Date/Time	`O` or `o`	`2017-09-15T06:07:08.1230000-06:00`
RFC1123	`R` or `r`	`Fri, 15 Sep 2017 06:07:08 GMT`
Sortable Date/Time	`s`	`2017-09-15T06:07:08`
Short Time	`t`	`6:07 AM`
Long Time	`T`	`6:07:08 AM`
Universal Sortable Date/Time	`u`	`2017-09-15 06:07:08Z`
Universal full Date/Time	`U`	`Friday, September 15, 2017 12:07:08 PM`

Element	Format Pattern	Output
Month, Year	`Y`	`September, 2017`
Month	`MM`	`09`
Month	`MMM`	`Sep`
Month	`MMMM`	`September`
Day	`dd`	`15`
Day	`ddd`	`Fri`
Day	`ddddd`	`Friday`
Hour	`hh`	`06`
Minutes	`mm`	`07`
Seconds	`ss`	`08`
Milliseconds	`MMM`	`123`
AM/PM	`tt`	`AM`
Timezone offset	`zz`	`-06`
Timezone offset	`zzz`	`-06:00`

NOTE: This function returns lowercase month and day names for non-US culture codes by default.

Here are a few examples of format patterns, given a number of `-0.8967`:

Element	Format Pattern	Output
Currency	`C` or `c`	`($0.90)`
Decimal	`D` or `d`	`-0.8967`
Exponential (scientific)	`E` or `e`	`-8.967000E-001`
Fixed-point	`F` of `f`	`-0.90`
General	`G` or `g`	`-0.8967`
Number	`N` or `n`	`-0.90`
Percent	`P` or `p`	`-89.67 %`

Here are a few examples of custom format patterns, given a number of **-1.8967**:

Element	Format Pattern	Example	Output
Zero placeholder	0	"0000"	-0002
Digit placeholder	#	"###0"	-2
Decimal point	.	"#0.00"	-1.90
Group separator and scaling	,	"0,00#.##"	-0,001.9
Percentage placeholder	%	"#.00%"	-189.67%
Exponential notation	E0, E+0, e0 or e+0	"#0.0e0"	-19.0e-1
Escape character	\	"\###0.000\#"	-#1.897#
Literal string delimiter	'string' or "string"	"#.##' points'"	-1.9 points
Section separator	;	"#0.00;(#0.00)"	(1.90)

Example 1

The following example illustrates date and time formats:

```
%%[

var @dateString, @timeString, @long, @short, @fullShortTime,
@fullShortTimeFR, @fullLongTime, @generalShortTime,
@generalLongTime, @monthDay, @roundTrip, @RFC1123,
@sortable, @shortTime, @longTime, @universalSortable,
@universalFull, @monthYear, @monthNumber, @monthShortName,
@monthFullName, @dayNumber, @dayFullName, @hour, @minute,
@seconds, @AMPM, @offsetHours, @offsetHoursMinutes

set @dateString = "2017-09-15T06:07:08.1230000-06:00"
set @timeString = "06:07:08.123 AM"

set @long = Format(@dateString,"D", "Date")
set @short = Format(@dateString,"d", "Date")
set @fullShortTime = Format(@dateString,"f", "Date")
set @fullShortTimeFR = ProperCase(Format(@dateString,"f",
"Date","fr-FR"))
set @fullLongTime = Format(@dateString,"F", "Date")
set @generalShortTime = Format(@dateString,"g", "Date")
```

```
set @generalLongTime = Format(@dateString,"G", "Date")
set @monthDay = Format(@dateString,"M", "Date")
set @roundTrip = Format(@dateString,"O", "Date")
set @RFC1123 = Format(@dateString,"R", "Date")
set @sortable = Format(@dateString,"s", "Date")
set @shortTime = Format(@dateString,"t", "Date")
set @longTime = Format(@dateString,"T", "Date")
set @universalSortable = Format(@dateString,"u", "Date")
set @universalFull = Format(@dateString,"U", "Date")
set @monthYear = Format(@dateString,"Y", "Date")

set @monthNumber = Format(@dateString,"MM","Date")
set @monthShortName = Format(@dateString,"MMM","Date")
set @monthFullName = Format(@dateString,"MMMM","Date")

set @dayNumber = Format(@dateString,"dd","Date")
set @dayShortName = Format(@dateString,"ddd","Date")
set @dayFullName = Format(@dateString,"ddddd","Date")

set @hour = Format(@timeString,"hh","Date")
set @minute = Format(@timeString,"mm","Date")
set @seconds = Format(@timeString, "ss","Date")
set @AMPM = Format(@timeString,"tt","Date")
set @offsetHours = Format(@dateString,"zz","Date")
set @offsetHoursMinutes = Format(@dateString,"zzz","Date")


]%%
dateString: %%=v(@dateString)=%%
<br><br>long: %%=v(@long)=%%
<br>short: %%=v(@short)=%%
<br>fullShortTime: %%=v(@fullShortTime)=%%
<br>fullShortTimeFR: %%=v(@fullShortTimeFR)=%%
<br>fullLongTime: %%=v(@fullLongTime)=%%
<br>generalShortTime: %%=v(@generalShortTime)=%%
<br>generalLongTime: %%=v(@generalLongTime)=%%
<br>monthDay: %%=v(@monthDay)=%%
<br>roundTrip: %%=v(@roundTrip)=%%
<br>RFC1123: %%=v(@RFC1123)=%%
<br>sortable: %%=v(@sortable)=%%
<br>shortTime: %%=v(@shortTime)=%%
<br>longTime: %%=v(@longTime)=%%
```

```
<br>universalSortable: %%=v(@universalSortable)=%%
<br>universalFull: %%=v(@universalFull)=%%
<br>monthYear: %%=v(@monthYear)=%%
<br><br>monthNumber: %%=v(@monthNumber)=%%
<br>monthShortName: %%=v(@monthShortName)=%%
<br>monthFullName: %%=v(@monthFullName)=%%
<br>dayNumber: %%=v(@dayNumber)=%%
<br>dayShortName: %%=v(@dayShortName)=%%
<br>dayFullName: %%=v(@dayFullName)=%%
<br><br>timeString: %%=v(@timeString)=%%
<br>hour: %%=v(@hour)=%%
<br>minute: %%=v(@minute)=%%
<br>seconds: %%=v(@seconds)=%%
<br>AMPM: %%=v(@AMPM)=%%
<br>offsetHours: %%=v(@offsetHours)=%%
<br>offsetHoursMinutes: %%=v(@offsetHoursMinutes)=%%
```

Output

```
dateString: 2017-09-15T06:07:08.1230000-06:00

long: Friday, September 15, 2017
short: 9/15/2017
fullShortTime: Friday, September 15, 2017 6:07 AM
fullShortTimeFR: Vendredi 15 Septembre 2017 06:07
fullLongTime: Friday, September 15, 2017 6:07:08 AM
generalShortTime: 9/15/2017 6:07 AM
generalLongTime: 9/15/2017 6:07:08 AM
monthDay: September 15
roundTrip: 2017-09-15T06:07:08.1230000-06:00
RFC1123: Fri, 15 Sep 2017 06:07:08 GMT
sortable: 2017-09-15T06:07:08
shortTime: 6:07 AM
longTime: 6:07:08 AM
universalSortable: 2017-09-15 06:07:08Z
universalFull: Friday, September 15, 2017 12:07:08 PM
monthYear: September, 2017

monthNumber: 09
monthShortName: Sep
monthFullName: September
dayNumber: 15
```

```
dayShortName: Fri
dayFullName: Friday

timeString: 06:07:08.123 AM
hour: 06
minute: 07
seconds: 08
AMPM: AM
offsetHours: -06
offsetHoursMinutes: -06:00
```

Example 2

The following example illustrates the standard number formats:

```
%%[

var @num
var @Currency
var @Currency3
var @Decimal
var @Exponential
var @Fixed
var @Fixed3
var @General
var @Number
var @Number3
var @Percent

set @num = "-0.8967"

set @Currency = Format(@num, "C")
set @Currency3 = Format(@num, "C3")
set @Decimal = Format(@num, "D")
set @Exponential = Format(@num, "E")
set @Fixed = Format(@num, "F")
set @Fixed3 = Format(@num, "F3")
set @General = Format(@num, "G")
set @Number = Format(@num, "N")
set @Number3 = Format(@num, "N3")
set @Percent = Format(@num, "P")
```

```
]%%
num: %%=v(@num)=%%
<br><br>Currency: %%=v(@Currency)=%%
<br>Currency3: %%=v(@Currency3)=%%
<br>Decimal: %%=v(@Decimal)=%%
<br>Exponential: %%=v(@Exponential)=%%
<br>Fixed: %%=v(@Fixed)=%%
<br>Fixed3: %%=v(@Fixed3)=%%
<br>General: %%=v(@General)=%%
<br>Number: %%=v(@Number)=%%
<br>Number3: %%=v(@Number3)=%%
<br>Percent: %%=v(@Percent)=%%
```

Output

```
num: -0.8967

Currency: ($0.90)
Currency3: ($0.897)
Decimal: -0.8967
Exponential: -8.967000E-001
Fixed: -0.90
Fixed3: -0.897
General: -0.8967
Number: -0.90
Number3: -0.897
Percent: -89.67 %
```

Example 3

The following example illustrates the custom number formats:

```
%%[

var @num
var @ZeroPlaceholder
var @DigitPlaceholder
var @DecimalPoint
var @GroupSeparator
var @PercentagePlaceholder
var @Exponential
var @EscapeCharacter
var @LiteralDelimiter
```

```
var @SectionSeparator


set @num = "-1.8967"

set @ZeroPlaceholder = format(@num,"0000")
set @DigitPlaceholder = format(@num,"###0")
set @DecimalPoint = format(@num,"#0.00")
set @GroupSeparator = format(@num,"0,00#.##")
set @PercentagePlaceholder = format(@num,"#.00%")
set @Exponential = format(@num,"#0.0e0")
set @EscapeCharacter = format(@num,"\###0.000\#")
set @LiteralDelimiter = format(@num,"#.##' points'")
set @SectionSeparator = format(@num,"#0.00;(#0.00)")


]%%
num: %%=v(@num)=%%
<br><br>ZeroPlaceholder: %%=v(@ZeroPlaceholder)=%%
<br>DigitPlaceholder: %%=v(@DigitPlaceholder)=%%
<br>DecimalPoint: %%=v(@DecimalPoint)=%%
<br>GroupSeparator: %%=v(@GroupSeparator)=%%
<br>PercentagePlaceholder: %%=v(@PercentagePlaceholder)=%%
<br>Exponential: %%=v(@Exponential)=%%
<br>EscapeCharacter: %%=v(@EscapeCharacter)=%%
<br>LiteralDelimiter: %%=v(@LiteralDelimiter)=%%
<br>SectionSeparator: %%=v(@SectionSeparator)=%%
```

Output

```
num: -1.8967

ZeroPlaceholder: -0002
DigitPlaceholder: -2
DecimalPoint: -1.90
GroupSeparator: -0,001.9
PercentagePlaceholder: -189.67%
Exponential: -19.0e-1
EscapeCharacter: -#1.897#
LiteralDelimiter: -1.9 points
SectionSeparator: (1.90)
```

FormatCurrency

This function formats a string as a currency for the specified locale.

> **NOTE:** By default, this function rounds half up to two decimal places.

Arguments

`FormatCurrency(1,2,3,4)`

Ordinal	Type	Required	Description
1	String	True	Currency string to format
2	String	True	ISO locale code for the currency unit
3	Number	False	Decimal places to include in the output
4	String	False	Currency symbol for output. This overrides the currency symbol specified by the ISO locale code

Example 1

```
%%[

var @num
var @currency
var @locale

set @num = "123.45678"
set @locale = "en-US"
set @currency  = FormatCurrency(@num, @locale)

]%%
num: %%=v(@num)=%%
<br>locale: %%=v(@locale)=%%
<br>currency: %%=v(@currency)=%%
```

Output

```
num: 123.45678
locale: en-US
currency: $123.46
```

Example 1

```
%%[

var @num
var @currency
var @locale

set @num = "123.45678"
set @locale = "fr-FR"
set @currency  = FormatCurrency(@num, @locale)

]%%
num: %%=v(@num)=%%
<br>locale: %%=v(@locale)=%%
<br>currency: %%=v(@currency)=%%
```

Output

```
num: 123.45678
locale: fr-FR
currency: 123,46 €
```

Example 2

```
%%[

var @num
var @currency
var @locale

set @num = "123.45678"
set @locale = "de-DE"
set @currency  = FormatCurrency(@num, @locale, 3, "~$~")

]%%
num: %%=v(@num)=%%
<br>locale: %%=v(@locale)=%%
<br>currency: %%=v(@currency)=%%
```

Output

```
num: 123.45678
locale: de-DE
currency: 123,457 ~$~
```

FormatNumber
This function formats a string as a number.

Format patterns follow the C# format types outlined in the official Microsoft documentation:

- Standard Numeric Format Strings
- Standard Date and Time Format Strings

Some of these custom formats are supported:

- Custom Numeric Format Strings
- Custom Date and Time Format Strings

> **NOTE:** By default, this function rounds half up to two decimal places.

Arguments
`FormatNumber(1,2,3)`

Ordinal	Type	Required	Description
1	String	True	The number string to format
2	String	True	The output format pattern (see table below for values)
3	String	False	ISO code for locale-specific pattern elements

Here are a few examples of format patterns, given a number of `123`:

Element	Format Pattern	Output
Currency	`C` or `c`	`$123.00`
Decimal	`D` or `d`	`123`
Exponential (scientific)	`E` or `e`	`1.230000E+002`
Fixed-point	`F` of `f`	`123.00`
General	`G` or `g`	`123`
Number	`N` or `n`	`123.00`
Percent	`P` or `p`	`12,300.00 %`
Hexadecimal	`X` or `x`	`7B`

NOTE: The `D` pattern requires an integer for input.

Here are a few examples of custom format patterns, given a number of `-1.8967`:

Element	Format Pattern	Example	Output
Zero placeholder	0	`"0000"`	`-0002`
Digit placeholder	#	`"###0"`	`-2`
Decimal point	.	`"#0.00"`	`-1.90`
Group separator and scaling	,	`"0,00#.##"`	`-0,001.9`
Percentage placeholder	%	`"#.00%"`	`-189.67%`
Exponential notation	`E0`, `E+0`, `e0` or `e+0`	`"#0.0e0"`	`-19.0e-1`
Escape character	\	`"\###0.000\#"`	`-#1.897#`
Literal string delimiter	`'string'` or `"string"`	`"#.##' points'"`	`-1.9 points`
Section separator	;	`"#0.00;(#0.00)"`	`(1.90)`

Example 1

```
%%[

var @num
var @Currency
var @Currency3
var @Decimal
var @Exponential
var @Fixed
var @Fixed3
var @General
var @Number
var @Number3
var @Percent
var @Hex

set @num = "123"

set @Currency = FormatNumber(@num, "C")
set @Currency3 = FormatNumber(@num, "C3")
set @Decimal = FormatNumber(@num, "D")
set @Exponential = FormatNumber(@num, "E")
set @Fixed = FormatNumber(@num, "F")
set @Fixed3 = FormatNumber(@num, "F3")
set @General = FormatNumber(@num, "G")
set @Number = FormatNumber(@num, "N")
set @Number3 = FormatNumber(@num, "N3")
set @Percent = FormatNumber(@num, "P")
set @Hex = FormatNumber(@num, "X")

]%%
num: %%=v(@num)=%%
<br><br>Currency: %%=v(@Currency)=%%
<br>Currency3: %%=v(@Currency3)=%%
<br>Decimal: %%=v(@Decimal)=%%
<br>Exponential: %%=v(@Exponential)=%%
<br>Fixed: %%=v(@Fixed)=%%
<br>Fixed3: %%=v(@Fixed3)=%%
<br>General: %%=v(@General)=%%
<br>Number: %%=v(@Number)=%%
<br>Number3: %%=v(@Number3)=%%
```

```
<br>Percent: %%=v(@Percent)=%%
<br>Hex: %%=v(@Hex)=%%
```

Output

```
num: 123

Currency: $123.00
Currency3: $123.000
Decimal: 123
Exponential: 1.230000E+002
Fixed: 123.00
Fixed3: 123.000
General: 123
Number: 123.00
Number3: 123.000
Percent: 12,300.00 %
Hex: 7B
```

Example 2

```
%%[

var @num
var @ZeroPlaceholder
var @DigitPlaceholder
var @DecimalPoint
var @GroupSeparator
var @PercentagePlaceholder
var @Exponential
var @EscapeCharacter
var @LiteralDelimiter
var @SectionSeparator


set @num = "-1.8967"

set @ZeroPlaceholder = FormatNumber(@num,"0000")
set @DigitPlaceholder = FormatNumber(@num,"###0")
set @DecimalPoint = FormatNumber(@num,"#0.00")
set @GroupSeparator = FormatNumber(@num,"0,00#.##")
set @PercentagePlaceholder = FormatNumber(@num,"#.00%")
```

```
set @Exponential = FormatNumber(@num,"#0.0e0")
set @EscapeCharacter = FormatNumber(@num,"\###0.000\#")
set @LiteralDelimiter = FormatNumber(@num,"#.##' points'")
set @SectionSeparator = FormatNumber(@num,"#0.00;(#0.00)")


]%%
num: %%=v(@num)=%%
<br><br>ZeroPlaceholder: %%=v(@ZeroPlaceholder)=%%
<br>DigitPlaceholder: %%=v(@DigitPlaceholder)=%%
<br>DecimalPoint: %%=v(@DecimalPoint)=%%
<br>GroupSeparator: %%=v(@GroupSeparator)=%%
<br>PercentagePlaceholder: %%=v(@PercentagePlaceholder)=%%
<br>Exponential: %%=v(@Exponential)=%%
<br>EscapeCharacter: %%=v(@EscapeCharacter)=%%
<br>LiteralDelimiter: %%=v(@LiteralDelimiter)=%%
<br>SectionSeparator: %%=v(@SectionSeparator)=%%
```

Output

```
num: -1.8967

ZeroPlaceholder: -0002
DigitPlaceholder: -2
DecimalPoint: -1.90
GroupSeparator: -0,001.9
PercentagePlaceholder: -189.67%
Exponential: -19.0e-1
EscapeCharacter: -#1.897#
LiteralDelimiter: -1.9 points
SectionSeparator: (1.90)
```

Example 3

```
%%[

var @num
var @Number

set @num = "123.456"
```

```
set @Number3 = FormatNumber(@num, "N3", "fr-FR")

]%%
num: %%=v(@num)=%%
<br>Number3: %%=v(@Number3)=%%
```

Output

```
num: 123.456
Number3: 123,456
```

GUID

This function returns a 36-character global unique identifier (GUID) string.

Arguments

GUID()

This function does not accept any arguments.

Example 1

```
GUID: %%=GUID()=%%
```

Output

```
24c97bbd-9f6e-4da7-94e5-d4b0ac7c2229
```

IIf

This in-line IF function returns the value of the second argument if the value for the first argument evaluates as true.

Arguments

IIf(1,2,3)

Ordinal	Type	Required	Description
1	String	True	Conditional expression that returns a true or false
2	String	True	Value to return of the conditional expression returns true
3	String	True	Value to return of the conditional expression returns false

Example 1

```
%%[

var @greeting
var @firstName
set @firstName = AttributeValue("firstName")
set @greeting = Iif(not Empty(@firstName), @firstName,
"Member")

]%%
Dear %%=v(@greeting)=%%,
```

Output

```
Dear Member,
```

IsEmailAddress

This function confirms whether or not a value matches a valid email syntax. The function returns **`true`** if the syntax is valid or **`false`** if it's not.

> **NOTE:** The function only provides syntax validation. It does not indicate whether the email address is deliverable. For example, the function will not check whether an MX record exists for the domain or whether the email address is a role-based email.

Argument

`IsEmailAddress(1)`

Ordinal	Type	Required	Description
1	String	True	Email address to validate

Example

When a landing page form is submitted, an **`email`** form field is validated and an alert message is displayed if the email value is invalid.

```
%%=Iif(IsEmailAddress(RequestParameter('email'))==false,'<div
class="alert">You have entered an invalid email address</
div>','')=%%
```

Output

A value of **james@limedash** will return the following output.

```
<div class="alert">You have entered an invalid email
address</div>
```

IsNull

Similar to the Empty function, this function provides a conditional evaluation of an expression. If the expression evaluates as **null**, the function will output **true**, otherwise it will output **false**.

> **NOTE:** This function only evaluates Data Extension field values. When used to evaluate other contexts, it will output **false**.

Argument

IsNull(1)

Ordinal	Type	Required	Description
1	String	True	A variable or nested function to evaluate

Example

In the following example, a form is displayed on a personalized landing page and the code conditionally displays a field.

```
%%[

var @phone
set @phone = Lookup("Members","Phone","Subscriber
Key", _subscriberKey)

if IsNull(@phone) then

]%%

<label>Phone</label> <input type="text" name="phone">

%%[ endif ]%%
```

Output

If the Data Extension **Phone** field does not contain a value for a Subscriber, the IsNull function will evaluate to **true** and an input field will be displayed on the form.

```
<label>Phone</label> <input type="text" name="phone">
```

IsPhoneNumber

This function confirms whether or not a value is a valid US phone number. The function returns **true** if the syntax is valid or **false** if it's not. Any non-numeric characters are ignored on evaluation.

Sample phone number strings and their resulting evaluation by the function are provided below.

Phone Number	Result
234-235-5678	true
234 235 5678	true
(541) 754-3010	true
+1-541-754-3010	false
1234567890	false

> **NOTE:** This function will only validate US phone numbers. Other country formats will return a **false** result.

Argument

IsPhoneNumber(1)

Ordinal	Type	Required	Description
1	String	True	Phone number to validate

Example

When a landing page form is submitted, an **phone** form field is validated and an alert message is displayed if the syntax is invalid.

```
%%=Iif(IsPhoneNumber(RequestParameter('phone'))==false,'<div
class="alert">You have entered an invalid US phone number</
div>','')=%%
```

Output
A value of **0402 123 456** will return the following output.

```
<div class="alert">You have entered an invalid US phone
number</div>
```

Output

While code within an AMPscript block does not display output where the block appears in an email on a page, the Output function enables variable values to be output at the location where the code block appears.

This function is convenient when debugging AMPscript, as it enables variables or function values to be output in an email, message or page, without the requirement to output the code in an inline AMPscript function.

> **NOTE:** This function will only return a result from nested functions. It will not return a result if only a variable is used as an argument. For example **`Output(@firstName)`** will not output a value, even if the variable has been set within the code block.

Argument
`Output(1)`

Ordinal	Type	Required	Description
1	String	True	Evaluated function to display

Example 1
The following example outputs a **`@firstName`** variable from a Data Extension field, concatenated with a descriptive string:

```
%%[

var @firstName
set @firstName = Lookup("Members", "First Name", "Email",
emailaddr)

Output(Concat("First Name: ", @firstName))

]%%
```

Output

A field value of **Nora** will return the following output:

```
First Name: Nora
```

Example 2

The following example outputs the domain of a Subscriber's email address:

```
%%[

Output(Domain(emailaddr))

]%%
```

Output

An email address value of **leon@limedash.com** will return the following output:

```
limedash.com
```

OutputLine

This function is similar to the Output function, but it inserts a line feed character after the result.

This function is convenient when there is a requirement to output multiple functions results from a code block, as each result will be displayed on a separate line, whereas multiple Output functions in a single code block will display each result on the same line.

> **NOTE:** This function will only return a result from nested functions. It will not return a result if only a variable is used as an argument.

Argument
OutputLine(1)

Ordinal	Type	Required	Description
1	String	True	Evaluated function to display

Example
The following example outputs Data Extension fields (for a Subscriber) as separate lines concatenated with a descriptive string:

```
%%[

var @rows, @row, @firstName, @lastName, @email, @phone

set @rows = LookupRows("Members", "Subscriber Key",
_subscriberKey)
set @row = Row(@rows, 1) /* there is only one row per
member */
set @firstName = Field(@row, "First Name")
set @lastName = Field(@row, "Last Name")
set @email = Field(@row, "Email")
set @phone = Field(@row, "Phone Number")

OutputLine(Concat("First Name: ", @firstName))
OutputLine(Concat("Last Name: ", @lastName))
OutputLine(Concat("Email: ", @email))
OutputLine(Concat("Phone: ", @phone))

]%%
```

Output
Each OutputLine result will be displayed on a new line.

```
First Name: Doug
Last Name: Smith
Email: doug@limedash.com
Phone: 234 235 5678
```

RaiseError

This function enables the suppression or cancellation of an email send. It is useful for exception handling in your code, if an unexpected result occurs.

> **NOTE:** This function still counts as an email send, even if an email was not sent to a Subscriber. Only use this function for exception handling, not for segmenting or excluding a large number of Subscribers.

Arguments

`RaiseError(1,2,3,4,5)`

Ordinal	Type	Required	Description
1	String	True	Error message to display or log (see note)
2	Boolean	False	Indicates whether the function skips the send for current Subscriber and continues or stops. A value of `true` skips the send for current Subscriber and moves to next Subscriber. A value of `false` stops the send and returns an error. The default value is `false`.
3	String	False	User defined API error code (see note)
4	Number	False	User defined API error number (see note)
5	Boolean	False	Indicates whether the function preserves Data Extension rows inserted, updated, or deleted by AMPscript functions before error occurs, even if the process skips the Subscriber. A value of `1` will preserve data operations to Data Extensions before the error is raised, even if the Subscriber is skipped. A value of `0` does not preserve operations before the error.

> **NOTE:** Arguments 1, 3 and 4 output by the function are not available from Send Tracking in Email Studio. Marketing Cloud Support will be able to advise of the function output.

Example 1

The following example uses the ClaimRow function to allocate a coupon code value from a Data Extension to a Subscriber, if a coupon is available and not already assigned to the Subscriber's email address. If the coupon has previously been assigned to the Subscriber, then the previously allocated coupon code is returned.

```
%%[

var @email, @couponRow, @couponCode

/* include the send context attributes or columns to record
here */
set @email = AttributeValue("emailAddr")

set @couponRow = ClaimRow("CouponCodes", "IsClaimed",
"EmailAddress", @email)

if not empty(@couponRow) then

  set @couponCode = Field(@couponRow, "CouponCode")

else

  RaiseError("No coupons available")

endif

]%%
```

```
Coupon code: %%=v(@couponCode)=%%
```

Output

If no coupon codes are available, the following message appears when previewing an email and the email send is aborted.

```
No coupons available
```

Example 2

The following example is a variation from the first, but in this scenario, the email send is skipped for the current Subscriber.

```
%%[

var @email, @couponRow, @couponCode

/* include the send context attributes or columns to record
here */
set @email = AttributeValue("emailAddr")

set @couponRow = ClaimRow("CouponCodes", "IsClaimed",
"EmailAddress", @email)

if not empty(@couponRow) then

  set @couponCode = Field(@couponRow, "CouponCode")

else

  RaiseError("No coupons available", true)

endif

]%%

Coupon code: %%=v(@couponCode)=%%
```

V

This function outputs the value of a variable. It is commonly used when a variable is defined within a code block and the result is displayed in an email, message or web page.

Argument

V(1)

Ordinal	Type	Required	Description
1	String	True	Variable value to output

Example

The following example returns the result of a variable from a code block and displays it inline within an HTML tag.

```
%%[

var @firstName, @displayName

set @firstName = AttributeValue("First Name")

if empty(@firstName) then
  set @displayName = "friend"
else
  set @displayName = @firstName
endif

]%%
<p>Hello %%=v(@displayName)=%%,</p>
```

Output

The function will output the value of the variable. For a Sendable Data Extension containing the **First Name** field value **Barb**, the following output will be displayed:

```
<p>Hello Barb,</p>
```

Exclusion Scripts

Overview
Exclusion scripts enable Subscribers to be conditionally excluded from being sent an email, based on a logical test.

This feature is available in the following Marketing Cloud applications:

1. Content Builder
2. Journey Builder
3. Triggered Sends
4. Automation Studio

Syntax
Exclusion scripts use AMPscript expressions which, if they evaluate to **`true`**, suppress the sending of an email to the respective Subscriber. The following requirements apply to exclusion scripts:

1. AMPscript blocks or inline AMPscript cannot be included
2. Scripts cannot span multiple lines
3. Variables cannot be set
4. The expression must evaluate to **`true`** or **`false`**

Exclusion scripts are evaluated in the context of the Subscriber they are sent to, so they can include attributes or personalization strings.

> **NOTE:** You should only use exclusion scripts for exception handling, not for segmenting or excluding a large number of subscribers.

> **TIP:** Use Exclusion Scripts instead of the RaiseError function for excluding Subscribers. Emails excluded from sending by the RaiseError function will count as a Super Message and should be reserved for exception handling.

Example 1

The following expression will suppress the sending of an email to a Subscriber if they do not have a points balance.

```
Empty(AttributeValue("Points"))
```

Output

1. A 'Points' value is returned by the AttributeValue function, based on the data source context of the Contact or Subscriber that the email is sent to.
2. An Empty function checks if the points value is null or empty.

If this test evaluates to **`true`**, then the email will not be sent.

Example 2

The following expression can be used when sending an email to an internal list for review.

```
Domain(emailaddr) != "mycompany.com"
```

Output

1. The Domain AMPscript function returns the associated domain of the Subscriber email, based on the email address personalization string.
2. A comparison operator checks if the domain is not equal to the constant **`"mycompany.com"`**.

If this test evaluates to **`true`**, then the email will not be sent.

Example 3

The following expression can be used to skip sending a promotional email to a Subscriber if their promotion date has ended.

```
FormatDate(SystemDateToLocalDate(Now()), "YYYYMMDD")
< AttributeValue("End Date")
```

Output

1. The SystemDateToLocalDate function converts the current system time (from the Now function) into the account locale.
2. The resulting expression is converted into the **`YYYYMMDD`** format using the FormatDate function.
3. An 'End Date' attribute is returned by the AttributeValue function, based on the data source context of the Contact or Subscriber that the email is sent to.

If the current date and time (as defined by the account locale) is later than the 'End Date' attribute, the email will not be sent.

AMPscript & Guide Template Language

Overview

Marketing Cloud provides templating features through Guide Template Language (also referred to as 'Guide' or 'GTL') which is based on the Mustache and Handlebars.js template engines.

Mustache, aptly named after its curly brace syntax that resembles a sideways mustache, is a popular template engine that is widely available across different languages and runtimes. Built on a simple syntax, Mustache provides a 'logic-less' approach to templating, as it lacks explicit control flow statements like 'if' and 'else' conditionals or 'loops'; however, both looping and conditional evaluation can be achieved using built-in block helpers.

Handlebars is a superset of Mustache and uses helpers, literals and partials to add extensibility and minimal logic to Mustache.

Using these two template engines, Guide provides a declarative syntax that leverages the advantages of template-based content architecture, while also retaining interoperability with AMPscript and Server Side JavaScript (SSJS) scripting languages. Guide can be used in any platform application that publishes personalized content, including:

- Email messages
- SMS messages
- Mobile Push notifications
- CloudPage landing pages

> **NOTE:** Guide is not a scripting language. Rather, it's a templating language. While simple conditional statements and process loops can be achieved in Guide through built-in block helpers, it's not designed as a replacement for AMPscript.

Syntax

Guide uses tags to define where data or content should appear on a page. The most basic type of tag is a Simple Tag. Referred to as a 'variable' in Mustache or an 'expression' in Handlebars, a Simple Tag is represented in curly braces; for example, **`{{name}}`**. When rendered, the Simple Tag will be replaced by the corresponding value from the context.

A **`{{name}}`** tag in a basic template will try to find the name key in the current data source context. If there is no name key, the parent contexts will be checked recursively. If the top context is reached and the name key is still not found, nothing will be rendered.

> **TIP:** You can use tags as a substitute for attribute personalization strings. For example, a personalization string named **`%%FirstName%%`** can be substituted with **`{{FirstName}}`** to retrieve a value from a data source context.

AMPscript and Guide

AMPscript functions can be included as inline functions in Guide tags. To include an AMPscript function in a Guide tag, prefix the function with a **=** character.

> **NOTE:** When using Guide in CloudPages with AMPscript, it is necessary to escape OMM delimiters for the Guide tags to be interpreted. This is achieved by adding a **`%%{={{ }}=}%%`** string immediately before or after a closing AMPscript block.

Example 1

The following example retrieves an 'Order Total' value from a Sendable Data Extension and is formatted using the FormatCurrency function:

```
{{=FormatCurrency([Order Total],'en-GB',2)}}
```

Output

For a value of **23.99**, the function will render the following string:

```
£23.99
```

Example 2

The following example formats a credit card expiry month and date in an **MM/YY** format, based on numeric values from a Data Extension using an Iif function, and with Length and Concat nested functions:

```
{{=iif(Length([Expiry Month])==1,Concat(0,[Expiry
Month]),[Expiry Month])}}/{{[Expiry Year]}}
```

Output

For an 'Expiry Month' value of **7** and an 'Expiry Year' value of **21**, the function will render the following string:

```
07/21
```

AMPscript & Server-Side JavaScript

Overview

Marketing Cloud's Server-Side JavaScript (SSJS) has several advantages over AMPscript. First, JavaScript is more mainstream and familiar to developers. Marketing Cloud SSJS also includes additional features that do not exist in AMPscript, like arrays, array functions and JSON parsing tools.

On the flip side, the Marketing Cloud SSJS is not maintained like AMPscript, so most newer AMPscript functions have no SSJS equivalent. The use of SSJS is generally discouraged by Marketing Cloud Support due to additional overhead that adversely affects platform performance.

If an advanced development scenario aligns with the capabilities of SSJS, you will probably need to leverage the features and advantages of AMPscript too. Fortunately, there are two SSJS functions that allow you to get and set variables in AMPscript.

GetValue

This function returns the value of the specified AMPscript variable.

Argument

`GetValue(1)`

Ordinal	Type	Required	Description
1	String	True	AMPscript variable from which to return a value

Example

```
%%[

var @firstName

set @firstName = AttributeValue("firstName") /* value from
attribute or DE column in send context */
set @firstName = "Leon" /* or a literal value */

]%%
<script runat="server">

Platform.Load("core","1.1.5");

var firstName = Variable.GetValue("@firstName");

Write("<br>firstName: " + firstName);

</script>
```

Output

```
firstName: Leon
```

SetValue

This function sets the value of an AMPscript variable inside a block.

Arguments

`SetValue(1,2)`

Ordinal	Type	Required	Description
1	String	True	AMPscript variable name
2	String	True	AMPscript variable value

Example

```
<script runat="server">

Platform.Load("core","1.1.5");

var firstName = Attribute.GetValue("FirstName"); /* value
from attribute or DE column in send context */
firstName = "Lily"; /* or a literal value */

Variable.SetValue("@firstName", firstName);

</script>
firstName: %%=v(@firstName)=%%
```

Output

```
firstName: Lily
```

Content Syndication

Overview

Content syndication enables content from external, publicly accessible HTTP sources to be included in emails and landing pages.

Applications include embedding the following content in emails and landing pages:

- news feeds
- dynamically generated content (for example, personalized images)
- product information from an e-commerce or content management system (CMS) platform
- personalized maps
- personalized charts
- localized content based on a Subscriber's location (for example, content in different languages)

Optionally, syndicated content can also be cached, whereby retrieved content for the duration of an email send.

> **NOTE:** There are several best practices to consider when using syndicated content. Refer to Content Syndication Best Practices.

Syntax

The content syndication syntax uses an **`HTTPGet`** command suffixed with a URL. This string should be contained within **`%%`** delimiters. The syndicated content will be returned where the string appears in the email or landing page.

> **NOTE:** Content Syndication is only supported on HTTP port 80 and HTTPS port 443. The use of non-standard ports will result in an error.

Example

The following string is used on a landing page:

```
%%httpget "https://httpbin.org/html"%%
```

Output

This string will output the content from the URL on the landing page:

```
<!DOCTYPE html>
<html>
  <head>
  </head>
  <body>
      <h1>Herman Melville - Moby-Dick</h1>
      <div>
        <p>
          Availing himself of the mild, summer-cool weather
that now reigned in these latitudes, and in preparation for
the peculiarly active pursuits ... Hadst thou taken this old
blacksmith to thyself ere his full ruin came upon him, then
had the young widow had a delicious grief, and her orphans
a truly venerable, legendary sire to dream of in their
after years; and all of them a care-killing competency.
        </p>
      </div>
  </body>
</html>
```

Variables & Functions

AMPscript variables or inline functions are not supported in syndicated content URLs. The URL should be a constant. To set the URL based on a logical condition, use **`if`** and **`elseif`** statements to output the respective content syndication string.

> **NOTE:** A Subscriber's email address and email send job identifier can included in the syndicated content URL. Refer to Content Syndication Variables.

Example

```
%%[

var @tier
set @tier = AttributeValue("Tier")

if @tier == "gold" then
]%%
  %%httpget "https://httpbin.org/html?tier=gold"%%
%%[ elseif @tier == "silver" then ]%%
  %%httpget "https://httpbin.org/html?tier=silver"%%
%%[ else ]%%
  %%httpget "https://httpbin.org/html?tier=bronze"%%
%%[ endif ]%%
```

Output

If the 'Tier' value for a Subscriber is **`gold`** within a contextual data source, the email will retrieve content from the following URL:

```
https://httpbin.org/html?tier=gold
```

Syndicated content URLs can include an email job identifier or Subscriber's email address as a variable, by including a **`[jobid]`** or **`[email address]`** string in the URL. Other variables are not supported.

This feature is useful for logging email sends in external platforms, or retrieving personalized content.

Example 1

The following string is included in an email and is requested once the email has been sent:

```
%%After;HTTPGet "https://limedash.com/webhook/
sent?id=[jobid]"%%
```

Output

An HTTP GET request is made to the URL once the email has been sent. For an email Job ID of **`5678`**, the following URL will be requested:

```
https://limedash.com/webhook/sent?id=5678
```

Example 2

The following string is included in an email:

```
%%HTTPGet "https://httpbin.org/get?email=[email address]"%%
```

Output

The HTTP GET request resolves to the following URL for a Subscriber with an email address of **barb@limedash.com**, which can be used to retrieve personalized content for the Subscriber from the external platform.

```
https://httpbin.org/get?email=barb@limedash.com
```

HTTPGetWrap Command

Prefixing an **href** attribute value in syndicated content with **HTTPGetWrap|** will track links in an email.

Example

An **href** attribute is prefixed with a **HTTPGetWrap|** string in the external syndicated content.

```
<!DOCTYPE html>
<html>
  <head>
  </head>
  <body>
      <h1>Herman Melville - Moby-Dick</h1>
      <div>
        <p>Hadst thou taken this old <a
href="HTTPGetWrap|http://limedash.com/blacksmith">blacksmith</
a> to thyself ere his full ruin came upon him.</p>
      </div>
  </body>
</html>
```

> **NOTE:** The **httpgetwrap|** prefix must be enabled by Marketing Cloud Support. The special business rule is called **WRAP_HTTPGET_URLS**.

Before HTTPGet Command

Prefixing **`HTTPGet`** with a **`Before;`** string will retrieve the content once, at the beginning of an email send.

> **TIP:** Use this command if the syndicated content in an email send does not change.

Example

```
%%Before;HTTPGet "https://limedash.com/webhook/sending"%%
```

After HTTPGet Command

Prefixing **`HTTPGet`** with an **`After;`** string will send a request to the specified URL. This command will not output any content in the email. This command is useful as a webhook, to indicate that an email has been sent.

> **NOTE:** This command cannot be used with triggered email sends, as a triggered email send job does not end after an email is sent.

Example

```
%%After;HTTPGet "https://limedash.com/webhook/sent"%%
```

Empty Return Handling Options

If the syndicated content URL returns empty content, the platform assumes there is no syndicated content relevant to the context of the email, and continues the email send. This behavior can be changed by appending a number delimited by a semicolon to the **`HTTPGet`** string.

The following values are supported.

Value	Result
0	Continues processing (default value)
1	Stops processing the email send and returns an error
2	Skips sending the email to the respective Subscriber for the **`HTTPGet`** command, or stops processing the email send and returns an error for the **`Before;HTTPGet`** command

> **NOTE:** This flag is ignored if used with the **`After;HTTPGet`** command.

Example 1

The following string is included in an email and the resolved URL returns an empty response for a Subscriber.

```
%%HTTPGet;1 "https://limedash.com/content?email=[email
address]"%%
```

Output

The email send is cancelled and an error is raised.

```
A subscriber level HTTPGET call completed but returned no
content. This HTTPGET call is configured to stop the job
when this happens.
```

Example 2

The following string is included in an email and the URL returns an empty response.

```
%%Before;HTTPGet;2 "https://limedash.com/content"%%
```

Output

The email send is cancelled and an error is raised.

```
A BEFORE HTTPGET call completed but returned no content.
This HTTPGET call is configured to stop the job when this
happens.
```

Best Practices

Script Block Organization

Taking time to organize your AMPscript code blocks has many advantages. Most importantly, it makes your code much easier to debug. It's also a show of goodwill (and expertise) to those coming after you who will need to make sense of your code. Some of these practices aren't specific to AMPscript:

- It is good practice to place the majority of your AMPscript code at the top of the email or web page. This will make your code easier to find and maintain.
- Do not try to hide your AMPscript code with HTML comments or blocks. This often leads to inadvertent code inclusion.
- Use descriptive variable names and match them exactly to your send context field names where possible. As you get into more complex scripting scenarios, this will make a big difference.
- Take the time to add comments to your AMPscript code. Sometimes it's helpful to rough out the logic of your solution with comments and fill in the code afterward.
- Align opening and closing script block tags: **`%%[`** and **`]%%`**.
- Align **`if`**, **`else`** and **`endif`** elements as well as your **`for`** and **`next`** blocks.
- Instead of using a string of nested, in-line AMPscript functions to display a variable value in the body of your email or web page, create a variable for it at the top of the email or web page and reference it with a short **`v()`** function. This organization technique keeps the logic centralized and the body less cluttered.

You will note that that the Marketing Cloud visual editors (WYSIWYG) are not optimized for displaying nicely formatted AMPscript code. The built-in indention and parsing is still not perfect and may undo your code formatting efforts. This can be mitigated by not using the visual editor content blocks and sticking with HTML-only ones.

Coding Defensively

Leveraging the AttributeValue and Empty Functions

It is good practice to assume that any of the contextual personalization variables/strings in an email or web page might not exist or be blank. If you reference a Profile Attribute or Data Extension column name that does not exist in your sending audience, your send will terminate with a runtime error. To minimize that possibility, you can use the AttributeValue function to proactively check those contextual variables.

With that in mind, unless you are leveraging a built-in personalization string (for example, **`_subscriberKey`**, **`memberid`** etc.), you should be using a combination of AttributeValue and Empty to ensure that your variables exist or have a value.

Proactively Using RaiseError

Often in the development stage, the primary sending audiences are incomplete or based completely on fictitious data. Making assumptions about sending audience attributes and external data can get you into trouble. One way to approach this in code is to commit to adding extra conditionals to handle any aberrations that may come up in your data. A *good* assumption is to expect data to be bad or missing. If those attributes do not exist or are not in the format you expect, then check them with a conditional and use the RaiseError function to ensure that the email does not get sent. RaiseError allows you to either abort the email send entirely or to skip a particular Subscriber where these specific error conditions exist. It is generally better to abort the send or skip the Subscriber to send a broken email to Subscribers.

Debugging

If your code isn't working the way you think it should, there are a few techniques you can use to narrow the problem.

Leveraging the Toolbar Validate in Classic Content

Often overlooked, the Validate button in Classic Content will provide additional details on any syntactical issues. Starting there is a good plan.

In Content Builder, this syntax validation is built-in. It's displayed in red in the Preview and Test step.

Writing Variable Values

If your syntax is fine and you are dealing with runtime errors, you can strip out all HTML in your email or web page leaving just your AMPscript. If that does not give you some direction, reduce your code to the least amount that works, then slowly add to it until it breaks. While this is repetitive, it can get you to the problem area quickly.

Sometimes, reducing to only AMPscript isn't a reasonable approach. Another useful technique is to output variable values in the flow of your code:

```
%%[

/* some other AMPscript here */

output(concat("<br>region: ", @region))

/* some other AMPscript here */

]%%
```

Here are some good places for displaying debug values:

- directly after variables set from values in the sending audience (Profile Attributes or Data Extension columns)
- before any conditional statements
- inside any loops

Using a SSJS Try/Catch to Trap AMPscript Errors

For those elusive AMPscript runtime errors, you can get some additional details of the error by trapping exceptions with a SSJS **`try/catch`** block.

```
<script runat="server">

Platform.Load("core","1.1.5");

try {
</script>
%%[

/* Your AMPscript goes here */

]%%
```

```
<script runat="server">
} catch (e) {
  Write("<br>" + Stringify(e))
}

</script>
```

Modularization

Code reuse is a universal programming best practice. Projects that include highly personalized messages that leverage data from multiple sources are good candidates for breaking out components into reusable blocks.

Shared Content Areas

Suppose you have a loyalty email campaign that includes a section above the footer displaying the current reward level. If that element needs to be included in *all* of the loyalty messaging, the block would be a good candidate isolation as a component Content Area.

Instead of creating a copy of it in your email, you can simply reference it by Customer/External Key or by path in your email template:

Content Builder (Customer/External Key reference)

```
%%=ContentBlockByKey("RewardStatus")=%%
```

Classic Content (directory path reference)

```
%%=ContentAreaByName("My Contents\Loyalty\RewardStatus")=%%
```

Including code like this will enable you to make a single code change that alters content across multiple emails.

> **NOTE:** While it's possible to have Content Areas and Blocks include other Content Areas and Blocks, it's best to not go more than two levels deep. If your content blocks have multiple children, it makes them much harder to maintain.

Dynamic Content Area Paths

Taking the Shared Content Areas concept a bit further, you can also 'calculate' the key or path to a specific Content Area dynamically. One advantage this has over the previous method, is that it's more explicit in intent within the email.

Suppose you have several versions of the **RewardStatus** Content Block mentioned above – ones that vary by locale/language. You can utilize the Concat function to build the key or path:

Content Builder (Customer/External Key reference)

```
%%[

var @locale
var @defaultLocale
var @contentBlockKey

set @locale = AttributeValue("locale")
set @defaultLocale = "en-us"

if not empty(@locale) then
    set @contentBlockKey = concat("RewardStatus _ ", @locale)
else
    set @contentBlockKey = concat("RewardStatus _ ",
@defaultLocale)
endif

]%%
%%=ContentBlockByKey(@contentBlockKey)=%%
```

Classic Content (directory path reference)

```
%%[

var @locale
var @defaultLocale
var @contentAreaPath

set @locale = AttributeValue("locale")
set @defaultLocale = "en-us"
```

```
if not empty(@locale) then
    set @contentAreaPath = concat("My Contents\Loyalty\
RewardStatus _ ", @locale)
else
    set @contentAreaPath = concat("My Contents\Loyalty\
RewardStatus _ ", @defaultLocale)
endif

]%%
%%=ContentAreaByName(@contentAreaPath)=%%
```

Content Syndication

As the content syndication feature executes external HTTP requests, there are implications if the feature is used excessively. You should consider the following guidelines when using content syndication.

Occurrences

Limit the number of content syndication occurrences to three or less. More occurrences may impact an email job send speed or landing page response time.

Caching

If the syndicated content is the same for all Subscribers for an email send, use **`Before;HTTPGet`** to cache the syndicated content, instead of making separate requests for each email.

Audience Size

Keep your audience size under 1000 Subscribers for sends. If your audience size is larger than 1000, segment your list or Data Extension to smaller audiences and use several email sends.

Function Index

Notes

Notes

Notes

Notes

Notes

Notes

Notes

Notes